LITERATURE, ANALYTICALLY SPEAKING

*Cognitive Approaches to Literature and Culture Series*
*Edited by Frederick Luis Aldama, Arturo J. Aldama, and*
*Patrick Colm Hogan*

*Cognitive Approaches to Literature and Culture includes*
*monographs and edited volumes that incorporate cutting-edge*
*research in cognitive science, neuroscience, psychology, linguis-*
*tics, narrative theory, and related fields, exploring how this*
*research bears on and illuminates cultural phenomena such as,*
*but not limited to, literature, film, drama, music, dance, visual*
*art, digital media, and comics. The volumes published in this*
*series represent both specialized scholarship and interdisciplin-*
*ary investigations that are deeply sensitive to cultural specif-*
*ics and grounded in a cross-cultural understanding of shared*
*emotive and cognitive principles.*

# Literature,
# Analytically Speaking

EXPLORATIONS IN THE THEORY OF
INTERPRETATION, ANALYTIC AESTHETICS,
AND EVOLUTION

*Peter Swirski*

UNIVERSITY OF TEXAS PRESS
*Austin*

Requests for permission to reproduce material from this work
should be sent to:
　Permissions
　University of Texas Press
　P.O. Box 7819
　Austin, TX 78713–7819
　www.utexas.edu/utpress/about/bpermission.html

♾ The paper used in this book meets the minimum requirements
of ANSI/NISO z39.48–1992 (R1997) (Permanence of Paper).

Library of Congress Cataloging-in-Publication Data

Swirski, Peter.
　Literature, analytically speaking : explorations in the theory of
interpretation, analytic aesthetics, and evolution / Peter Swirski.
　　　p.　　　cm.—(Cognitive approaches to literature and culture)
　Includes bibliographical references and index.
　ISBN 978-0-292-72178-4 (cloth : alk. paper)
　1. Literature—Philosophy.　I. Title.
　PN49.S874　2010
　801—dc22

2009024365

*This book is dedicated to Joseph Carroll, Brian Boyd, Jerrold Levinson, Paisley Livingston, and other evolutionary-literary scholars and analytic aestheticians.*

# CONTENTS

LITERATURE, ANALYTICALLY SPEAKING

One      ANALYTIC AESTHETICS

*And for those who are still interested in pronouncing judgments as to aesthetic value, it is only by identifying, tracking down, and laying bare the supreme workings of style that we are able to say why a given work is beautiful, why it has enjoyed different kinds of reception in the course of time, and why, although it follows models and sometimes even precepts that are scattered far and wide in the sea of intertextuality, it has been able to gather those legacies and make them blossom in such a way as to give life to something original.*

UMBERTO ECO, *ON LITERATURE*

# A BOOK OF LITERARY THEORY

*If there is a discipline called Poetics, it . . . will have to deal with one of the dimensions of language, and in that sense it will be the proper object of the critic, just like poetry is the object of the poet.*
UMBERTO ECO, *ON LITERATURE*

This is a book of literary theory, written by a literary theorist for literary theorists. My aim here is fourfold. First and foremost, I seek to integrate contemporary analytic aesthetics together with certain of its concepts and methods into literary studies. Conversely, by virtue of scrutinizing aspects of narrative fiction with an intensity uncommon in philosophy, I seek to enrich and complexify the understanding of *belles lettres* among our natural allies: aestheticians of philosophical persuasion. Either way, I aim to throw a bridge between literary studies and the domain that shares so much of its subject matter yet lies so far apart in its research program and methodology.

Moving down, I aim to rehearse, and in some cases refine, the solutions to several problems in aesthetics that bear directly on the interpretation of literature. The general tenets and many specific theses elaborated herein have been worked out over the past three decades or so by philosophers like Arthur Danto, David Lewis, Kendall Walton, Gregory Currie, Jerrold Levinson, Peter Lamarque, Stein Olsen, Stephen Davies, Robert Stecker, Gary Iseminger, Dennis Dutton, Paisley Livingston, and many others. However, given that their work remains practically unknown in literary studies, *Literature, Analytically Speaking* highlights their findings and tailors them to our field-specific needs.

Preoccupied with theory, analytic philosophers are occasionally wont to overlook the forest of art for the trees. Bearing this in mind, I draw from all this theorizing a set of practical guidelines for critics in the interpretive trenches. Bringing aesthetic theory and critical praxis together, I aim to enhance interdisciplinary knowledge of—and the methods of disciplinary research into—the fundamentals of literary-aesthetic study. For, as I contend, both of these goals can be profitably pursued by adopting, and when necessary adapting, not just the specific postulates but the very philosophy that underlies the analytic approach.

Problems of interpretation continue to occupy theorists of literature, partly because they are the most pressing and partly because they are the most difficult on our agenda. Alas, like the McCartneys' divorce attorneys, scholars who labor to rationalize the principles of literary-critical interpretation seem only to agree to disagree on almost everything under the sun. Indeed, in the words of one eminent thinker, this "great variety of Taste, as well as of opinion which prevails in the world, is too obvious not to have fallen under every one's observation."[1] It is a sobering thought that David Hume's summation from 1757 has lost nothing of its punch in our day.

While there have long existed competing schools of textual exegesis, amid today's cornucopia of positions and oppositions theorists of literature cannot even agree on the foundational principles according to which research should be organized. The variety of textual moves and anti-intentionalist movements known collectively as postmodernism has only exacerbated this balkanization. Alas, if the maturity of a research discipline is to be judged by the emergence of a shared program of study driven by a methodology contiguous with other areas of inquiry, literary theory—viewed not as a heterogeneous body of metacritical commentary but as a *research* discipline—is still in its infancy.[2]

Recognizing this, I turn to analytic philosophy in pursuit of a cogent and principled methodology. Although in itself the interdisciplinarity turn is nothing new, the extent to which literary scholarship actually practices what it preaches is another matter. Richard Levin's "The New Interdisciplinarity in Literary Criticism" (1993) thoroughly documents, in fact, that cross-campus standards in critical theory and practice remain for the most part skin deep. This may in turn explain why, on the jacket of a 1999 critical anthology, Mieke Bal felt the need to defend herself against "the common assumption that interdisciplinarity makes the object of inquiry vague and the methodology muddled."[3]

The partition that separates literary criticism from neighboring disciplines such as analytic aesthetics or pragmatics may be invisible but is none the less real. It is a pretty safe bet, for example, that when it comes to speech-act theory—an area of inquiry shared by analytic aesthetics and linguistics—few story scholars could sketch it even in broad strokes, let alone track its significance for the analysis of ontology of fiction in general and narrative fiction in particular.[4] Ditto for the so-called problem of fictional truth and a host of other topics pursued with analytic rigor and success in a discipline of which many have only a vague and often not entirely favorable notion.

This is where *Literature, Analytically Speaking* comes in. Taking both the specific findings and the general methods of analytic aesthetics to belong squarely to literary scholarship, I set out to formulate an alternative to some of the notions embraced by the current generation of critical inquirers. The central of those is the denial to authorial intentions their rightful place in the study of the reception of literature. "Rightful," I hurry to point out, should *not* be taken to imply any kind of sacrosanct status. My approach to human agency is entirely more moderate, not to say commonsensical—taking intentions to be a vital, if not always fully accessible or even reliable, facet of literary interpretation.[5]

Likewise, contesting critical and metacritical evocations of the "literary text," I argue that to the extent "literary" entails anything like "aesthetic," the term is a conceptual oxymoron and as such a primary candidate for disciplinary reassessment. To this end I marshal a series of case studies designed to bring out categorical—both ontological and art-interpretive—distinctions between texts and works. Arguing against the centrality of the notion of text and thus against the concomitant marginalization of the concept of work, I advance an alternative to the theories of interpretation associated chiefly with poststructuralism.

To facilitate this, the book is structured conceptually like an hourglass. It opens with a basic inquiry into the ontology of literary art and follows with the analysis of the principles of aesthetic interpretation. It then narrows the scope to investigate the nature of narrative fiction as well as the interpretive guidelines for "fleshing out" story contents (the problem of fictional truth). Toward the end it fans out again to revisit a broader set of methodological points about intentions and interpretations before closing with a look at the evolutionary implications for the notion of the aesthetic and for aesthetics *tout court*.

Since it would not do to talk about the principles of interpretation before determining what it is that we are interpreting in the first place, Chapter 2 opens with the identity of literary artworks. Literary theory today may be agog with polemics on sundry aspects of interpretation, but amid these metacritical thrusts and parries surprisingly little effort is directed at the most fundamental research category of all. Yet, recalcitrant as it has proven to be, the concept of an artwork lies at the heart of the entire critical enterprise, not least because of its ramifications for the ways in which we (should) interact with literature.

On the other hand, little of such reticence is in evidence among analytic philosophers who clearly consider themselves equal to the task of clarifying what it is that artists bring into being. Consequently, my analysis rides coattails on the work of aestheticians who analyze the nature of art, of which literature forms a natural phylum. Taking ontological identity and aesthetic function to be distinct items—*contra* proponents of functionalism, of whom I will have more to say as I go along—I thus separate inquiries into "What Artworks Are" (identity) from "How to Tell Artworks from One Another" (individuation).[6]

Having said that, I do not extend these ontological investigations to other forms of art. Limitations of space, coherence, and not least knowledge dictate that I restrict myself to the only corner of the art world of which I can speak with some confidence. My purpose is thus to clarify matters pertaining to the analysis of narrative fiction, passing over other forms of art, such as painting, music, sculpture, and stage performance. Fortunately, as we shall see in Chapter 2, ontological theses devised for artworks in general prove to be disciplined yet flexible enough to capture what is essential about works of literature.

With the question of identity out of the way, I look at a couple of concepts typically twinned without a moment's hesitation. "Works" and "texts" are terms so ingrained in contemporary critical discourse that many scholars take them to be pretheoretical and, as such, in little need of elucidation. Many, as a matter of fact, employ them interchangeably (sort of like "cell phone" and "mobile"), begging the question of whether we could dispense with one of them without any loss. Indeed, poststructuralism—which in many ways still drives the disciplinary paradigm—typically privileges the notion of text, although, as conclusively demonstrated by textual scholars proper, without much reflection on what this move entails.[7]

Critics who do distinguish works from texts, on the other hand, often omit to tell us why this ought to be so. Filling this crucial lacuna, in Chapter 3 I disambiguate the concepts of work and text, supply a chain of reasoning for why they are not identical, and elaborate the framework for applying either concept en route to individuating artworks. I devote especial consideration to the concept of text, this catch-all of so much critical and metacritical discourse. I detail not only how complex it is but also how it is yoked to contexts where we really speak of work. Loosely speaking, literary texts can be—and frequently are—used synonymously with literary works, but this substitutiveness does not extend to contexts where the difference *is* of consequence.

In Chapters 4 and 5 I take under the microscope the category that forms the interpretive bread and butter for most literary critics and scholars: narrative fiction. The very fact of asking what makes fiction *fiction* signals a significant departure from colloquial parlance whereby fiction is assumed to be synonymous with literature. Analytically speaking they are, naturally, anything but. Bertrand Russell's *Autobiography* is magnificent literature but not fiction. Andrew Wiles's proof of Fermat's last "theorem" is a magnificent nonfiction but hardly a work of literature—not, at least, in any widespread sense of the term.[8]

Armed with a constellation of arguments grounded in speech-act theory, I thus distinguish fiction ("made-up stories, usually in prose") from nonfiction ("prose that has not been made up"), as per a recent, unintentionally hilarious handbook for creative writers.[9] Then, in Chapter 6 I take on the problem of fictional truth. The matter is deceptively simple and concerns the assumptions *all* readers must make to fill in ubiquitous semantic gaps in the stories they read. The solution involves an intricate, if for the most part tacit, type of reflexive interaction (game) between the author and the reader conducted principally by means of the text—though not only.

While unraveling the inner workings of this interpretive *pas de deux,* I revisit the notion of agency to demonstrate how a moderate appeal to authorial intentions overcomes a range of theoretical and practical obstacles in anchoring interpretation in literary works. This part of my analysis might help some literary theorists overcome the interpretive split-personality syndrome frequently exhibited in contacts with literature. A characteristic symptom is the discrepancy between their sometimes wildly implausible theories and the sensible (not to say commonsensical) practical aesthetics they fall back on when face to face with a story.

Who could forget Roland Barthes and Michel Foucault, who propounded the death of the author in books that never failed to ascribe their authorship? Or Jacques Derrida, who breezily endorsed the intertextual playfulness of contextless referents while protesting that his numerous debunkers failed to get *his* message right? Indeed, the chasm between their words and deeds was so pronounced that even Paul de Man—himself no stranger to deconstruction—reproached his self-defeating colleagues:

> In all of them a paradoxical discrepancy appears between the general statements they make about the nature of literature (statements on which they base their critical methods) and the actual results of their interpretations.[10]

Moving on, to get a better grasp on the role of intentions in interpretation, Chapter 7 revisits the standard objections raised against intentionalism in the context of literary study. My task is made easier by the fact that the conceptual map for skirting the Scylla of radical intentionalism and the Charybdis of radical anti-intentionalism already will have been put in place in the preceding chapters. As such, I contrast work-directed interpretations and textual readings, fortifying this theoretical distinction with the analysis of a genre-busting novel from one of the most aesthetically versatile American writers, the late Thomas M. Disch.

Finally, to cap the book, evolution. Despite prodigious amounts of print on the nature of literature and literary-critical axiology, there is as yet little consensus on how to approach the analysis of beauty and truth. Beauty or, *pace* Longinus, sublimity has traditionally been yoked to the truth of representation, whether naturalistically mimetic, self-reflexively impressionistic, or any other. Taking stock of the recent work in evolutionary and evolutionary-literary studies, I argue that a promising approach to the analysis of narrative truth emerges from the work on behavioral veracity within the neo-Darwinian paradigm—thus bringing us full circle to the questions of methodology and disciplinary research.

## A MODEL FOR A SCIENCE OF LITERATURE

*One can construct a theory of literature, and use individual works as documents, and one can read individual works in the light of a theory of literature, or, rather, in an attempt to make the very principles of a theory of literature emerge from the examination of individual works.*
UMBERTO ECO, *ON LITERATURE*

Taking *Poetics* as a model for a science of literature, Lubomir Doležel proposed that Aristotle's efforts can be construed in two distinct, though not unrelated, ways.[11] First of all, *Poetics* is a volume of practical criticism replete with staging advice for the working dramatist that advances structural and, by derivation, aesthetic judgments about the works to which it refers. On the other hand, it is distinctly more philosophical in flavor, laying down a succession of normative postulates of inquiry into the aesthetics of tragedy, comedy, epic poetry, and dithyrambic poetry.

Either way, Aristotle's vision is much more analytical and empirical than any conception of criticism as the foundry of value judgments or of metacriticism as the study of literary beauty. In view of these differences, before jumping into the thick of argument and counterargument, it may help to distinguish aesthetics as it had been understood historically from aesthetics in the analytic vein. After all, in its original context, the ancient Greek *aisthesis* or *aesthesis* signified no more than perception or sensation, being conspicuously mute on the subject of the sublime.

Although metacritical interest in the arts goes back to the Babylonians, modern aesthetics and the philosophy of art did not come into their own until the publication of Kant's *Critique of Judgement* in 1790. As far as analytic aesthetics is concerned, it has even been argued that it did not coalesce into a professional discipline until the 1940s, roughly co-extensive with the birth of the American Society for Aesthetics and the launch of *Journal of Aesthetics and Art Criticism*. To complicate matters further, debates rage nowadays whether there even exists a set of judgments that could be marked off as strictly aesthetic, that is, categorically separate from artistic, cognitive, or ethical.[12]

Be that as it may, the conceptual nucleus of modern aesthetics centers on the heterogeneous, not to say interdisciplinary, inquiry into the philosophy of art. This, in turn, entails inquiry into the assortment of beliefs, concepts, and theories that impinge on our contacts with phenomena that involve aesthetic experience and value. Given how broad and inclusive this characterization is, it invites an obvious rejoinder. Aesthetic values and art have been intimately associated with each other in virtually all human cultures. Why, then, differentiate aesthetics from the philosophy of art at all?

The reasons are twofold. On the one hand, not all aesthetic encounters and judgments necessarily involve art. For many people naturescapes— or, for me, the fastidious creations of bower birds—can be a source of wondrous beauty. On the other hand, not all judgments about art are aesthetic in character. Cognitive, moral, functional, even institutional considerations play a role in contacts with artworks on a regular basis. It is for no other reason that in 1964 Arthur Danto coined the term "artwork" to detach analysis of aesthetic creations from their implicit

Art or nature? Exquisite bower design. *On the one hand, not all aesthetic encounters and judgments necessarily involve art. For many people naturescapes—or, for me, the fastidious creations of bower birds—can be a source of wondrous beauty.*

valuation as "Art." In sum, instead of mapping one to one, aesthetics and the philosophy of art only cross-sect each other's domains.

If modern aesthetics is only a little more than two centuries old, analytic philosophy is younger still by about a century, evolving from the work of Frege, Russell, Wittgenstein, and the logical positivists of the Vienna Circle. One needs to distinguish here the *school* of analytic philosophy associated with the Vienna Circle—which largely dissipated in the 1960s after Quine and others had battered its methodological premises—and the *type* of philosophy descended from that tradition. In this book I am naturally interested in the latter, not least because even in its short history the analytic orientation has proven immensely fruitful.

Surveying its meteoric career in the opening chapter of *Blackwell Companion to Philosophy,* John Searle gives it an enthusiastic two thumbs up. Nothing in the history of philosophy, he contends, has come close to the analytic method in "rigour, clarity, intelligence and, above all, its intellectual content" (1996a, 23). Audacious as the assertion is, it would be difficult to contest (not that such has not been tried). The principal mode of doing philosophy in the United States, Canada, Great Britain, Australia, New Zealand, Scandinavia, Germany, and more and more in other parts of Europe and South America is indeed analytic. So much so, points out Searle, that scholars in the nonanalytic tradition "feel it necessary to define their position in relation to analytic philosophy" (1).

If analytic philosophy can be said to deal with the analysis of meaning, analytic aesthetics can be said to deal with the meaning of art and aesthetic experience. Meaning here ought to be understood inclusively—from the ontology of art, the nature of fiction, the nature of representation, and the mechanisms of emotional response to art to the nature of aesthetic properties and their relation to artistic, cognitive, or moral ones. That even this limited inventory is a far cry from the historical conception of aesthetics as the study of beauty is no accident. In a legacy of John Passmore's crusade against wild-goose chasing after essentialist traits of *all* art, research today is typically limited to narrowly defined problems within a single art form—as it is in my case.[13]

The rationale behind this methodological modesty is simple. In the spirit of analytic philosophy *tout court,* it is felt that only by proceeding systematically and piecemeal does work in aesthetics stand a chance of maturing into a coherent, cumulative research paradigm. Indeed, contends Bernard Williams in the second prologue to the above-mentioned *Companion to Philosophy,* this is the analysts' recipe for success—"as opposed to work done in their local departments of literature" (26). Even as with other literary scholars and critics I mutter "Ouch," this disciplinary dis is worth a pause with regard to what it implies about research in literary and cultural studies.

For better or—as I had opportunity to demonstrate in *Between Literature and Science* (2000) and *Of Literature and Knowledge* (2007)—for worse, such condemnations are for the most part well deserved.[14] Their repercussions for the task at hand transcend, however, the occasional oddities professed by professors of literature in the name of this or that methodological fiat. When a half-century ago C. P. Snow bemoaned the schism between the Two Cultures, he certainly did not envision a situation where two neighboring disciplines, such as literary studies and analytic aesthetics, could be so estranged from each other.

And yet, even as philosophers habitually lay siege to problems in literary theory, few critics are aware of the work conducted under the banner of analytic aesthetics. How many of us are conversant with, for instance, David Lewis's Reality and Mutual Belief principles? Or with their roles in defining the agenda for the analysis of fictional truth—that is, for the interpretation of implicit story content, indispensable to the grasp of all narratives? The sad truth is that, despite vows of interdisciplinarity, theorists today remain almost completely negligent of analytic aesthetics.

Nor is this disciplinary isolation a latter-day phenomenon. Twenty years ago Anita Silvers took stock of the situation in an essay whose Age of Aquarius title, "Letting the Sunshine In," evoked the spirit of harmony and understanding. Even so, upon surveying the would-be cross-currents between art criticism and aesthetics, her verdict was far from sanguine. With the one possible exception of Wimsatt and Beardsley's "Intentional Fallacy," she wrote, "historians and critics of the arts treated the work of the analytic aestheticians at best as irrelevant, but sometimes as malevolent" (1987, 137).

Twenty years thence, the Modern Language Association's 2007 *MLA International Bibliography* has its own statistical story to tell. A keyword search for "analytic" and "aesthetics" yields all of 22 hits, only half of which are actually devoted to analytic aesthetics. The disparity with the disciplinary mainstream is stark: "literary theory" registers more than 38,000 hits, "aesthetics" and "literature" more than 8,000, and "aesthetics" and "literary theory" more than 2,000. "Literary theory" and "analytic aesthetics" renders all of 3. On the authority of this completest database in literary studies, the conclusion is hard to avoid: while aesthetics is quite popular, analytic aesthetics is not.

This lack of rapport may be symptomatic of a broader tendency within the humanities toward disciplinary autarchy. The recent rise of molecular genetics, neurophysiology, sociobiology, psychophysics, or biomechanics, to name a few, attests to the fusion of scientific research across disparate fields of inquiry. Given their common subject (the arts), research arsenal (linguistic and counterfactual analysis), and interest (theory of interpretation), it is therefore hard to understand why, as the editor of the 1998 *Encyclopedia of Aesthetics* rues, so "many people concerned with art and culture today seem to want to distance themselves from aesthetics."[15]

Like a Serengeti waterhole that can nurture fish, reptiles, mammals, and fowl alike, analytic aesthetics is capable of nurturing scholars from departments other than philosophy. After all, its object of study—any and all modes of artistic creation—is intrinsically comparative. In this it is mirrored by the discipline itself for, in the quintessentially cross-campus fashion, aesthetics lies on the cusp of literary studies, art history, evolutionary studies, translation theory, linguistics, pragmatics, semiotics, philosophy of language, philosophy of mind, metaphysics, cognitive science, sociology, psychology, and law and ethics, to name a few.

Literary studies itself, with its multiple subdomains such as epistemology, narratology, and genre theory, typifies a multidisciplinary environment, but the same can be said of the visual and performance arts. One of the venerable topics in aesthetics is, in fact, the extension of ontological, stylistic, or structural regularities from one form of art into others. Cutting through the traditional ways of looking at artworks—be it according to historical period, nationality, mode of narration, modality of expression, or any other—aesthetics prides itself on being inherently interdisciplinary and comparative.

## THE STATE OF THE ART IN AESTHETICS AND ART CRITICISM

*Unfortunately, "postmodern" is a term bon a tout faire. I have the impression that it is applied today to anything the user of the term happens to like.*
UMBERTO ECO, *POSTSCRIPT TO THE NAME OF THE ROSE*

Against this backdrop, it may not be amiss to pause over the recent endeavor to summarize the state of the art in aesthetics and art criticism. The above-mentioned *Encyclopedia of Aesthetics* casts itself in this very light, as an effort to define the field and the research in the field for the twenty-first century. As such, it implicitly invites comparison with other leading "chains of knowledge" of the past. Diderot and D'Alambert's *Encyclopédie* was, after all, not just a collection of knowledge from antiquity on but also a method of bringing order to it. The legendary eleventh edition of the *Britannica* was not a mere litany of facts but a reasoned summary of the practical and speculative research of its era.

In keeping with the hyperexplosion and consequent fragmentation of knowledge in the present age, one might suppose the goals before the *Encyclopedia of Aesthetics* to be somewhat less assuming. Not so. According to the editors, this

> first English-language reference work on this scale devoted
> to aesthetics offers a combination of historical reference
> material and critical discussions of contemporary aesthetics
> intended for general readers and experts alike.[16]

This, in other words, is it—more than two thousand pages on the ways in which we interpret works of art and the culture in which they are embedded. In the same spirit, the four volumes bring together not only philosophers (analytic and otherwise) but also art historians, sociologists, psychologists, anthropologists, and other theorists and metatheorists of art and culture. Given these claims to comprehensiveness, one may be allowed a quick tour of the encyclopedia insofar as, in many ways, it makes for an instructive foil for my own project.

To begin, the publication that prides itself on being *the* reference work in aesthetics—and which actually indexes the distinction between works and texts—continues to conflate and, as such, confuse these fundamental concepts. Evidently the bulk of the encyclopedists are ignorant of, or simply ignore, the categorical distinction between a (fair) text and an intentional aesthetic construct such as the work.[17] The neglect of research by philosophers in the analytic tradition is, in fact, the norm rather than the exception. The seemingly comprehensive chapter on fiction contains not a word on the problem of fictional truth, a central and widely debated topic in analytic aesthetics.

Equally striking is the lack of an entry on evolution, which is implicated in so many spheres of cultural activity, including literature.[18] Connections between literary aesthetics and literary epistemology are so plentiful that they give renewed credence to arguments that aesthetic values employed to define *belles lettres* may, indeed, need to include a distinct sort of cognitive value. Given that all cognitive theories rest at the bottom on the modern evolutionary synthesis, this is a startling oversight. Not even the article on empirical aesthetics—a growing subfield that combines philosophical analysis, literary theory, and psychometric experiments— makes any note of neo-Darwinian theory, including theory of mind.[19]

Theory of mind (commonly shortened as TOM) refers to our astonishing and astonishingly successful ability to read people's minds—or more precisely to read minds off people's behavioral and linguistic cues, often provided for that purpose. Such mind reading has nothing to do with ESP or any other paranormal mumbo jumbo. It is a normal, universal, and indispensable component of our innate folk psychology by means of which we attribute mental states (beliefs, desires, intentions) to other beings and have mental states attributed to us. Theory of mind, in short, is a process of hypothesis formation about one another's mind to make sense of one another's behavior.

If formal research into mental representations of the world can be said to have begun with Piaget, its contemporary renaissance is usually traced to David Premack and Guy Woodruff's 1978 article "Does the Chimpanzee Have a Theory of Mind?"[20] Since then theory of mind has surged to the foreground in fields such as psychopathology (studies of autism, for example), neurology, primatology, evolutionary ecology, and—not least—analytic philosophy of mind and language. Indeed, thirty years on the investigative circle seems to have closed, inasmuch as theory of mind today informs a growing number of inquiries into the intentional stance one needs to adopt to interpret artworks. As such, it forms the empirical backbone behind my analytic approach.

Theory of mind is all about recognizing the role of cognition and intentions in our biological and cultural lives. It is about recognizing purposes and goals—whether in real life or in fiction—within a framework of human behavior. Ultimately, it is about recognizing other people as intentional agents. As such, research into TOM provides the latest and final nail in the coffin of poststructuralist criticism defined by anti-authorial and anti-intentionalist dogmas. And apparently for this very reason, theory of mind and other evolutionary and literary-evolutionary topics are conspicuously absent from the *Encyclopedia of Aesthetics*. Instead, the editors prefer to genuflect to cognitive and interpretive relativism.

It is more than a mere question of poststructuralist aesthetics occupying a disproportionate amount of headroom. More to the point, one detects a calculated endeavor *not* to channel debate according to the best available research but, in a triumph of plurality over argumentative evidence, to compile a list of mutually critiquing choruses instead. Pointedly, the editors concede as much in the preface. In a homage to postmodern skepticism about cognition they "to incorporate the contemporary doubts about the encyclopedia into its very structure."[21] This open abdication of intellectual responsibility is especially striking in a discipline such as aesthetics, in which theories are in many cases a matter of ongoing work and which could benefit from a judicious pruning of branches that have failed to bear fruit.

The contrast with the principles of literary study enunciated already two and a half thousand years ago in *Poetics* could scarcely be starker. "Thought," counseled Aristotle, "is found where something is proved to be or not to be" (64). The gulf between his stress on rigorous argument and today's duty-free theorizing speaks for itself. In a more contemporary environment, his point is eloquently reiterated in "From Small Beginnings: Literary Theorists Encounter Analytic Philosophy" (1990). In this rare example of informed philosophical anatomy from a professor of English, David Gorman reviews one of the rare encounters between story scholars and analytic aestheticians.

Setting the record straight on what it means for literary theorists to add to—and thus to contest—the work in analytic philosophy, his verdict is decidedly unflattering. Addressing himself to a collection of essays on analytic philosophy, deconstruction, and literary theory, Gorman's running theme is the critics' refusal or plain inability to do their philosophical homework. In fact, his diagnosis could in many ways serve as the motto for *Literature, Analytically Speaking*: "The main problem afflicting modern literary theory lies in the remarkable willingess of most theorists to accept, with little examination, dicta of the philosophical authorities who have impressed them for some reason, as opposed to thinking through such ideas critically" (650).

The point is simple but worth reiterating: the power of analytic philosophy rests in its methodology rather than in any one of its specific formulations. The latter, by analogy with the sciences, may be superseded by subsequent research—conducted, significantly, along methodologically sound lines. Literary critics who aspire to tackle issues in philosophy, writes Gorman, or who wish to tackle issues in critical theory in a manner respected by philosophers must therefore recognize that "exegesis cannot substitute for argument" (655). To this Rule Number One of Interdisciplinary Scholarship I can only append Rule Number Two: "Learn Fast Rule Number One."

Unfortunately, in the wider world of knowledge hunters, the research credentials of literary and cultural studies remain shaky at best. There is no need to reinvoke Bernard Williams's opprobrium from the previous section, either. A 1989 bestseller in the philosophy of science disparages the most egregious methodological excesses as none other than "Research by Literary Interpretation." The hallmark of the pseudoscientists, points out the author, is to "focus upon the words, not on the underlying facts and reasons. In this regard the pseudoscientists act like lawyers gathering precedents and using these as arguments, rather than attending to what has actually been communicated."[22]

These censures do not seem to bother literary theorists, the better known of whom actually boasts that his kind of analysis "seeks not to find the foundation and the conditions of truth."[23] To be fair, such attitudes are not confined to literary criticism. Laments in classical studies about intellectual damage inflicted by "new historicism, or history without facts" are picked up in anthropology whose sorry state is attributed to its theoretical apparatus, drawn "alas, from cultural studies." Historians themselves are up in arms against the so-called New History, according to which "'Mickey Mouse may in fact be more important to an understanding of the 1930s than Franklin Roosevelt."

In this context, the 2006 special issue of the *Yearbook of English Studies,* published under the aegis of the Modern Humanities Research Association, may mark the beginning of the end of such laissez-faire practices. Traditional in content (Victorian literature), it is anything but traditional in its methodological orientation. Conspicuously gone is the constructivist/deconstructivist element that has given literary studies a bad name with recondite theorizing and inscrutable jargon. Indeed, if the imprint of this leading research association in the humanities can be taken as the harbinger of things to come, agency and intentionality are making a comeback at the expense of postmodernist theory and theorese.

## NEW VISTAS FOR LOOKING AT ART

*We thus find ourselves facing not an opposition (as was long thought) between a normative poetics and an aesthetics . . . but, rather, the oscillation between a descriptive theory and a critical practice that presuppose each other in turn.*
UMBERTO ECO, *ON LITERATURE*

Over the past two decades or so, a series of pivotal books in analytic aesthetics opened new vistas for looking at art and, for that matter, at the discipline itself. Confined to philosophy, this disciplinary renaissance did little, however, to bring literary scholars into the analytic program. Arguably the only book-length study that comes close to combining the tools of analytic philosophy and the interests of literary theory is Peter Lamarque and Stein Olsen's *Truth, Fiction, and Literature* (1994). However, despite its length, their investigation is directed almost entirely at the problem of fictional truth and, as such, is of limited value to story scholars searching for a broader paradigm.

Even more to the point, although they are preoccupied with literature and literary analysis, Lamarque and Olsen write strictly with the trained philosopher rather than the literary theorist in mind. The consequences are predictable, insofar as one would look in vain for any response from literary critics to what is, after all, a major contribution to the field. In short, much as one might wish it were otherwise, the gulf that divides literary metacriticism and philosophical aesthetics remains today as deep as ever. Be that as it may, my interest in analytic aesthetics is proportional precisely to the extent that some of its recent studies can serve as signposts on the road to interdisciplinary fence mending.

Here are a few examples of the research program I have in mind: Richard Shusterman's *Analytic Aesthetics* (1989); Gregory Currie's *The Nature of Fiction* (1990); Kendall Walton's *Mimesis as Make-Believe* (1990); Stephen Davies's *Definitions of Art* (1991); Gary Iseminger's *Intention and Interpretation* (1992); Jerrold Levinson's *The Pleasures of Aesthetics* (1996); Robert Stecker's *Artworks* (1996); Joseph Margolis's *What, After All, Is a Work of Art?* (1999); Nöel Carroll's *Theories of Art Today* (2000); Michael Krausz's *Is There a Single Right Interpretation?* (2002); Paisley Livingston and Berys Gaut's *The Creation of Art* (2003); and Livingston's *Art and Intention* (2005).

Naturally, this is only a short list of philosophical publications devoted to disentangling the web of aesthetic and sociocultural practices known as art. Appearing at the end of a century during which analytic aesthetics emerged as a research discipline and setting the agenda for the century in which I write, they map the continuities and discontinuities between the historical views on art and the current endeavors to theorize them. Offering a portal onto the history, methodology, and the cutting edge of the field, they pursue a number of inquiries homologous to those at the heart of literary studies.

Not to look too far, one can mention inquiries into the nature of works of fiction (such as their ontology), the significance of authorial intentions in interpretation, or the nature of aesthetic appreciation. However, in contrast to the still prevalent mode of doing literary and cultural studies, by and large analytic philosophers refrain from methodological fiats and sweeping generalizations on (postmodern) society, culture, language, or art. Instead, they take on systematically defined problems and dissect them with a view to internal cogency and critical practice.

By and large, this is also the path on which I embark. Weighing the theoretical pros and cons, I mount a series of arguments in support of what I consider to be compelling accounts of the identity and individuation of artworks, the text/work distinction, the nature of fiction, the problem of fictional truth, the relation of authorial intentions to critical interpretations, and the evolutionary roots of some aesthetic judgments. Given how unfamiliar all this philosophizing may be to at least some critics and students of literature, at every step I copiously illustrate my discussions with literary examples and case studies.

All the same, a lingering doubt may rear its hydra head at this point. Why devote time and energy at all to what might, after all, be construed as merely another addition to the already crowded supermarket in literary theory? One, the skeptic might persevere, that does not even properly belong to literary studies, as the word "philosophy," which graces more than one subtitle of the books on aesthetics, would suggest? Although seldom couched in such parochial terms, this variant on *ignoramus et ignorabimus* is widespread enough to warrant a brief response.

The object of such skepticism is a neighboring discipline whose research program bears on a range of topics of immediate concern to us. For decades now, with analytical and evidentiary transparency rarely evinced in literary theory, the philosophers have advanced the understanding of some long-standing, not to say foundational, principles of interpreting artworks. Notwithstanding the often bone-dry and esoteric style of their analyses, some even keep an eye on the practical consequences of adopting their proposals in critical and classroom practice.[24]

To take the first example off the shelf, in the chapter on "Intention and Interpretation of Literature" in *The Pleasures of Aesthetics*, Jerrold Levinson sets out to dispel doubts about one type of intention-driven approach to interpretation (hypothetical intentionalism) and, by extension, about all and any intention-driven approaches to interpretation *period*. Indeed, his series of arguments leaves little doubt that—however alien the notion may be to the avatars of Barthes or Derrida—some moderate form of intentionalism is an inalienable part of our contacts with works of literature.

Yet one would look in vain for a concerted response from literary critics to this explicit contribution, and implicit challenge, to their patterns of inquiry—unless, that is, steadfast ignorance is the response. If so, however, it is a highly inopportune one, given how ongoing research in analytic aesthetics offers hope for the eventual emergence of a coherent and cumulative program of inquiry into sundry problems of literary interpretation. Indeed, the progressive character of such work provides the best justification of its centrality within Anglo-American aesthetics and within philosophy in general.

It is in this spirit that Joseph Margolis exhorted his colleagues in the 1990s to exorcise the dreariness of aesthetics. In the context, the dreariness had less to do with hair-splitting dullness than with revitalizing the discipline, partly via infusion of ideas from nonanalytically minded critics and partly by adopting a less reverential stance to the disciplinary pantheon. There is little to gain, chided the philosopher, from deferring to the sages of the past whenever research has already surpassed them. One should not hesitate to admit that a "considerable part of current Anglo-American aesthetics is simply superannuated" (1993, 134).

One does not have to imagine the reaction from literary theorists on being told that a considerable part of *their* professional lore is simply superannuated. The howls of outrage that greeted the Sokal hoax from humanists loath to forgo genuflections to deconstructive, psychoanalytic, and other disciplinary authorities were certainly eloquent enough.[25] Yet this is exactly what I propose—a different methodological apparatus in the service of a different research paradigm. And the extent to which I feel justified in turning to analytic aesthetics is the extent to which it is driven by argument and not exegesis.

For these reasons, I find it hard to accept the (qualitative) remonstrations that literary studies and analytic aesthetics are incommensurate in their research or the (quantitative) defense that the inundation of print precludes *rapprochement* with research outside lit crit. "Who has the leisure to master other-disciplinary paradigms when there is no time to read even a fraction of what is published in one's own profession?" goes the not wholly unjustified plaint. Yet, even if only by virtue of appropriation of inquiries traditionally in the provenance of literary-critical theory, analytic aesthetics *is* a part of the profession.

Preoccupied as it is with critical and metacritical theory directed at textual and contextual interpretation, literary scholarship has little to lose in the bargain except poor methodological habits and disciplinary isolation. At the same time, by keeping abreast of the discipline whose findings bear straightforwardly on our own domain, literary scholars can cross-pollinate and thus revitalize joint inquiry into any number of recalcitrant interpretive conundra. It is with this expectation that, in the chapters to follow, I take a look at literature through the lens framed by analytic aesthetics.

It would be foolish to think that any one book can cut through the Gordian knots of theory that have eluded thinkers from Aristotle on. Accordingly, *Literature, Analytically Speaking* should not be confused with a kind of definitive, not to say megalomaniacal, *Principia Literaria*. Some of its formulations are bound to be challenged by subsequent researchers—as they ought to be. Given the disputes among generations of literary critics from Horace, Plotinus, Sidney, Pope, Arnold, Taine, and Propp to Wellek, Warren, Beardsley, Frye, Todorov, Hirsch, Fish, Eco, and innumerable others, anything else would be unthinkable.

That said, I do advance a series of precepts that aim to capture the ways in which literary fictions are actually interpreted—never mind the theoretical bumper stickers. For reasons defended in the chapters that follow, these are also the ways that *ought to* inform any coherent theory of interpretation. Certain aspects of our contacts with literature, in other words, I take to be rationally secure, even as many problems remain in need of refinement or full-scale analysis. Identifying some of those as I go along, I hope that this analytically driven effort entices literary scholars to join the fray, with disciplinary and interdisciplinary benefits to all.

As in all interdisciplinary bridge building, selections and simplifications are inevitable. There is nothing wrong with that—as long as they do not amount to gross distortions. Although building on one another, each of the book's eight chapters forms therefore a complete whole. Each building block of each argument is made as systematic and transparent as I can make it, so that each can be considered on its own merit. When important theoretical beliefs and interpretive practices are challenged, justification is required at every step of the way, and readers will be justified in taking their time to ponder every argumentative twist and turn. Only this can provide the confidence that the path taken is, indeed, the correct one.

In the end, some philosophers may find the exposition too plodding or too simplified for their liking. Conversely, some literary theorists may feel that it leaves too many stepping-stones unstepped on while complicating what is plain and simple. Perils of this nature cannot be entirely avoided insofar as they come with the interdisciplinary territory. To the philosophers I can only respond that a literary-critical study that corroborates the work in analytic aesthetics shows that both are on the right track. To the critics I can only say that many of the matters considered here *are* complex and knotty and once again encourage them to stay the course in the hope that, overall, the methodological pros outweigh the cons.

In his classic essays Francis Bacon taught that truth emerges more readily from error than from confusion. Even if one's findings are in error, he observed, it is the lucidity of the arguments outfitted in their support that permits one to deduce that it is so and rectify the error. Thus, to the extent that *Literature, Analytically Speaking* speaks analytically, it speaks the language of Bacon. For in the spirit of scientific analysis—in the sense of conforming to the basic criteria common to all rational inquiry—it foregrounds its analytic premises as a way of inviting *you* to put them to the critical test.

*Two*    A R T W O R K

> *These literary entities are here among us. They were not there from the beginning of time as (perhaps) square roots and Pythagoras's theorems were, but now that they have been created by literature and nourished by our emotional investment in them, they do exist and we have to come to terms with them.*
>
> UMBERTO ECO, *ON LITERATURE*

# WHAT IS ART?

*That depends on the format of our ontology.*
UMBERTO ECO, *ON LITERATURE*

Over the ages there has been no shortage of critical manifestos on the order of Horace's *Ars Poetica,* Sidney's *Defence of Poesie,* Wordsworth's preface to *Lyrical Ballads,* or Tolstoy's "What Is Art?" As rationalizations for the class of writing practiced by their exponents, they are widely and justly famous. As ontological propositions, however, they are rather straightforward flops. Take, for example, the recollection of emotion in tranquility. The stipulation is hardly sufficient insofar as a statement to the police, post facto pressing charges for a traumatic assault, need hardly be art. Nor is it necessary, insofar as it rules out art—for example, Keith Jarrett's *Sun Bear* improvisations—created extempore.

Whatever the reason, literary scholars have by and large ceded questions of ontology to philosophers. Indeed, outside of Wellek and Warren's *Theory of Literature* (1949), little effort seems to have been expanded on inquiries into the nature of literary creations. For that matter, not even Wellek and Warren live up to the promise expressed in the title of their Chapter 12, "The Mode of Existence of a Literary Work of Art." The lion's share of their discussion goes, after all, to disproving that a literary work is a physical object (printed page), a succession of sounds when recited, or an experience in the mind of the author or reader.[1]

When it comes, however, to telling us what a literary artwork is, the two critics are decidedly less forthcoming. Promisingly, they begin with an intimation that a poem is "a structure of norms" (151), which is presumably a structure that bears certain aesthetic characteristics. When it comes, however, to elucidating the nature of these structures and characteristics, the authors shortchange us with a banality—they have "a special ontological status" (157)—never to return to it again. The analysis ends, in other words, where it ought to begin.

Not much appears to have changed during the intervening decades. One would indeed be hard pressed to find more than a trace of ontological analysis even in comprehensive introductions to modern literary theory. Steven Connor's 1997 *Postmodernist Culture: An Introduction to Theories of the Contemporary* provides literally a textbook example. Its one and only reference to the subject, namely that "the ontological character of the postmodernist novel is shown in its concern with the making of autonomous worlds" (130), only manages to muddle the distinction between storyworlds and possible worlds (see Chapter 7).

To be fair, when it comes to questions of identity and individuation, the pickings among philosophers outside the analytic tradition turn out to be equally slim. To take one example, on the authority of one of the more lucid exegetes of Deleuze and Guattari, a work of art is—before all else—a sensation. For scholars inclined to wonder how the sensation of having one's teeth scaled constitutes an artwork, the exegete elaborates the concept in the following gem of precision. A work of art is a sensation that "does nothing if it does not restore us to our constitutive infinity by creating the world anew."[2]

Another critic, who valiantly tries to extract Maurice Blanchot's ontology of art, concedes that Blanchot's ontology "excludes very little, almost nothing, not even people."[3] Outside of Neil LaBute's unforgettable film *The Shape of Things,* I assume you are as baffled—albeit flattered—as I am to be judged an artwork. In yet another misapprehension of the issues at stake, Judith R. Blau expatiates on "postontological art," an oxymoron intelligible only in view of her theoretical underpinnings—which come from Lyotard—and her odd conception of aesthetics mainly as "a specialty of moral philosophy" (2001, 191).

Examples of postmodern misconceptions about ontology can be multiplied almost at will. In *After Ontology* (2001), William D. Melaney takes an extreme position by dismissing the subject altogether with "metaphysics has been 'deconstructed'" (7). In its place he offers alternatives on the order of "Heidegger's ontological approach to Kant suggests that the role of the imagination as the nonrational root of synthesis contains the promise for a new understanding of truth" (25). All such "ontologies" are inherently irrefutable and as such vacuous. What they actually prove is that metaphysical speculation is, indeed, a genre apart from logical analysis.

Given all this confusion, it is important to make clear right from the start what we are after. The most straightforward way to understand ontology may be as a classificatory—value-neutral—schema to help scholars determine which entities in the world outside are, and which are not, artworks. More precisely, for any *x*, the theory should tell us if *x* is an artwork (identity condition) and distinguish it from other works (individuation). Pointedly, it is not designed to tell us if *x* is a particularly good or particularly bad work of art, though it may help us select the criteria for forming such opinions.

In short, ontologies of art are not to be confused with theories of art, which are meant to account for artworks' aesthetic value, institutional status, and such like. To be sure, all ontologies have ramifications for the type of criteria according to which aesthetic values are decided. But in and of themselves, they have little to say about artworks' value, status, and/or rank. Bearing these preliminaries in mind, we can now compare two popular yet contrasting accounts of the nature of artworks to emerge during the past two decades. Both are staunchly antifunctionalist in that both deny that art becomes art by dint of its function in the community—typically by being a (rich) source of aesthetic experience.[4]

Jerrold Levinson made his original stab at the ontology of art in "What a Musical Work Is," reprinted in his *Music, Art, and Metaphysics* (1990).[5] Gregory Currie's theses, conceived in part as a counter to Levinson, were spelled out in *An Ontology of Art* (1989), in a chapter titled "Art Works as Action Types," to which Levinson responded with a new round of refinements. A good place to start may be by taking a closer look at Currie's definition of an artwork. An apparent believer that good things come in small sizes, on page 66 in *An Ontology of Art* the aesthetician defines the core of his theory in eight words: "a work of art is an action type."[6]

Currie elaborates this Action Type Hypothesis (ATH) several pages on. A work of art is an action type by means of which the artist "instantiates the event type, *discovering of S via H*" (75). Of the variables *S* and *H*, only the latter is conceptually new. *S* denotes the structure of the artwork in question—in a literary work equivalent to the text. *H*, on the other hand, is a novel concept in aesthetics. It refers to the heuristic—roughly, the norms and guidelines that assist in the process of scientific discovery—which the aesthetician imports from the philosophy of science.[7]

One can see right away what is distinctive about this approach. A work of art is no longer defined in the familiar terms of an object or structural pattern. It is not, in other words, something to touch and trace the texture of, as we oftentimes do with sculptures. Nor is an artwork something that can be listened to, tracking Bach's counterpoint between

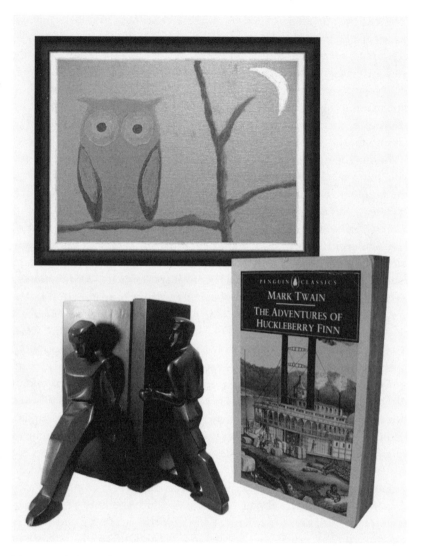

Not artworks? A sculpture, a painting, a narrative. Courtesy of Selina Lai. *A work of art is no longer defined in the familiar terms of an object or structural pattern. It is not, in other words, something to touch and trace the texture of, as we oftentimes do with sculptures.*

different melody lines. Nor is it something to gaze at, following the traces of brushwork as they dissolve into continuous blotches of color. Nor, when it comes to stories, is it something to read and emote with.

What a work of art *is*, according to the aesthetician, is an action type. Before we move on, let me quickly rehash the distinction between type and token.[8] An action type, as the name implies, is a class of actions that can be instantiated by different individuals at different times. For instance, "novel writing" is an action type. At one point or another, both Herman Melville and Herman Wouk instantiated an action type of "writing a novel." In contrast, a given performance of such action—for example, the composition of the specific novel that opens with "Call me Ishmael"—is only a token (individual instance) of the action type.

On the thesis before us, the artist "instantiates the event type, *discovering of S via H.*" In other words, when a novel is brought into being, the artist performs the action of producing its structure—the text—via a certain heuristic path. Tautologically, such an action will always involve a person (one can assume for simplicity's sake that it is not a joint effort, as in the case of the four writers using the pen name Luther Blissett or the Oulipo group, among others). Strangely, however, the identity of the artist is posited to be irrelevant to the identity of the work. Only the structure and the heuristic are said to matter.

This is counterintuitive. According to Currie, although Sinclair Lewis and no one else wrote *It Can't Happen Here* in 1936, Lewis's identity is not relevant to the identity of his work. Even more oddly, not even Lewis's act of composition of the novel is constitutive of its identity. Instead, only the action *type*—the generic action of novel-writing—is said to define the nature of *It Can't Happen Here*. Significantly, Currie's stance seems to be mirrored by Ellen Dissanayake, a researcher into the theory of art from the evolutionary perspective. Over the past twenty years or so Dissanayake has argued forcefully that the definition of art should be linked not to artifacts but rather to a type of action that she calls "making-special." My answer (in the next section) to the philosopher may, therefore, be relevant to the evolutionary scholar.

If what Currie argues seems vexing and confusing, it is the price he is willing to pay for avoiding the errors of those who approach identity solely in terms of local (perceptual) properties. The latter claim, simplified somewhat, that all that counts toward the identity of an artwork is what can be seen, touched, or heard. Indeed, the Action Type Hypothesis is probably best appreciated as a system designed above all to avoid the pitfalls that plague localist ontologies. Localist ontologies are intended to identify and individuate literary works exclusively in terms of local—that is, nonrelational—properties of the text. Nothing brings this goal out as concisely as the avowal from one eminent proponent of ontological localism: a literary work "is the text or script itself."[9]

Inasmuch as I devote much of the next chapter to refuting this assertion, here I shall only flag the doubts raised by claims of the ontological equivalence of works and texts. The Bible exemplifies them quite vividly. Which is *the* biblical text? Is it the synoptic gospels, and if so, in which transcription: Aramaic, Coptic, Greek, or Latin? Or is it some synthetic reconstruction thereof, and if so, does it include the apocrypha, the Nag Hammadi Gnostic codices, or the Dead Sea scrolls? On any localist ontology there appear to be as many Bibles as one cares to enumerate (to say nothing of the *real* problem of individuation, on which more in Chapter 3). Ad hoc appeals to some canonical text do not help either. Even the Authorized King James Bible, commonly believed to preserve the original 1611 orthography, in fact reprints the 1769 modernized text.[10]

In general, typesetter errors, revisions, missing pages, oral literature (no text), and a bevy of other factors confound any straightforward localist ontology. If a literary work is the text itself, was Whitman revising *Leaves of Grass,* or was he creating a new poem every time he added a line? To ward off the idea that such dilemmas crop up only in *belles lettres,* consider the classic sculpture *Laocoön.* Which is *the* structure to be identified with this artwork: the perished Hellenic original, the first-century Roman marbles, the sixteenth-century restoration, or the contemporary re-restoration in line with the artist's reconstructed intentions?[11]

## CURRIE'S ONTOLOGY

*Let us even say, to avoid ontological and metaphysical discussions, that they [literary entities] exist like a cultural habitus, a social disposition.*
UMBERTO ECO, *ON LITERATURE*

Immune to the above quandaries, Currie's ontology clearly improves on localist theories that reduce artworks to their structures (or literary works to texts). Unfortunately, its relative merits are not enough to carry the day. The Action Type Hypothesis suffers from several major and minor drawbacks.

1. The most objectionable part of the ATH is Currie's *rejection of the view that works of art are created*—and, as a corollary, that the identity of the artist is essential to the identity of the work. Both propositions contradict our entrenched beliefs about art. Even in ancient Greek, the language in which some of our first coherent philosophies of art survive, the word for poet meant "maker"—maker of things that did not exist before.

Not accidentally, the identity of the artist who brings into existence a previously nonexistent artifact underpins our socio-aesthetic canons and practices. Copyright laws, intellectual property regulations, and original-ity lawsuits filed to determine authorship of artistic property testify to the cultural recognition of the umbilical link of creators to artworks. It is for no other reason that George Harrison had to fork over a half-million dol-lars to The Chiffons for plagiarizing their tune in "My Sweet Lord"—a suit the ATH would render groundless. It is for no other reason that Para-mount had to settle for an undisclosed sum with Art Buchwald and Alain Bernheim for plagiarizing their storyline in *Coming to America*.[12]

All this is no news to Currie, who admits not only that the "over-whelming majority of us think that works are created" but that "the best explanation of this convergence of opinion is that works are created"![13] My point is that since the philosopher routinely appeals to common practices and commonsense intuitions when critiquing rival theories, he is answerable to them as well. After all, his is not a normative but a descriptive ontology that pledges to be "not unfaithful to our [real life] data" (3). As it stands, however, the ATH gainsays the attitudes of most creators, consumers, and critics of art.

2. In Currie's view, *people can never interact with a work of art,* since a work is posited to be an action type rather than an object to contem-plate, read, or otherwise enjoy. In this he resembles Croce, Lewis, Col-lingwood, and Richards (to say nothing of Plato), all of whom, insisting that art is purely mental in nature, eliminate it from the realm of what is accessible to and sharable among consumers. If, however, your mental architecture is anything like my own, the proposal that we can never interact with a work of art seems too much to ask.

There is probably no more fundamental belief about art than that of the activity in which people create things. Currie himself exemplifies this point when he continues to refer to a painting not as an action type but as a *"result"* or "outcome" of such action.[14] Such usage, acceptable in normal parlance, is at odds with his thesis. While the ATH usefully foregrounds the centrality of the artist's action (type) to the identity of his work, it ends up throwing out the baby with the bathwater. Undoubtedly, the making of art is a type of action, and undoubtedly, artists' actions must be factored into judgments about what they accomplish. But the point about artworks is not so much the action type but the result of a specific action, manifest in the end structure.[15]

3. Since in its original context the heuristic refers to the scientific norms and guidelines that aid the construction of a theory, Currie's espousal of the concept places his ontology in difficulty. The aesthetician actually flip-flops between two different definitions. At first the heuristic is simply the process by which the artwork was created (think, for instance, of the twists and turns that chart the writing of a novel). Thereafter, however, the heuristic becomes a set of *aesthetically relevant facts* about the genesis of a work.[16]

The latter is, of course, a sensible definition of the art-historical context. But then, why not call it such? It is, at the very least, misleading to pin the label "heuristic" on the strategies, methods, and whatever else determines the artist's path to creation—and even more so to pin it on aesthetically relevant facts that fall outside it. Curiously, even though the heuristic lies at the heart of the ATH, Currie expressly declines to describe it in any but the broadest terms, leaving open how much exactly we can know about art. After all, if a work-as-action-type is instantiated by a text attained via a heuristic and if the latter is shrouded in ontological mist, it is anybody's guess what an artwork actually is.

Criticisms of this nature prompted Currie to revise the extension of the heuristic and limit it only to what is pertinent to the path to creation. Oddly, however, now he extends it to factors the artist may have known only in principle—that is, those of which he may actually have been unaware. Causally unconnected facts and events cannot now be ruled out by some minimal interpretation of the heuristic, for example, that it include only those the artist actually knew about. As a result, the historical path to structure needed to identify an artwork must include the sum total of all and any countless things that the artist could have known in principle.[17]

Whatever Currie is talking about at this point clashes not only with any standard conception of heuristic but also with his own definition of it as the artist's path to structure. In the end, according to the ATH, we are not only forever barred from contact with artworks—since they are action types, not tangible tokens—but confront insuperable hurdles when faced with the tokens. Only omniscience, after all, could trace the heuristic that the artist may have known in principle. All this begs the question of what exactly we do perceive and appreciate when we go to a museum, to a concert, or to bed with the dog-eared copy of *A Canticle for Leibowitz*.

4. The ATH stresses the importance of the path to creation with regard to self-referential art such as Duchamp's *Fountain,* an exhibited urinal, or Rauschenberg's *Erased De Kooning Drawing,* from which a drawing by De Kooning was erased to leave a blank. The point is that the structure (text) alone does not determine the relevant properties of an artwork. The structure of a run-of-the-mill urinal and Duchamp's exhibit is identical, but their historical provenance and thus some of their aesthetic features are not.

Some aestheticians question the relevance of such far-out stunts to what is universal about the ontology of art. In the words of one reviewer, making art its own subject matter "may tell us something interesting or amusing but cannot enlighten us about the essential nature of those artworks which are not self-referential (viz. the vast majority)."[18] My caveat is different. Currie is absolutely right to underscore that works of art are determined not only by their structural (textual) properties but equally by relational (nonlocalist) ones. But while his diagnosis of the failings of localist ontologies is correct, his remedy is not.

The ATH is hardly the best tool to fix what is missing from localist ontologies. To the already mentioned difficulties one might add the rash of ontological entities in the vicinity of works of art. We have now not only the elusive works-as-action-types but their multiple instantiations (action tokens of the action type)—a questionable complication. To cap it all, Currie concedes on page 75 that the metaphysical nature of action types is anything but clear and settled. Perhaps there are ways of salvaging the theory, but the price exacted by its apparent drawbacks seems too steep not to look for an alternative.

## ONE OF THE REMIXES ADVANCED BY LEVINSON

*For an extreme example, let us imagine we had to read the* Don Quixote *that was rewritten by Borges' Pierre Menard (and that Menard's text can be interpreted differently from Cervantes's text, at least to the extent Borges claimed).*
UMBERTO ECO, *ON LITERATURE*

I submit that one of the remixes advanced by Levinson is not only more tenable than the ATH but comes close to reflecting common critical practice. In general, Levinson's approach is designed to avoid two kinds of problems. The first is Currie's identification of works with action types (rather than with the end results of artists' actions). The other is the familiar family of problems crippling localist (textualist) ontologies. For this he marshals the concept of determined or indicated structures. Their difference from "pure" structures such as birds, rocks, or clouds is crucial but simple. Indicated structures come into existence by virtue of intentional human actions that yield "an exemplar of the structure involved, or a blueprint of it."[19]

No intentional agency is responsible for rocks, clouds, or sparrows, hence their "unindicated" nature. Things that come into being as a result of intentional acts are of a different feather altogether. Naturally an indicated structure is not yet a work of art. Architectural blueprints, take-home exams, or the results of selective breeding such as Holstein milkers or Chihuahuas are all intentionally created but are not artworks. Necessity, in other words, does not entail sufficiency. To be a work of art, the created structure needs to possess other traits that will distinguish it from non-art.

Paradigmatically, the composition of a novel—say, *Picture This* by Joseph Heller—is an example of intentional action and the text of *Picture This* of an indicated structure. Here, however, we run into the problem of drafts. At which point does the text become indicated: with the final full stop of the first draft, the final corrigendum of the proofs, the printing of a revised edition, or some other subsequent or intermediate stage? Versions (drafts) of works are clearly works as they stood in a given moment, but the conceptual and empirical nature of works in progress could benefit from closer analysis—not least because they impinge on the time of composition in all the proposals considered below.[20]

A different set of questions is entailed by ready-made or "found" art. Does a piece of driftwood become driftwood art by virtue of being indicated and/or exhibited by a human agent? I return to this matter at the end of this chapter. For now, let us get a feel for Levinson's approach. The first formula considered by the aesthetician is very simple. The identity of a work of art is determined only by the identity of the artist and the time at which he created (intentionally indicated) the text:

$$W = A + t$$

The symbolic notation is used here to clarify the syntax and facilitate comparison with subsequent versions. It is pretty straightforward anyway: "W" denotes Work, "A" denotes the Artist (or Author), and "t" indicates the time of composition. The symbol "+" does not mean a mathematical sum or a logical operator but simply the necessity of each of the disparate factors involved, be it the artist, the time of composition, the relevant art-historical context, or any other.[21]

Levinson's second formula is even more straightforward:

$$W = C$$

where "C" stands for the total art-historical Context up to the time of creation.

We thus have two preliminary answers to "What is an artwork?" Since both are advanced in "What a Musical Work Is," Levinson calls the first one MW (for Musical Work) and the second MW' and proceeds to analyze their respective merits. Although he rehearses three distinct arguments for preferring the first formula, none is in my view satisfying. Skipping the two less important ones, let me focus here on the central argument.[22] It posits two works, $W_1$ and $W_2$, created independently by two artists in the same art-historical context, which have exactly the same structure. Imagine two poets who enter a writing contest that rigidly prescribes subject matter, imagery, and so forth, and who independently compose identical haikus.

There are countless thought experiments of this nature, none more celebrated than the fictional case of "Pierre Menard, Author of *The Quixote*." As Borges relates it, during an inventory of posthumous papers of an obscure French *auteur,* the literary executors discover what appear to be copies of lengthy parts of *Don Quixote*. Incredibly enough, they are not. Having apparently immersed himself in early seventeenth-century literature, culture, language, life, mindset, and what not, Menard *independently* created chapters identical word for word with Cervantes's.

Levinson argues that, identical texts notwithstanding, artworks $W_1$ and $W_2$ created by artists A and B would differ. While I concur with the conclusion, I am not convinced by his argument. A better reason for rejecting MW' is simply that it flunks individuation.

As it stands, any number of structures created independently in the same art-historical context are *one and the same* work of art. In the case of our two poets, they would write the same and not just an identically texted haiku. A friend of Duchamp who lugged a look-alike urinal to the Armory could bask in the dubious glory of having created *Foun-*

*tain,* and so on. Such results not only obliterate the causal independence of individual paths to creation but obscure the aesthetic differences between the creations themselves.

In the end, Levinson settles on a remix of MW. An artwork is defined as a Structure as determined by Artist at "t"—symbolically W = S + A + t. The creator of a work is essential to the identity and individuation of that work, maintains the aesthetician, by providing the assurance that the creator's works are his alone. This remix has been criticized by Currie on four counts, the first three of which, together with my emendations, take up the rest of this section.

1. The presence of indicated structures leads to a metaphysical *embarras de richesses.* Currie spells it out in his review of Levinson's *Music, Art, and Metaphysics:* there is "S as indicated by Smith at *t,* S as not indicated by me at *t,* S as thought about by Levinson at *t',* my desk as illuminated by my lamp at . . . , and so on."[23] Also, Levinson appears at times to suggest that artistic structures are Platonic entities that, when they are indicated by the artist, are discovered rather than created. The latter self-contradiction can be voided by approaching indication of structures as genuine creation.

The answer to the former objection comes from Levinson's proviso that indicated structures be restricted to instances when an exemplar or blueprint is created. This rules out most cases of the "S not indicated by me at *t*" and "S thought about by Levinson at *t'*" variety. Some situations, however, call for more nuance. What if I think artistically and creatively—say compose a poem in my head, as gulag-incarcerated Solzhenitsyn did? Do I then create a structure, perhaps in the hardwiring of synapses, which enables the recall of the poem? *Prima facie,* the answer seems to be Yes. A desk illuminated by a lamp is, however, an easier case. Light patterns reflected by a desk lamp do come into existence, and light patterns as a form of art are "indicated" by shadow-theater troupes worldwide.

2. Time and structure factors suffer from unreasonable narrowness (this applies equally to the ATH). In the present form, the most trivial deviation in the art-historical context or the misplacement of an immaterial syntactic comma results in a different work (think back to the problem of drafts). This objection is relatively easy to meet. The time factor should be relaxed to include situations where *no relevant changes* occur in the art-historical context, and the structural factor should permit variations within a correct instance of the text.

3. In *An Ontology of Art* Currie tries to raise doubts about MW by means of a couple of Twin Earth scenarios. These thought experiments involve a planet indistinguishable from our own that exhibits identical physical and cultural characteristics while lying in another region of the universe. "All the actions and achievements accomplished on earth, including all the artistic ones, are duplicated on Twin Earth. In particular, Beethoven has a twin on Twin Earth."[24] The upshot, according to Currie, is that if both composers come up with the same musical structure, it proves that they do not create it—unless the identity of the work is entailed by the identity of the artist. As it happens, it *is,* allowing Levinson to rebut the Twin Earth counterfactuals in his 1992 review of *An Ontology of Art.*

All the same, let me highlight a broader methodological problem with putative planets and Twin Beethovens that are to elicit intuitions about artworks from our everyday context. The unstated premise behind such scenarios is that as long as they satisfy the formal rules of logic, their cultural validity is thereby established. Although the use of counterfactuals is a legitimate philosophical and scientific practice, I have doubts about indiscriminate evocations of possible world scenarios, starting with the fact that logical coherence does not entail truth or pertinence. Outrageous falsehoods can be no less coherent than truths.[25]

Thermodynamic improbabilities such as resurrection of the dead are also not logically impossible, yet we do not see corpses rising up in front of our eyes and do not expect to. Although Currie's Martians, Twin Earth Beethovens, or societies with chairlike nose rests are all flawless from a logical standpoint, they are hard to accept as the last word on our reality. In this view I find an unlikely ally in the aesthetician himself, who allows that the "only way to make sense of our judgements of aesthetic value in this and other cases is to interpret them as being relative to the class of human works of art. The scale that *we* use is the scale defined by the kinds of artistic abilities found in *our* communities."[26]

In sum, I doubt that Currie's extreme doppelgänger cases have the upshot he had in mind—not, at least, if our ontology is to reflect our critical practice. If we accept that out yonder lies a planet indistinguishable from our own, Currie's argument will follow (although, as I note above, not his conclusion). Is it a legitimate supposition, though? I think not. For one, the Twin Earth cases—which are his main weapon against the type of theory proposed by Levinson—founder on the premise of twinness, or indistinguishability, of the two earths.

I can show it by a *reductio* of the major premise. If the Twin Earth is to be somewhere in space—be it another cluster, galaxy, or nebula—then the position, distribution, and magnitude of stars on its firmament will by definition differ from ours. Under such conditions, works of astrological poetry inspired by these constellations will differ from our astrological poetry when describing the position, distribution, or magnitude of stars in its firmament. Different artworks entail different art histories; different art histories entail different cultures; different cultures entail different planets. QED.

"Very cogent!" applauded Douglas Hofstadter, who in his latest book, *I Am a Strange Loop,* also expressed reservations about Twin Earth counterfactuals. "I doubt, however," he continued after reading my proof, "that it would in the least sway a philosopher inclined toward such thought experiments, who would simply throw in the extra postulate that all stars in the sky were always seen in identical positions to those on earth. Once you've postulated something as extreme as twin earth, you might as well go whole hog."[27]

I am not sure, however, that the extra fiat that all stars everywhere look the same saves the day for the recalcitrant philosopher. While insisting that this far-out counterfactual addresses our concerns, he removes its subject outside our universe—for only this would permit a Twin Earth to be in the same position with regard to all stars in the universe. Astronomers have mapped so many stars, galaxies, nebulae, and clusters from this corner of the visible universe that there is simply little room for another planet out yonder with the exactly same distribution of stars, galaxies, nebulae, and clusters. So the choice is stark: either drop the Twin Earth scenario or drop the claim that the counterfactual bears on *this* world (by being actual, rather than merely logically, possible in it).

## A CLINCHING ARGUMENT

*And it is clear that at this stage, if the work of art is form, the way of giving form involves more than just lexis or syntax.*
UMBERTO ECO, *ON LITERATURE*

There is, however, a clinching argument against W = S + A + t. It is this: a work created in a significantly different art-historical context would not be the same as a work indistinguishable from it in all the respects stipulated by Levinson (text, author, time). Here is why. Suppose Tom Wolfe and Truman Capote never lived or never experimented with New Journalism or nonfiction novels. In this impoverished art-historical context Heller's 1988 "faction," *Picture This,* would be *more original, experimental, and daring* than it is now. Same author, same text, same time of composition but different aesthetic properties and, as a result, different literary works. In short, MW does not individuate as it should.

The objection is fundamental enough to preclude a quick fix. In order to render it invulnerable to this kind of counterexample, our ontology must include the art-historical context.[28] Recognizing this, in 1992 Levinson fused MW and MW' into a formula he calls MW+. Schematically, this last remix represents a work as a Structure (text) created by the Author in an art-historical Context at a time "t":

$$W = S + A + C + \text{"t"}$$

In this shape the remix finally fulfills the requirements of identity, individuation, and aesthetic sensitivity. In other words, it tells us what an artwork is, and—as we shall see in Chapter 3—it differentiates any two works by differentiating their aesthetic properties. Moreover, it reflects the views on creatability and the role of the artist that are difficult to contravene. If artists indeed create (indicate) novels, paintings, and such, then these are necessarily intentional artifacts embedded in determinate art-historical settings.

However, to the extent that the remix stipulates only the necessary but not the sufficient conditions, it suffers from overambitiousness. Alongside artworks, MW+ snags countless other entities from areas of life where it is not immediately obvious that it is needed, for instance, from science or philosophy. Scientists also determine new structures, both theoretical, in the form of laws and theorems, and physical, as in the synthesis of completely new elements such as technetium. The remix is powerless to separate such cases from instances of artistic/aesthetic creation for which it was marshaled.[29]

According to MW+, new ontological entities are born every time scientific or philosophical research leads to a new blueprint or exemplar, from technetium as synthesized by Perrier and Segre in 1937 to the lab apparatus that enabled the synthesis or even the indication of MW+ in 1992. What is one to do with this cornucopia? Levinson stands by his findings, stating that "even if historiography of science doesn't appear to require such postulations at this point, I claim it is otherwise with the theory of artistic phenomena."[30] I think the ground on which he stands may actually be firmer than it might seem.

Even if science does not, the history of science does, after all, recognize structures as indicated by creators. One example among many is the independent and simultaneous discovery of the calculus by Newton and Leibnitz. Even though the mathematical structure was the same (with minor differences in notation), the identity of the creator was far from immaterial, as evidenced by the acrimonious strife as to whose formulation predated the other's.[31] Much for the same reasons, journals in science and philosophy print the dates of first and revised submissions in the service of documenting priority and thus identity of discovery.

I am the first to admit, however, that the answer I just gave, while valid in its own right, evades the fundamental question that neither Levinson nor Currie attempts to tackle. Yet the question cannot be evaded for too long, simply because it is fundamental to all attempts to fashion a viable ontology of art. Levinson's strictures apply to science because they offer no limits on their extension. What is needed is a constraint on the ontology that will confine it to *artistic* activity. Here is my proposal for such a stopping rule.

To be a work of art, an item must satisfy this additional clause: its creation must have been guided by the primary (or at least equally important) intention of achieving aesthetic ends. Aesthetic ends, to be sure, need not be pursued to the exclusion of others. Authors routinely pursue any number of goals directed at art, knowledge, edification, entertainment, fame, money, and other ends. Having said that, the primacy of aesthetic goals is inviolable since any relaxation of the clause—for example, that aesthetic goals play only a conspicuous role—would net all kinds of religious, philosophical, and other works.

Note that being (created as) art is not at all the same as being approached as art. Most of the time we pay scarcely any attention to the distinction insofar as the two, indeed, correlate to a high degree. When a novel is successfully executed with the primary intention of achieving aesthetic ends—common among which is that it be regarded as an artwork in the community—in a reflexive recognition of this fact the novel functions as art in the community. But that does not mean that *being* a literary artwork is the same as *functioning* as one.

The most obvious examples in which identity and function of art diverge are prehistoric idols, religious iconography, ancient potsherds, and such like. All are structures not created primarily, or even at all, with aesthetic intentions. Yet some idols, icons, or potsherds are separated from their context of creation and treated (displayed in museums) as artworks. Personal letters or diaries—some, unlike those of Pepys or the

Goncourts, of scant aesthetic value—also enter the domain of literature in complete editions of their writers' *oeuvres*.[32] Conversely, works *known* to have been created as art may not function as such owing, for instance, to envy or ideological repression.

This is not to downplay practical difficulties in rendering judgments about creative intentions. For starters, defining the aesthetic component may not always be easy given the presumptive lack of essentialist features common to all and only art. Furthermore, reconstructing intentions is, by definition, a task fraught with the possibility of getting it wrong or just not knowing the answer. But these are facts of life common to all endeavors of knowing the world that in no way dispute the conceptual point that the identity of art is *not* determined by its function, no matter how often the two converge.[33]

So much for limiting our ontology to artworks alone. Coming back to Levinson's proposal, I would like to suggest three modifications. Augmented by the sufficiency clause, the last remix defines an artwork as an *aesthetic* structure created by the artist in a historical context at a given time: $W = aS + A + C + \text{"t."}$ The time component is superfluous at this point, since it is already covered by the art-historical context. The definition can thus be simplified to $W = aS + A + C$, with the time requirement deleted altogether.[34]

Second, the case of Newton versus Leibnitz persuades that the path to creation can at times hold the key to the identity of the created structure. Newton's path to creation was certainly different from Leibnitz's insofar as the Englishman needed to create calculus for his laws of mechanics, while the German did not. The wrangle about who founded calculus suggests that the path to creation, a factor not strictly covered by the historical context, can sometimes be relevant to the identity of a work of art. My second modification is thus explicitly to subsume the path to creation into the art-historical context and extend both to the work's completion.

Finally, aesthetically relevant factors are not those potentially known to the writer but those that actually figured in the execution of the work—although not necessarily with full deliberation. These *executive* factors, together with the *executive* path to creation taken by the writer, comprise the influence of relevant art/social institutions, as defined by institutional theories of art.[35] Incorporating the suggested modification to the extension of the context, the remix redux is now $W = aS + A + eC$.

However, in the new, modified sense, the person of an artist is also incorporated into the art-historical context. Since the latter includes the creative path taken by the specific author at a specific time up until the work's completion, it contains all the elements necessary for individuation.[36] Schematically this can be represented as $W = aS + eC$, with the proviso that aesthetic Structure and executive Context are no longer the structure and context they were in Levinson's theory.

One advantage of this formulation is that it breaks with the residual elitism of institutional ontologies of art. In those, artworks are said to become artworks by virtue of being recognized as such by people with institutionalized (or just authorized) positions in the art world. Another advantage is that the last remix is immune to the incipient functionalism that cripples the more demotic versions of institutionalism, whereby anyone and his agent are said to be so authorized.[37]

Only time will tell whether the remix redux will stand. I am encouraged, however, by Levinson's indication of support for my theses. I draw further support from the coincidence of my conclusions with those of other aestheticians. Robert Stecker, for one, concludes that a "literary work offers up to us a text produced by a certain individual in a particular historical context" (1994, 196). Gary Iseminger writes that a literary work "is a textually embodied conceptual structure, whose conceptual component is (identical to) the structure—compatible with its text—which its author intended (meant) in composing it" (1992, 92–93).

I wish to point out that the remix does not mean the end of idiosyncratic, transgressive, or playful readings that may or may not aim at maximizing the aesthetic value of the text.[38] The remix redux does not mean that New Critics who read literature with a view to organic unity—or structuralists who read with a view to binary dialectics—or Marxists who read with a view to class oppression—or New Historicists who read with a view to power hierarchy—or deconstructionists who read with a view to free-for-all *jouissance*—got it all wrong. All it means is that to the extent they ignored the authors' intentions, they did not interpret the works but only the texts. In other words, they did not interpret aesthetically.

That this commonsensical point is at odds with much of literary-critical theory and practice says a lot about the discipline in which post-structuralism and contextless "close reading" are still the norm. In contrast to criticism in which anything not contradicted by the text "goes," the remix redux only constrains what can be asserted in the course of interpreting art *qua* art. Indeed, as Mary Louise Pratt reminds us, contextual—as opposed to textual—interpretation is even implicit in the very view of literature as a speech act:

> Far from being autonomous, self-contained, self-motivating, context-free objects which exist independently from the "pragmatic" concerns of "everyday" discourse, literary works take place in a context, and like any other utterance they cannot be described apart from that context. (1977, 115)

So, what about driftwood art? What about bird bowers, seascapes, and other aesthetically appealing ready-mades with which nature abounds? What about monkeys banging out the collected plays of Shakespeare? What about third-order computers spontaneously generating coherent and meaningful texts?[39] If our ontology works as it should, it ought to spit out sensible answers for all such "artificating" scenarios, contrived or not. Indeed it does, in all cases indexing the answer to intentions in action.

A hunk of driftwood or a urinal does become an artwork if it is indicated with nondeceptively aesthetic intentions. I take it here as a matter of course that aesthetic intentions comprise those of "merely" entertaining and not just edifying, making my ontology again more "nobrow" than those limited to high art only. In the case of our hunk of driftwood, it might be presented with the self-reflexively ironic intentions of making a statement about the nature of creativity (or impossibility thereof)—thus corresponding to Duchamp's statement about the power hierarchy of the art world in 1913. Making the driftwood "interpretable," such intentions make it an artwork.[40]

On the other hand, the answer is No if no such intentions are at work. A handsome piece of driftwood carried home to serve as a bookend does not thereby become art. Nor does a ready-made found at an exhibition when it involves fraud, a joke, or an error. Fluorescent tubing, concrete boxes, piles of felt, or even cans of excrement—notorious conceptual art all—could, after all, be inadvertently left behind by the museum work crew.[41] Remember: the remix redux does not render judgments about the value of such art (if it did, I for one would call it "art"). Still, ontology should mesh with aesthetic appreciation/interpretation, the subject to which we are now ready to turn.

Three    WORK AND TEXT

*So called texts of poetics are not always useful in understand-*
*ing the work that inspired them, but they help us understand*
*how to solve the technical problem which is the production of*
*the work.*
UMBERTO ECO, *ON LITERATURE*

## ARTWORKS ARE NOT EQUIVALENT TO THEIR STRUCTURES

*A text is like a musical score.*
UMBERTO ECO, *ON LITERATURE*

Artworks are not equivalent to their structures from the standpoint of identity. But what about individuation? If literary works are not equivalent to texts, what *is* the relation between creations that boast identical texts? What is the relation between individuation and appreciation of artworks or more generally between ontology and axiology? The merits of any analytic proposal can be ascertained by how well it handles these questions vis-à-vis common sense, common aesthetic intuitions, and critical practice.

A good benchmark for my own theses is once again provided by localists. If you recall from Chapter 2, the localist approach to identity was alluringly simple: artworks are equivalent to their texts. By now we know why this is not so. But localists also propose that artworks are equivalent to their structures as far as *individuation* is concerned. In other words, they propose that all aesthetic features of an artwork needed for individuation reside exclusively in its structure. If so, it would mean that all evidence for art interpretation would come from the direct evidence of the critic's senses. In this picture life is indeed easy: the context does not matter, and an identical text is always one and the same text.

The localists do concede that artworks may exhibit properties other than directly perceptible ones. However, according to them, these have zero bearing on aesthetic properties and thus on interpretation. Specifically, aesthetic properties of an artwork are said to be independent of its history of creation, including the crucial subset of this history bracketed by the artist's intentions. Work-related facts from the artist's path to creation or from the historical context would, after all, take the critic outside the directly perceived "art-ifact."

The variant of localism specific to literary studies is textualism—the belief that literary works are identical to their texts. Textualists are scholars who would do away with the concept of a work altogether and those who merely confuse the reading of texts with the interpretation of literary works.[1] We need to distinguish textualism from other variants of localism because, when it comes to literature, straightforward localism is not possible. Unlike interpretation of music, painting, or sculpture, in which we can directly perceive at least such properties of the works in question as sound, color, or texture, the aesthetic interpretation of a novel must perforce be preceded by linguistic comprehension.

In passing, I should flag an interesting question about the synaesthetic qualities of literature, that is, those shared with other arts such as musical or pictorial compositions. Poetry and prose display, after all, a number of musical qualities, such as rhythm, rhyme, syncopation, and onomatopoeia, perceivable as directly as are the musical qualities of Chopin's polonaises or Zappa's xenochronies. At the same time, literature displays pictorial qualities, most apparently in shaped poetry. This aspect of the relation between the aesthetics of textualism and localism could benefit from study in its own right.

In literary studies the most influential textualist manifestos were Wimsatt and Beardsley's "The Intentional Fallacy" (1946) and Frye's *The Anatomy of Criticism* (1957). Oddly enough, these pillars of New Criticism remain in remarkable accord with the more modern theories of interpretation. The advent of deconstruction has not, after all, dulled the edge of textualist pronouncements. Quite the contrary. Paul de Man's *Blindness and Insight,* which professes his "interest in primary literary texts" (1983, viii), is a good example insofar as "literary text" is, strictly speaking, a contradiction in terms. One cannot appreciate literary attributes such as influence, genre, and originality without stepping outside the text to the work.[2]

The same confusion underpins another collection of essays that has shaped postmodernist thought for more than a quarter-century: *Deconstruction and Criticism* (1979). Harold Bloom typifies it with the following fiat: "There are *no* texts but only interpretations."[3] Insofar as there *are* texts—strings of phonemes or letters that form utterances—this is arrant nonsense, unless by "texts" he means works. In the same volume, Derrida's characterization of a text as "a differential network, a fabric of traces referring endlessly to something other than itself" is similarly problematic. It clearly takes him outside brute text—that is, the sequence of letters on the page—to the fabric of aesthetic traces that constitutes the work.

The most egregious illustration comes, however, from J. Hillis Miller. His simile "The poem, like all texts, is 'unreadable'" quite simply equivocates texts and works, even though only the art-historical context—from the conventions of free verse and prose poetry to the author's intentions—can identify a text as a poem. Prose lyrics can, after all, be textually indistinguishable from lyrical prose. Although Michael Ondatjee's *The Collected Works of Billy the Kid* used to be classified as a novel, now the poet-novelist lists this imagistic and fragmentary narrative among his volumes of poetry. The point is, whichever it is, one could never divine it from the text alone.

Textualism also has attracted vigorous support in some analytic quarters. In 1988 a full-scale endorsement of textualist aesthetics was advanced by Nelson Goodman and Catherine Elgin in *Reconceptions in Philosophy and Other Arts and Sciences*. There, in even more uncompromising terms than in Goodman's earlier *Languages of Art*, the matter was restated: works and texts "one-to-one correlated, and the work can alternatively be identified with the text" (56). In most cases we do, of course, individuate works by reference to their texts because, in most cases, this is all that is needed. Can one, however, imagine circumstances in which localism will not do?

For an answer I turn first to Kendall Walton, who offers a simple rebuttal to the equation of texts and works. In the widely cited "Categories of Art" (1970), the aesthetician argues that aesthetic traits are not fixed by structural properties but by these properties as seen through the work's category. To make his point, he pictures a society that makes *guernicas*, works just like Picasso's Cubist painting, only in bas-relief. Next to these three-dimensional creations, the painting on a flat canvas would exhibit different aesthetic traits inasmuch as some of its features are dependent on its genre. Thus Picasso's masterpiece might seem violent, dynamic, disturbing to us. But it would probably strike the makers of bas-relief *guernicas* "as cold, stark, lifeless . . . but in any case *not* violent, dynamic and vital" (347).[4]

Aesthetic attributes of any work depend, in other words, on the attributes of other works in the genre. And being dependent on the generic matrix, they are emphatically nonlocal. Aware of problems with reducing artworks interpretively to their structures, Frank Sibley sought to overcome them by means of the so-called supervenience thesis. Conceding that aesthetic qualities are not equivalent to pictorial ones—in itself a dramatic retrenchment from full-blown localism—Sibley argued that they supervene on the latter without being reducible to them.

But here the localist finds himself in a quandary. He claims, after all, that the context of a work's creation is irrelevant to the grasp of its aesthetic qualities, and Walton's counterfactual demonstrates why this will not work. Therefore, to avoid the charge of bootstrapping, Sibley needs to find another source for making the necessary aesthetic distinctions. With this in mind, he invokes the notion of taste, which might allow contemplators of art to map strictly pictorial properties onto aesthetic ones. His entire theoretical edifice rests, therefore, on the faculty of taste, defined as the *inherent* ability to discern aesthetic features of art.

Are there reasons for rejecting this new and improved localist theory of interpretation? I think so. The simplest one is that the very notion, not to mention the exercise, of taste entails knowledge of art-historical context—knowledge that is emphatically nonlocal. Notwithstanding the evolutionary roots of some aspects of aesthetics, good taste is not a congenital faculty but a "nurtured" one. To acquire it involves a prolonged exposure to art as well as knowledge of many nonlocal aspects of its history: creation, reception, influence, genre, and so forth.[5]

The acquisition and exercise of taste is thus an inherently contextual and comparative process, in contradistinction to the contextless tenets of the aesthetic localist. Similar arguments, developed with a literary audience in mind, have led other critics to similar conclusions. Taste, concludes David Daiches in "Literary Evaluations" (1969), is always a developed faculty, being "the sum of discriminations made available by attentive reading in a large variety of literary modes" (177). Thus *contra* supervenience, tasteful mapping of pictorial attributes onto aesthetic ones is not a direct but always a comparative—nonlocal—process.

In fact, although Walton himself never makes the point, the very concept of genre implies one's extratextual awareness of the genre's synchronic and diachronic extensions in order to appreciate the interplay of convention and invention in any given work. At the same time, category-based arguments are only a limiting case of a much wider range of counterexamples to textualism. Genre is, after all, only one of many extratextual determinants of a literary work's aesthetic properties. Other refutations of textualism occur when the text and genre remain the same but other art-historical factors effect a change in aesthetic properties.

A conclusive refutation of aesthetic equivalence between a work and its structure comes from a familiar source: Levinson's "What a Musical Work Is." The philosopher provides three distinct counters to localism, based on the respective exclusion of the event of creation, the art-historical context, and the musical performance means.[6]

Levinson's first argument can be expressed as a quasi-theorem. If literary works were just texts, they would not be creatable since—at least if Platonism is true—ontological structures (such as texts) are types that exist at all times. Logically speaking, the text of Truman Capote's *In Cold Blood* could have been written before 1965, hence its text type also must have existed prior to 1965. From this it would follow that if artists create their works—in the strong sense of bringing them into existence—the said works cannot be equivalent to their structures.

One conceivable objection to this argument would be to question the very notion of artistic creation. Nevertheless, notwithstanding the rhetorical tropes of *nihil novi,* such objections would quickly find themselves on shaky ground. The creability of art is perhaps the single most incontrovertible creed associated with the activity of artists in society. The entire Western tradition in art is rooted in the concept of artworks that did not exist prior to their creation. A great deal of the status, importance, and symbolic value bestowed on art owes to its being brought into existence. If, however, like me you find the Platonism of the first refutation a little hard to swallow, there is a different class of arguments to show that artworks acquire most of their aesthetic properties from their contexts.

In what follows I assume that properties such as originality, complexity, and influence are all aesthetic in nature. One could, I suppose, demur that Levinson's examples below make the case for differences in artistic but not aesthetic traits. In this case, however, the burden of proof falls on the skeptic insofar as judgments about artistry have been part and parcel of aesthetic judgments throughout history. Art criticism would, indeed, not be what it is if one could not appreciate Raymond Chandler as a virtuoso of the simile in the course of aesthetically appreciating his prose. Moreover, if there are essentialist distinctions between artistic and aesthetic properties, it remains to be seen what they are, especially in view of the historical difficulties in articulating the latter (which begs the question of how exactly these two are to be teased apart).

In any case, my own real-life case studies that follow Levinson's three counterfactuals below are immune to skeptical objections of this sort.

## THE ART–HISTORICAL CONTEXT

*But then the problem is solved at the writer's desk as he inter-*
*rogates the material on which he is working—material that*
*reveals natural laws of its own, but at the same time contains*
*the recollection of the culture with which it is loaded (the echo*
*of intertextuality).*
UMBERTO ECO, *POSTSCRIPT TO THE NAME*
*OF THE ROSE*

Within the art-historical context we can discern two
groups of factors: those specific to the overall environment in which a
work was composed and those specific, even idiosyncratic, to the creating individual. The first group comprises pertinent factors from sociocultural context up to the conclusion of the process of creation, including the artist's antecedents and contemporaries, dominant styles and/or
influences, and such like. Group two may include the creator's indebt-
edness to other artists, his current and past repertoire, or his style and
artistic achievement.

Levinson's thesis is straightforward: different contexts entail different
aesthetic features, and different aesthetic features entail different works
(whose texts might even be identical).[7] Since his counterfactuals all derive from music, let me adapt them to literature.

1.  A work textually identical to Capote's *In Cold Blood* (1965)
    but created by Norman Mailer in 1995 would be aesthetically
    different from Capote's work. For one, as a Mailer creation, *In
    Cold Blood* would no longer be contemporaneous with Tom
    Wolfe's New Journalistic *The Kandy Kolored Tangerine Flake
    Streamlined Baby.* It also would be derivative, coming after
    Mailer's *The Executioner's Song* (1979), which itself is indebted
    to Capote's *In Cold Blood.* Under these conditions, Mailer's *In
    Cold Blood* would be less daring and disturbing—not to men-
    tion less topical—than Capote's, being created in a literary
    context that has by then largely absorbed the techniques of
    the nonfiction novel of the 1960s.

2.  Ernest Hemingway's *In Our Time* (1924) is held to be a highly
    original work of fiction. Its lean, sparse, understated prose,
    pulsing with violence and stoicism, is an avatar of the novel
    hard-boiled American style. But a story collection from 1964

with the same text as Hemingway's would be stylistically
unoriginal, mining the by then familiar hard-boiled
tradition.

3.      Mailer's *The Naked and the Dead* (1948) is strongly influenced
by Dos Passos's *U.S.A.* (1936). Yet a work textually identical
with Mailer's but produced by Jack London (or even by Dos
Passos in the 1920s) would no longer be *U.S.A.*-influenced.
And, written long before *U.S.A.*, it would be highly experimental, which is no longer the case with the more imitative
work by Mailer.

Individually and jointly, the above examples reveal the untenabil-
ity of textualism with regard to aesthetic interpretation and individuation. To forestall objections that they are cooked-up counterfactuals
out of touch with reality—such as those made by Benjamin Tilghman
against whatever may be deduced from the travails of the fictional Pierre
Menard—let me turn to some real-life examples.[8]

In Hemingway's case, for instance, it may be argued that the credit
for the hard-boiled American style—lean, sparse, understated, pulsing
with violence and stoicism—belongs to Dashiell Hammett instead. The
latter's first Continental Op story appeared in October 1923, a full year
before the first edition of *In Our Time*. Critical *integrati* and *apocalittici*, to
fall back on Eco's parlance, may wish to resolve this paternity suit differently.[9] But either way, questions of originality, priority, influence, and so
forth cannot be decided on the basis of either text alone. For that, even
poststructuralists need to go outside the text to the larger context.

An even more vivid illustration of this principle comes from Homer's
*Iliad*. The story of the Achaean siege led by Agamemnon and his brother
Menelaus against the Trojans, among them Hector "of the flashing helmet," is famous the world over. Two passages, from Books 4 and 6, contrast the moods and feelings on either side of this epic strife. Passage
one is narrated by Agamemnon after Menelaus is struck by an arrow.
Fearing for his brother's life, the Greek commander consoles him with
words full of confidence and optimism about the ultimate outcome of
the war and the defeat of Troy.

Passage two is narrated by Hector to his wife, Andromache. To her
plea that he withdraw from the battlefield, the warrior declines with
words full of honor and courage yet resigned and pessimistic about the
ultimate outcome of the war and the defeat of Troy. Thus Agamemnon's
*optimistic* speech reads as follows:

> For of a surety know I this in heart and soul:
> the day shall come when sacred Ilios shall be laid low,
> and Priam, and the people of Priam, with goodly spear
> of ash.

Hector's *pessimistic* speech reads as follows:

> For of a surety know I this in heart and soul:
> the day shall come when sacred Ilios shall be laid low,
> and Priam, and the people of Priam, with goodly spear
> of ash.[10]

Note that not even a die-hard textualist can object that my counterexample does not involve aesthetic attributes of works, only of their creators. Even though there are traits equally attributable to writers and their works—being innovative or contemporaneous, for example—some aesthetic features cannot be reduced to statements about authors. It makes no sense to call the author of the *Iliad* archaic or skillfully plotted, even though his epic is both. In sum, identical texts in different contexts will yield different aesthetic attributes, and different aesthetic attributes will yield different works: *quod erat probandum.*

In "The Lottery at Babylon" Borges illustrates the same principle, albeit along ontological rather than aesthetic lines. The universal lottery gradually erases the distinction between Chance and Order so that, even though any train of events remains intact, its nature changes profoundly. This leads to paradoxes like that of a thief who steals a ticket that credits him with a burning of his tongue, which happens to be the legal penalty for the theft of a ticket. Thus some Babylonians can argue that "he deserved the burning irons in his status of a thief; others, generously, that the executioner should apply it to him because chance had determined it that way" (1964, 32).

Much as the ontology of Babylon is not deducible from events alone, the aesthetic attributes of literary works are not deducible from texts alone. Relevant historical context is indispensable to (ontological) individuation and (aesthetic) interpretation of any work of literature. And because ontological and aesthetic properties are relational—they do not reside in the text—one cannot equivocate literary works and texts. In fact, as we shall see in Chapter 6, the *dehors texte* is indispensable even at such a fundamental level of interpretation as grasping what happens in the story. Needless to say, all this directly contradicts Goodman and

οἶον προστήσας πρὸ Ἀχαιῶν Τρωσὶ μάχεσθαι,
ὥς σ' ἔβαλον Τρῶες, κατὰ δ' ὅρκια πιστὰ πάτησαν.
οὐ μέν πως ἅλιον πέλει ὅρκιον αἷμά τε ἀρνῶν
σπονδαί τ' ἄκρητοι καὶ δεξιαί, ἧς ἐπέπιθμεν.
160 εἴ περ γάρ τε καὶ αὐτίκ' Ὀλύμπιος οὐκ ἐτέλεσσεν,
ἔκ τε καὶ ὀψὲ τελεῖ, σύν τε μεγάλῳ ἀπέτισαν,
σὺν σφῆσιν κεφαλῇσι γυναιξί τε καὶ τεκέεσσιν.
εὖ γὰρ ἐγὼ τόδε οἶδα κατὰ φρένα καὶ κατὰ θυμόν·
ἔσσεται ἦμαρ ὅτ' ἄν ποτ' ὀλώλῃ Ἴλιος ἱρή
165 καὶ Πρίαμος καὶ λαὸς ἐϋμμελίω Πριάμοιο,
Ζεὺς δέ σφι Κρονίδης ὑψίζυγος, αἰθέρι ναίων,
αὐτὸς ἐπισσείῃσιν ἐρεμνὴν αἰγίδα πᾶσι
τῆσδ' ἀπάτης κοτέων· τὰ μὲν ἔσσεται οὐκ ἀτέλεστα·
ἀλλά μοι αἰνὸν ἄχος σέθεν ἔσσεται, ὦ Μενέλαε,
170 αἴ κε θάνῃς καὶ πότμον ἀναπλήσῃς βιότοιο.
καί κεν ἐλέγχιστος πολυδίψιον Ἄργος ἱκοίμην·
αὐτίκα γὰρ μνήσονται Ἀχαιοὶ πατρίδος αἴης·
κὰδ δέ κεν εὐχωλὴν Πριάμῳ καὶ Τρωσὶ λίποιμεν
Ἀργείην Ἑλένην· σέο δ' ὀστέα πύσει ἄρουρα
175 κειμένου ἐν Τροίῃ ἀτελευτήτῳ ἐπὶ ἔργῳ·
καί κέ τις ὧδ' ἐρέει Τρώων ὑπερηνορεόντων
τύμβῳ ἐπιθρῴσκων Μενελάου κυδαλίμοιο·
'αἴθ' οὕτως ἐπὶ πᾶσι χόλον τελέσει' Ἀγαμέμνων,
ὡς καὶ νῦν ἅλιον στρατὸν ἤγαγεν ἐνθάδ' Ἀχαιῶν,
180 καὶ δὴ ἔβη οἶκόνδε φίλην ἐς πατρίδα γαῖαν
σὺν κεινῇσιν νηυσί, λιπὼν ἀγαθὸν Μενέλαον.'
ὥς ποτέ τις ἐρέει· τότε μοι χάνοι εὐρεῖα χθών.

I swore this solemn oath, stationing you alone before the Achaeans to do battle with the Trojans, since the Trojans have thus struck you, and trodden under foot the oaths of faith. Yet in no way is an oath of no effect and the blood of lambs and drink offerings of unmixed wine and the handclasps in which we put our trust. For even if the Olympian does not immediately fulfill them, yet late and at length he will fulfill them, and with a heavy price do men make atonement, with their own heads and their wives and their children. For I know this well in my mind and heart; the day will come when sacred Ilios will be laid low, and Priam, and the people of Priam of the good ashen spear; and Zeus, son of Cronos, throned on high, who dwells in the sky, will himself shake over them all his dark aegis in anger for this deceit. These things will not fail of fulfillment; yet dreadful grief for you will be mine, Menelaus, if you die and fill up the measure of your fate. And as one most despised should I return to thirsty Argos, for immediately will the Achaeans take thought of their native land, and so should we leave Argive Helen as a boast to Priam and the Trojans. And your bones will the earth rot as you lie in the land of Troy with your task unfinished; and so will one of the arrogant Trojans say, as he leaps on the mound of glorious Menelaus: 'I wish that in every undertaking it may be thus that Agamemnon fulfills his wrath, just as now he has led here an army of the Achaeans in vain, and indeed he has gone away home to his dear native land with empty ships, and has left here noble Menelaus.' So will some man speak one day; on that day let the wide earth gape open for me."

⁹ πότμον Aristarchus: μοῖραν MSS.

430 ἠδὲ κασίγνητος, σὺ δέ μοι θαλερὸς παρακοίτης·
ἀλλ' ἄγε νῦν ἐλέαιρε καὶ αὐτοῦ μίμν' ἐπὶ πύργῳ,
μὴ παῖδ' ὀρφανικὸν θήῃς χήρην τε γυναῖκα·
λαὸν δὲ στῆσον παρ' ἐρινεόν, ἔνθα μάλιστα
ἀμβατός ἐστι πόλις καὶ ἐπίδρομον ἔπλετο τεῖχος.
435 τρὶς γὰρ τῇ γ' ἐλθόντες ἐπειρήσανθ' οἱ ἄριστοι
ἀμφ' Αἴαντε δύω καὶ ἀγακλυτὸν Ἰδομενῆα
ἠδ' ἀμφ' Ἀτρεΐδας καὶ Τυδέος ἄλκιμον υἱόν·
ἤ πού τίς σφιν ἔνισπε θεοπροπίων ἐῢ εἰδώς,
ἤ νυ καὶ αὐτῶν θυμὸς ἐποτρύνει καὶ ἀνώγει.
440 Τὴν δ' αὖτε προσέειπε μέγας κορυθαίολος Ἕκτωρ·
"ἦ καὶ ἐμοὶ τάδε πάντα μέλει, γύναι· ἀλλὰ μάλ' αἰνῶς
αἰδέομαι Τρῶας καὶ Τρῳάδας ἑλκεσιπέπλους,
αἴ κε κακὸς ὣς νόσφιν ἀλυσκάζω πολέμοιο·
445 οὐδέ με θυμὸς ἄνωγεν, ἐπεὶ μάθον ἔμμεναι ἐσθλὸς
αἰεὶ καὶ πρώτοισι μετὰ Τρώεσσι μάχεσθαι,
ἀρνύμενος πατρός τε μέγα κλέος ἠδ' ἐμὸν αὐτοῦ.
εὖ γὰρ ἐγὼ τόδε οἶδα κατὰ φρένα καὶ κατὰ θυμόν·
ἔσσεται ἦμαρ ὅτ' ἄν ποτ' ὀλώλῃ Ἴλιος ἱρή
450 καὶ Πρίαμος καὶ λαὸς ἐϋμμελίω Πριάμοιο.
ἀλλ' οὔ μοι Τρώων τόσσον μέλει ἄλγος ὀπίσσω,
οὔτ' αὐτῆς Ἑκάβης οὔτε Πριάμοιο ἄνακτος
οὔτε κασιγνήτων, οἵ κεν πολέες τε καὶ ἐσθλοὶ
ἐν κονίῃσι πέσοιεν ὑπ' ἀνδράσι δυσμενέεσσιν,
455 ὅσσον σεῦ, ὅτε κέν τις Ἀχαιῶν χαλκοχιτώνων
δακρυόεσσαν ἄγηται, ἐλεύθερον ἦμαρ ἀπούρας·
καί κεν ἐν Ἄργει ἐοῦσα πρὸς ἄλλης ἱστὸν ὑφαίνοις,
καί κεν ὕδωρ φορέοις Μεσσηΐδος ἤ Ὑπερείης

and you are my vigorous husband. Come now, have pity, and stay here on the wall, lest you make your son fatherless and your wife a widow. And for your army, station it by the wild fig tree, where the city may best be scaled, and the wall is open to assault. For thrice at this point came the best men in company with the two Aiantes and glorious Idomeneus and the sons of Atreus and the valiant son of Tydeus, and tried the walls: either someone well skilled in soothsaying told them, or perhaps their own heart urges and commands them to it."

Then spoke to her great Hector of the flashing helmet: "Woman, I too take thought of all this, but I dreadfully feel shame before the Trojans, and the Trojans' wives with trailing robes, if like a coward I skulk apart from the battle. Nor does my heart command it, since I have learnt to excel always and to fight among the foremost Trojans, striving to win great glory for my father and myself. For I know this well in my mind and heart: the day will come when sacred Ilios will fall, and Priam, and the people of Priam of the good ashen spear. But not so much does the grief that is to come to the Trojans move me, neither Hecabe's own, nor king Priam's, nor that of my brothers, many and noble, who will fall in the dust at the hands of their foes, as does your grief, when some bronze-clad Achaean will lead you away weeping and rob you of your day of freedom. Then perhaps in Argos will you ply the loom at another woman's bidding, or carry water from Messeïs or Hypereia, much

¹³ Lines 433–439 were rejected by Aristarchus.

Identical texts, different meanings. Excerpts from Books 4 and 6 of Homer's *Iliad* (translated by A. T. Murray, revised by William F. Wyatt). *In sum, identical texts in different contexts will yield different aesthetic attributes, and different aesthetic attributes will yield different works:* quod erat probandum.

Elgin's claim that "any inscription of the text, no matter who or what produced it, bears all the same interpretations as any other" (62).

The dispute between textualist and work-oriented theories of interpretation is, in the end, hardly a dispute at all. Only the art-historical context identifies and individuates the work. For that matter, even strictly textual meanings cannot be divorced from the wider contexts of the language in which they are written (suffice it to compare the meaning of "gay" ere and now). The concept of work is thus necessary for the aesthetic interpretation of the end result of artistic activity and sufficient for its identity and individuation. To coin a slogan, we get to *work through text-in-context.*

Literary interpretations are, of course, never uniquely determined by their contexts. There is no limit to interpretations of any work and no one best interpretation. Contexts for readers' interpretive economies fluctuate in response to the changing world, ensuring that a work's semantic potential can never be exhausted. In that sense, literary works truly are machines for generating meanings. Work through text-in-context is but a reflection of the fact that, in the words of a prominent textual critic, literary criticism is "necessarily a historical enterprise."[11]

This bring our ontological analyses to a conclusion, insofar as we can now identify an artwork and distinguish one artwork from another. All that remains is to conceptualize the nature of the text. This is easier said than done, not least because the term nowadays is a catch-all for anything at all that can sustain interpretation. In a textual largesse befitting the ur deconstructor, Derrida, for example, offers the world for the taking, contending that a text is "everything that was to be set up in opposition to writing: speech, life, the world, the real, history, and what not."[12] Not only is this vacuous—logically, if everything is a text, then nothing is—but also typical of literary studies in which scant attention is accorded to the identity and individuation of texts.

An instructive proof of where such complaisance can lead is furnished by F. O. Matthiessen's interpretation of Melville's *White Jacket* in the Constable Standard Edition. In the story, the narrator sinks into the sea in a trancelike state. But then, Melville writes, "some fashionless form brushed my side—some inert soiled fish of the sea."[13] Matthiessen rhapsodizes: "hardly anyone but Melville could have created the shudder that results from calling this frightening vagueness some 'soiled fish of the sea.'"[14] If only it were so. As the British and American first editions prove, Melville's word of choice in this passage was "coiled," which a typesetter's error changed to "soiled" in the Constable edition.

Excoriating such interpretive naiveté in *Textual and Literary Criticism,*

Fredson Bowers asks: "How far can we trust the ideas and methods of critics who think so little of analyzing the nature of the texts with which they work?" (1959, 3). Add to this the fact that poststructuralism has yet to remark that texts and works are birds of ontologically and aesthetically different feather, and the nature of texts—these cornerstones of literary studies—looms as elusive as that of unicorns. The textual fallacy has, in fact, gone so far that at some institutions literary criticism is now labeled "textual studies."[15]

When the classroom staple *Untying the Text: A Post-Structuralist Reader* purports to "concentrate on specific textual analyses," it is therefore guilty of two errors.[16] Not one of its assorted chapters deals in *textual* analysis, be it descriptive or analytical bibliography, codicology, palaeography, diplomatics, stemmatics, or other. Instead, they concentrate on matters of aesthetics, artistry, irony, referentiality (or lack thereof), originality, genre, and so on. Insofar as all of those presuppose extratextual knowledge, paradoxically the poststructuralists neither read texts nor interpret literary works.

In the context, one might be advised to listen to the text experts. Here is how, in *Textual Scholarship,* David Greetham demarcates their domain: "Textual scholars study *process* (the historical stages in the production, transmission, and reception of texts), not just *product* (the text resulting from such production, transmission, and reception)" (1994, 2). Informed by authorial intentions and historical process, the goals of textual scholarship turn out to be isomorphic with my theses on ontology and aesthetic interpretation. This convergence of independent lines of inquiry cannot but boost confidence in their respective methods and conclusions.

## GOOD OPERATIONAL GRASP

*However fluctuating, these [textual] scores are not unverifiable: anyone who claimed that Madame Bovary reconciles with Charles and lives happily ever after with him in the end would meet with the disapproval of people of sound common sense.*
UMBERTO ECO, *POSTSCRIPT TO THE NAME OF THE ROSE*

Researchers who work with texts, from "textuists" and literary critics to text linguists, psycholinguists, stylists, anthropologists, and others, certainly have a good operational grasp of what they study.[17]

Yet, as the successive editions of *The Encyclopedia of Language and Linguistics* make clear, the concept of the text has so far proven surprisingly elusive. In the thirteen years between Willie van Peer's (1993) and T. Sanders and J. Sanders' (2006) entries on the nature of text, the literature on the subject has exploded without necessarily settling the core issues.[18]

Given the seeming lack of consensus among specialists, let us begin with three intuitive notions of what a text is. Texts are commonly held to be documents or records, literary productions, or rhetorical compositions. However, all three definitions run counter to experience. The latter two, for example, are manifestly too restrictive. Conference guides are texts without being particularly literary or rhetorical. Readers who have yet to experience being processed through an academic symposium might just as well focus their attention on the annual income tax form, a text that will never be accused of being literary or rhetorical.

What is wrong with the definition of texts as documents? Not much, apart from failing the condition of necessity, inasmuch as oral texts have been with us from times immemorial. It is only through the intercession of the Athenian despot Peisistratus, after all, that the Homeric verses were written in mid–sixth century BCE for the first time. Most preliterate societies have employed professional Johnny Mnemonics to safeguard texts in memory, a task aided by our evolutionary predisposition to symmetry. (Rhyme, refrain, alliteration, dilation, or periphrasis are all species of symmetry.)[19]

Acknowledging oral texts does not seem like much of a conceptual hurdle. However, van Peer concedes as much, insisting that the definition falters in another way. According to him, "torn–up pages in a wastepaper basket" are not text, and a newspaper article cut up into sentences that are then pasted back at random would not even "be recognized as a text" (1993, 4565–4566). Surprisingly, the sole argument in support is an appeal to intuitions that, as it happens, squarely contradict the intuitions of everyone I canvassed. Equally, they also contradict the theory and practice of bibliographical reconstruction, in which fragmentation has no bearing on textual identity.[20]

It would, indeed, be an odd act of prestidigitation if, by dint of being torn or spliced in a different order, a text could be made ontologically to disappear. One may debate whether the fragmented text is the same text as before, but this is a question of individuation, not identity. The Sanderses' postulates on the nature of text also raise as many questions as they answer. Taking the semantic route, they argue that a text is more than a random set of utterances—"it shows connectedness" (2006, 598). But, they add, connectedness is a mental phenomenon—"it is not an inherent property of a text" (599).

The problem is, if it is the human mind that imposes coherence, there can be no incoherent text. Anything at all, no matter how random or disparate, can be connected in the mind, making the stipulation of connectedness meaningless. The following excerpts from *The Policeman's Beard Is Half Constructed* by Racter (short for Raconteur), a Z80 microcomputer with 64K RAM, adumbrate the point in question. Although they are far from coherent in the sense displayed by human writers, they are far from incoherent either. Their hilarity stems, in fact, from the reader's automatic attempts to impose coherence on their scattered semantics.[21]

> Awareness is like consciousness. Soul is like spirit. But soft is not like hard and weak is not like strong. A mechanic can be both soft and hard, and stewardess can be both weak and strong. This is called philosophy or world view.

> Many enraged psychiatrists are inciting a weary butcher. The butcher is weary and tired because he has cut meat and steak and lamb for hours and weeks. He does not desire to chant about anything with raving psychiatrists but he sings about his gingivectomist, he dreams about a single cosmologist, he thinks about his dog. The dog is named Herbert.

Incoherent though these passages may be (albeit flawless syntactically), I leave it to the reader to judge whether they form a text. Since I personally do not doubt that they do, I doubt whether coherence is necessary to have a text. The Sanderses insist it is, arguing—in defense of their semantic approach—that it "is hard, for instance, to make much sense of the idea of a structurally 'well-formed' but semantically anomalous text" (2006, 599). In lieu of a counterargument, let me quote from "Jabberwocky":

> 'Twas brillig, and the slithy toves
> Did gyre and gimble in the wabe:
> All mimsy were the borogoves,
> And the mome raths outgrabe.

The whole point of Carroll's poem is that it *is* structurally well formed and semantically anomalous. This rebuttal of the Sanderses' claims does not, of course, prove that the syntactic approach carries the day. Even though there is something to be said for Halliday and Hasan's minimalist definition of a text as "a unit of language in use" (1976, 1), it raises its own set of questions. Musicians, computer programmers, and mathematicians also produce texts, after all. In each case, however, the languages are distinct from Human Natural Languages (HNLs), such as English or Japanese, and from "conlangs" (constructed/artificial languages) such as Lingua Ignota or, more contemporarily, Esperanto or Ameslan.[22]

Or are they? After all, mathematical, musical, and computer-programming notational schemes are only convenient shorthand for normal linguistic encoding. "Square root of five plus sixteen factorial" makes perfect mathematical sense, much as "high C flat staccato" is understood by competent speakers of English who have adequate knowledge of music. In principle, one could express entire scores or proofs in longhand, although in practice they would be horrendously unwieldy and opaque. Hence, an interesting *marginalium:* Are mathematical and musical scores texts in the linguistic sense?

As literary critics we study linguistic structures (texts) in conventional alphabetic notation. Note that "structures" in this context avoids connotations of intentionality entailed by "utterances." Although Halliday and Hasan posit that texts come into existence only in a communicative context, texts can come about without human intervention—think of all those monkeys banging out *Macbeth* or wind eroding a rock face. Yet, although intriguing conceptually, counterfactuals of this nature have zero upshot for literary ontology inasmuch as literary *works* are always intentional. Moreover, there are good empirical reasons we should not lose sleep over these far-out scenarios.

Let us look closer at the dactylographic monkeys. In the original thought experiment, the French mathematician Emile Borel argued that a troop of typing monkeys would eventually reproduce, by the brute force of possible permutations, the entire French National Library.[23] To bring out the staggering leap of faith of this *Gedankenexperiment,* let me narrow it down to just a *single line of print.* Mathematically, the problem involves the combinatorial possibilities of filling the sixty-five spaces that make an average line. The variables are letters of the alphabet in lower and upper case, plus typographical signs—fifty in all. The solution is trivial, but the number is not:

$$50 \times 50 \times 50 \times \cdots \times 50 = 50^{65} = 10^{110}$$

Let us assume that every atom in the universe ($3^{75}$) is a printing press and that each has been printing nonstop since the beginning of time

($10^{14}$) at the rate of atomic vibrations ($10^{15}$ lines per second). By now they would have printed only $3^{75} \times 10^{14} \times 10^{15} = 3^{104}$ lines, or 0.00003 of the total. And this is for only one line of print with no repetitions—both restrictions waived by the Monkey Shakespeare Simulator. This computer program, aping a hundred simians banging away at a vastly accelerated rate, has so far managed to reproduce nineteen letters from *The Two Gentlemen of Verona* after only 42,162,500,000,000,000,000,000,000 monkey-years of labor.[24]

To go back to our starting point, the definition of text as a structure in a language does not look half so bad when you consider the alternatives. Not only is it not unduly restrictive, but it has the welcome consequence of bracketing off movies, operas, and other art forms with a linguistic component, not to mention poststructuralist pantextuality in which the whole world is a text.[25] But here a new quandary arises. Not all novels are solely language-based (in the HNL + conlang sense). There are music scores in Joyce, drawings in Vonnegut, computer graphs in Crichton, binary strings in Lem, chessboard problems in Perez-Reverte, and so forth.

At the other end of the spectrum are texts in children's stories, comic books, storyboards, and other types of sequential art in which the pictorial element is paramount. Since it is absurd to claim that Art Spiegelman's *Maus* is textless, we reach a conceptual fork in the road. Either the linguistic module alone makes up the text (excluding scores, drawings, diagrams, picture frames, and the like) or even a minimal linguistic module—the painter's name scribbled in the corner of the canvas, perhaps—confers the status of a text onto the entire structure. Since the first path is as plausible as the second implausible, it points a way forward.

This is not to exclude paralinguistic elements from critical analysis nor to overlook wholly nonlinguistic narratives: silent films, dance and mime, comic strips, or shadow theater.[26] Nonexistent comic strips can even be described, as in Calvino's *Cosmicomics,* and interpreted frame by imaginary frame. My only point is that, strictly speaking, the pictorial component falls outside the language base and thus the conceptual scope of language-based text. This accurately reflects the specificity of graphic novels or motion pictures that do lean on other media to convey their content.

Although van Peer concedes that the conception of text as a structure in a language is intuitively correct, he rejects it because linguists have as yet failed to "specify at least some minimal structural and functional characteristics of texts" (1993, 1). Be that as it may, a delimitation of a field of study must come before one can investigate it. One needs a working definition of text before sending linguists after its structural or functional characteristics, not to mention that extant text grammars fail to settle the questions of identity to everyone's satisfaction.

For example, the sentence-string syntactic approach and the cohesion-and-coherence semantic approach either propose unrealistic conditions (a text must be at least one sentence long) or otherwise fail to cohere with common experience.[27] The pragmatic approach favored by van Peer also has some odd consequences. One text can be "more" text than another, while conversations are deemed not to be texts at all. Despite reels upon reels of FBI-taped conversations between John Gotti and Sammy "The Bull" Gravano, all properly transcribed and analyzed in court, it is odd to be told they were not texts after all.

Assuming a text to be a structure in a language, textual identity is once again not a matter of direct perception, reducible to the apprehension of the structure alone. This is to say that one cannot determine on a perceptual basis only if a given structure is a text in a language or only scriptlike wallpaper. If the distinction seems odd, it is because in real life such distinctions are usually automatic since we bring a great deal of extratextual knowledge into the equation. That it can be far from inconsequential, however, is proven by the enigmatic Voynich manuscript.

In a scenario straight from the Twilight Zone, this illustrated codex has for four hundred years defied the world's best cryptographers, military code breakers, and now even supercomputers. Perplexingly, even though the Voynich manuscript may still prove to be gibberish, statistical analyses indicate that it is not! It has been demonstrated that it is written in at least two alternating "languages" that perfectly correspond to the distribution of its two scripts, A and B. And although some resemblance to Polynesian languages has been noted, nobody has any idea what this impenetrable script signifies—or even whether it is a script at all and not elaborate "textual" wallpaper.

## STRUCTURE IN A LANGUAGE

*Literary texts explicitly provide us with much that we will never cast doubt on, but also, unlike the real world they flag with supreme authority what we are to take as important in them, and what we must not take as a point of departure for freewheeling interpretations.*

UMBERTO ECO, *ON LITERATURE*

It seems that as far as textual identity is concerned, we keep coming back to the minimal definition of a structure in a language.[28] Yet this syntactic definition may not suffice for individuation. To gauge how difficult it may be to verify sameness or difference of a text (type or token), let us forget for a moment misspellings and other authorial deviations and focus on publishing practice. Is a type-facsimile edition that preserves the lineation and physical appearance of the original but in a different type setting the same text? What about the more common diplomatic transcript, which preserves not the appearance but only the textual content?

The editing standards inexorably steer us away from syntax and toward semantics by way of intended content. To set the issue in relief, let us begin with translations. Translations are semantically isomorphic to the original and may even involve self-renditions by an author like Samuel Beckett. Still, different contexts, different paths to creation, and not least different texts produce different works—exemplified by the familiar lines from Homer:

> Yes, for in my heart and soul I know this well:
> the day will come when sacred Troy must die,
> Priam must die and all his people with him;
> Priam who hurls the strong ash spear!
> (Translated by Robert Fagles, 1990, 150)

> The day will come—I know it in my heart of
> Hearts—when holy Illium will be destroyed,
> with Priam and the people of Priam of the good ashen spear
> (Translated by E. V. Rieu, 1953, 81)

> For this I know well in my heart and soul:
> the day must come when holy Illium
> is given to fire and sword, and Priam perishes
> good lance through he was, with all his people
> (Translated by Robert Fitzgerald, 1984, 61–62)

> For I know this well in my mind and heart:
> the day will come when sacred Ilios will be laid low, and Priam,
> and the people of Priam of the good ashen spear
> (Translated by A. T. Murray; revised by William F. Wyatt, 1999, 177)

These similar yet different editions provide a sharp illustration of what is at stake. When do differences between text tokens—which in drafts or versions may be minimal—amount to a different work, and when are they only variants of the same work? If one shreds a text and then pieces it together again with a tiny scrap missing or just in a different order, is it the same text? Or if a single letter is misplaced by the typesetter, as in the case of F. O. Matthiessen's misinterpretation, is it a different text? And if so, does one letter always make a difference?

The simplest and strictest proposals regarding textual individuation come from Goodman and Elgin, who in *Reconceptions in Philosophy* contend that any divergence whatsoever, no matter how small or insignificant, sets texts apart.[29] Conversely, if text tokens are identical, they are said to be tokens of the same text type, even in the case of polysemic words such as "set." Although "set" can have scores of meanings in English, on the syntactic approach favored by the philosophers, any instance of "set" always amounts to one and the same text.

To dispel any doubt, Goodman and Elgin make their position crystal clear in a comment on Borges. Pierre Menard's independent act of composition, they contend, produced nothing but an inscription of the text of Don Quixote that in all interpretive respects is identical with Cervantes's. All this is clear-cut—and too inflexible. One may insist that a missing comma yields a different text, but in most contexts this is an overly harsh judgment. Have I not read *1984* even if one of its commas evaporates in the print shop? On the other hand, although all commas are equal typographically, some are more equal than others aesthetically.

Recognizing this, Goodman and Elgin loosen their syntactic theses. Now when a monosyllabic text functions equally in more than one language (as "set" does in French, English, Polish, and so forth), it instantiates different texts. Thus individuation within a given language is based on syntax only (many "sets" = one text) but outside a language on semantics (many "sets" = many texts). Working in the same syntax-plus-semantics vein, another philosopher argues that two texts are identical when they share "the same semantic and syntactic properties" in a language.[30]

This allows considerable subtlety in individuation. Inadvertent scriptural elements such as misspellings, fickle orthography, and typos can now be rightfully rectified. Intentional deviance, on the other hand— Joyce's neologisms, Faulkner's Yoknapatawpha idiolects, bpNichol's typography—can be preserved.

But the openness (not to say vagueness) of this mixed approach invites its own share of difficulties. What is the degree of sameness that allows editorial reconstructors to alter the text and claim it is the same one? The lines spoken by Hector and Agamemnon are identical yet have different meanings. The answer does not seem to lie with pragmatics, which, even in single-word texts such as "set," multiplies ontological entities without end. Pragmatically, every change in meaning—whether on the semantic (locutionary) or contextual (illocutionary) level—would occasion not only a different work but a different text. Sensitivity to speech-act differences means that a single utterance could give rise to any number of text types, all looking exactly alike![31]

Since monosyllabic texts may leave one less than whelmed, let me turn to Alexandre Dumas for a typically colorful illustration. Here is one of his narrative scenarios stripped to bare bones. The French king's lover plays frigid as part of a political game: she wants him to get rid of his trusted adviser. The wily monarch gives his word that, yes, tomorrow he will finally thank the man for his services, and is rewarded by the lady. The next day, his entourage in attendance, the king indeed effusively thanks his adviser for his sterling performance. The one and the same speech has quite different meanings for the parties present: gratitude to the adviser, brush-off to the lady, and caution to the lady's backers that the king is on to them. One utterance—many texts?

Surveying the various competing proposals on textual individuation, one philosopher goes as far as to question whether any of them really corresponds to the intuitions said to underlie readerly and critical practice. "Although I have no systematic evidence to prove it," concludes Livingston, "informal experiments and experience incline me to believe that people do not share a framework of coherent intuitions" (1992b, 201). Given how volatile and sensitive to framing people's intuitions are, one might indeed have to admit that one's theses may be less factual descriptions than normative stipulations.

Keeping this in mind, I want nevertheless to argue that the reference to authorial intentions may suffice to resolve the problems of textual individuation. On my approach, a fair copy of the author's text is the matrix against which other variants are to be compared.[32] Thus the same text is one that *embodies its author's executive intentions,* allowing for textual variants occasioned by the evolving design, modernization, correction of unintended scriptural elements, and so forth. This is what I take Livingston has in mind when, in *Art and Intention,* he champions the "'locutionary' account of textual identity" (2005, 121).[33]

Linking textual individuation to the executive goals of the text's creator resolves the quandaries and unwanted consequences enumerated above. It avoids the proliferation of entities in the case of utterances that perform more than one speech act. It also avoids syntactic rigidity, allowing contextual data to guide scholars and critics while preserving the intuition that two works can share the same text type. For an example of such works, let us consider a situation in which a foreign-language speaker—say, the late Marcel Marceau—asks me for a text that means something else to him than to me in my own language.

I do not have a copy of *his* text, but I have an identical copy (text token) of mine. If I give him an English text of "chat" (as in an enjoinment to converse and exchange ideas), I think I also give him a French text of "chat" (encapsulating the feline abundance of purrs and meows). Naturally this substitutiveness does not extend to literary works, which are umbilically linked to their creators creating in historical contexts. But in the absence of any contextualizing data, faced with same-looking text exemplars, we may well conclude that both "chats" are tokens of the same text.

Significantly, linking textual individuation to intentions reflects common editorial principles whereby the reconstruction of an author's executive goals is "a prelude to the 'real' business of textual scholarship: the reconstruction of an author's intended text and/or the production of a critical edition displaying this intention."[34] Naturally, intentions are sometimes difficult to identify, and making informed conjectures about them can be tricky. Still, even in textual studies proper there is a world of difference between an intentionless script and a product of a deliberate design.

The mother of all questions is how much difference makes a difference—in other words, how much textual deviation flips over to another text? Notwithstanding millennia of editorial praxis and an inundation of theory, the long and short answer is that there is no answer. Textual relevance is irreducibly variable and nonalgorithmic (in terms of some putative percentage of deviance beyond which a text token no longer counts as an accurate copy). Textual verdicts are necessarily contingent, contextual, and case-specific.[35]

Admitting minor deviations among tokens of the same text accommodates corrections of authorial mistakes (spelling errors, malapropisms), modernizing of spelling or punctuation, reformatting in diplomatic editions, and other common editorial practices. Although "minor" will remain context-sensitive, one useful benchmark is provided by *Reader's Digest,* book-on-tape abridgments, Bowdlers of any stripe, or Big Brother expungers—major types all.

Bearing all this in mind, we can state more precisely what a literary work is, even as a good theory does not necessarily mean the end of practical problems during application:

> A literary work is an oral or written structure in a language (restored, if needed, according to its author's executive intentions), created in an art-historical context with a primary intention of realizing aesthetic/artistic properties.

One last issue is how this aesthetic, intentionalist, work-based definition compares to the sociohistorical approach favored by certain researchers. For Siegfried J. Schmidt, for example, the literary system is something quite different from a historically and aesthetically interpreted body of literary works. Tiered in a hierarchy of literary, metaliterary (critical), and meta-metaliterary (theoretical) pursuits, in his view "literature" is a class of social systems comprising not only literary artifacts but also their makers, mediators, critics, and other "processors."

Be that as it may, literary works form the core of any literary system. The inclusion of criticism and theory under the heading of "literary" may be valuable from a sociological perspective but has little to add aesthetically to what the term signifies. As implied by my discussion heretofore, the aesthetic appreciation of literary works lies at the center of any understanding of the literary system. This must be recognized by any ontology of literature, no matter what range of corollary activities it includes.

*Four*  FICTION AND NONFICTION

*This kind of novel chooses a "real" and recognizable past,
and, to make it recognizable, the novelist peoples it with characters already found in the encyclopedia (Richelieu, Mazarin),
making them perform actions that the encyclopedia does not
record (meeting Milady, consorting with a certain Bonacieux),
but which the encyclopedia does not contradict. Naturally,
to corroborate the illusion of reality, the historical characters
will also do what (as historiography concurs) they actually did
(besiege La Rochelle, have intimate relations with Anne of
Austria, deal with the Fronde).*
UMBERTO ECO, *POSTSCRIPT TO THE NAME
OF THE ROSE*

CRITICAL COMMON SENSE

*But let us try to approach a narrative work with common sense
and compare the assumptions we can make about it with those
we can make about the world.*
UMBERTO ECO, *ON LITERATURE*

In this inexhaustible source of philosophical insight and
critical common sense, Aristotle's *Poetics,* we find the following observation: "Homer and Empedocles have nothing in common but the meter,
so that it would be right to call the one poet, the other physicist rather
than poet."[1] The meaning of this passage is clear. The Greek philosopher
carefully distinguishes fiction, represented by epic poetry, from nonfiction, represented by science. Furthermore, he makes the distinction on
the basis of criteria other than the directly perceptible—but ultimately
superficial—factors, such as language, meter, and genre.

To ensure that his message does not get overlooked, a little further
on the philosopher restates the same principle in even more categorical
terms: "The poet and the historian differ not by writing in verse or in
prose. The work of Herodotus might be put into verse, and it would still
be a species of history, with meter no less than without it."[2] Here the
distinction is even more to the point. History, an enterprise more akin
to literature by virtue of its preoccupation with storytelling, is no less
separate from fiction than is the materialist physics of Empedocles.

There is no doubt that for Aristotle, much as for readers and scholars
during the intervening two and a half millennia, the discrimination between fiction and nonfiction was *a priori* in their contacts with literature.
If you told Venerable Bede or Thomas Aquinas that the chronicles or
theology they respectively wrote were fiction, they would have found

the proposition absurd in the extreme. During the past several decades, however, the more radical theorists have been renouncing, and on occasion even denouncing, the distinction between make-believe and assertion.

In some poststructuralist circles it has become downright trendy to question the distinction between fictional and, for example, historical discourse. Hayden White's *Metahistory: The Historical Imagination in Nineteenth-Century Europe* (1973) has long been notorious in its own discipline for precisely this reason. Professing that historiography is not so much a matter of evidence as of rhetorical tropes (metaphor, metonymy, synecdoche, and not least irony), White made a career of turning scholarly exhumation of the collective past into a relativistic exercise in literary interpretation.

These days, indeed, it seems to be par for the course in certain corners of literary and cultural studies to equivocate historical, journalistic, or even scientific works with fictions. Frank Lentricchia, for one, openly proclaims: "I conceive of theory as a type of rhetoric" (1983, 12). If one were to take him seriously, however, and accept his "theory" as merely rhetoric, there would be little reason to take him seriously—quite apart from the fact that much of poststructuralist rhetoric is only a pale reflection of the discursive sophistication of the Sophists or the analytic canons of Quintilian.

Not even philosophical aesthetics has proven immune to postmodern theory (or should it be postmodern rhetoric?). One of the staunchest declarations to the effect that the distinction between fiction and assertion is untenable was advanced by Hugh Wilder in "Intentions and the Very Idea of Fiction" (1988). Defining fiction in functionalist terms—fiction is what functions as fiction in a community—Wilder holds it to be a label of interpretive convenience rather than of the actual state of affairs. This is part of a broader historical claim of his that "fiction as a literary category was recognized as such only in the eighteenth and early nineteenth centuries" (72).

The implication of Wilder's thesis is remarkable: prior to the eighteenth century nobody realized that writers wrote fiction insofar as fiction as a literary category had not yet arisen. In this view, only the retrospective application of the concept fosters the illusion that Sappho, Menander, Virgil, Chaucer, Boccaccio, Cervantes, and thousands of other pre–eighteenth-century writers wrote fiction. Evidently Wilder has not heard of Aristotle's distinction between poetic fiction and the science of Empedocles or the history of Herodotus or of Plato's evocation of a categorical "quarrel between philosophy and poetry" (1999, 832) and the banishment of the latter from his *Republic*.

Wild assertions such as this notwithstanding, in everyday contacts with literature the distinction between fiction and nonfiction remains one of the central aspects of any work's identity. Without it we would find ourselves in the midst of conceptual anarchy with no grounds to tell Conan Doyle's *The Sign of Four* from Eco's *The Sign of Three*. Which is fiction and which is not? Which is detective make-believe and which pragmatic semiotics? Do both make believe or assert to an equal degree? And can we even meaningfully speak of degrees of fictionality or assertion in the first place?

If such inquiries appear too nit-picking or fanciful to be of consequence to anyone but academics, it is owing to the ease and assurance with which we can normally tell make-believe from belief. Literature is, of course, only one part of daily life in which, for the same reasons, discriminations between truth and falsehood are as significant as discriminations between assertion and make-believe in the stories we read. Not even the most avid postmodernist would accept a bank manager's "explanation" that since history is only rhetoric, his entire life's savings have been deconstructed into the account of the bank manager's.

The abject panic of 30 October 1938 perpetrated among thirty million CBS radio listeners by the misapprehension of Orson Welles's broadcast of H. G. Wells's *War of the Worlds* proves once and for all that the difference between fiction and nonfiction is far from inconsequential. Undoubtedly, the above episode is not a common one. We do not normally see people flee their homes, get soused, flock to the confessional, or attempt suicide as a result of failure to realize that a work of fiction is fiction. We do not normally see people call the *New York Times* to warn the public of the Martian attack, as almost a thousand individuals did that fateful Halloween Eve.[3]

It may be debatable whether this particular confusion of fiction with nonfiction was a freak occurrence. But it is clearly not debatable that the consequences of such confusion can be nothing short of disastrous. In his 1970 book, *The Panic Broadcast,* Howard Koch (who co-wrote the radio script with Welles) documents a couple of little-known historical footnotes to this notorious prank. The 1938 radio show was restaged in two subsequent South American incarnations, in 1944 in Chile and in 1949 in Ecuador. On both occasions it again triggered widespread agitation and panic, in the latter case tragically causing the deaths of fifteen people.

Fiction or nonfiction? Orson Welles's *Citizen Kane* was based on the life of
William Randolph Hearst. His broadcast of *War of the Worlds* terrified many
listeners who thought it was true. *The abject panic of 30 October 1938 perpetrated among
thirty million CBS radio listeners by the misapprehension of Orson Welles's broadcast of
H. G. Wells's* War of the Worlds *proves once and for all that the difference between fiction
and nonfiction is far from inconsequential.*

Human proclivity for confusing make-believe with reality has found a lasting expression in the fictional Madame Bovary, but, to paraphrase Flaubert, Madame Bovary *c'est bien nous*. Recent reports from South Korea dwell on the fate of players of the popular video game *Lineage* who got so wrapped up in the fiction that they starved themselves just to go on playing. In one gruesome development a player actually got killed when the sale of virtual Lineage swords did not turn out to the buyer's satisfaction. Closer to home, in the 1997 Heaven's Gate tragedy thirty-nine people committed suicide as a prequel to being whisked away in a spaceship said to be hiding behind the Hale-Bopp comet and carrying Jesus.

Making fiction bestows adaptive advantages, but life in the imagination also can give rise to any number of pathologies that are anything but adaptive. Still, the tendency of some people to confuse fiction with reality is well recorded. It is not even that the daily horoscope is the most popular section in most newspapers. More disturbingly, 30 percent of American high school biology *teachers* believe "in psychic powers and the ability to communicate with the dead."[4] A 2007 Gallup Poll of views on evolution found that 39 percent of adult Americans think it is unquestionably true and 27 percent probably true—a combined two-thirds of the total—that God created human beings in their present form within the last ten thousand years.[5]

In the 1990s, when *X-Files* agents Mulder and Scully owned the airwaves, James Alcock, a professor of psychology in Ontario, reported that one of the most cited sources of information among his students was—*The X-Files*. To his objections that it was only fiction they retorted: "Yes, but it's based on fact."[6] It is instructive to contrast this credulity with commentary from the show's creator, Chris Carter: "The thing you have to remember about *The X-Files* is this—it's a fiction." Pointedly, Carter added: "I don't know that it's my responsibility to say that I've just created a fiction that is a fiction."[7]

Around the same time Stephen Glass, a *New Republic* staff writer on social and political affairs, was caught making up quotations, websites, faxes, and whole organizations for his high-profile pieces. Jayson Blair of the *New York Times* resigned after plagiarizing quotes and fabricating fiction in dozens of his articles. Similar breaches led to the fall from journalistic grace of Janet Cooke of the *Washington Post,* Patricia Smith of the *Boston Globe,* and Jay Forman of *Slate.* The calumnies and apologies incited by their violations of professional ethics would be pointless if fact and fiction were one and the same thing—or if their nature was just a matter of consensual reception.

For the last word on what can go wrong if people confuse make-believe with reality I turn to Woody Allen. His droll take on the fiction/nonfiction distinction comes from "The Vodka Ad" skit from his early stand-up years. One day, says the comedian, he got a call from a vodka company with an offer of $50,000 to do publicity for it. After consulting his rabbi—who, as it later turned out, wanted to land the deal himself—he passed. Quipped Allen: "I must say it took great courage, 'cause I needed the money. I was writing, I needed to be free, creative . . . I was working on a nonfiction version of the Warren Report!"

Allen's joke highlights the perception of most Americans that fiction rubbed shoulders with nonfiction on almost every one of the 888 pages of the Warren Commission Report. But in typical Allen fashion, his joke has an interesting logical corollary. For only a categorical distinction between fiction and nonfiction makes his joke possible (that is to say, funny), much as only the distinction between fiction and nonfiction justifies the public outrage at the "lone assassin" theory. If the distinction between make-believe and assertion did not exist or if it was all contingent, there would be no joke to laugh at and no untruth to get excited about.

## MISCATEGORIZING FICTION

*The power of falsehood.*
UMBERTO ECO, *ON LITERATURE*

There is no need to dwell on the extreme examples of people dying as a result of miscategorizing fiction. The literary world is chock full of case studies of this nature, though few are as graphic as that of Art Spiegelman. When in 1991 the second installment of his category-busting masterpiece, *Maus II,* hit the *New York Times* bestseller list, it was in the category of fiction. The classification, inflected more by its genre (comic book) than its content (post-Holocaust biographical drama), was never contested by the readers who seemed perfectly at ease with the decision of the editors.[8]

After all, with Jews drawn as bewhiskered mice, Nazis as burly cats, the French as pot-bellied frogs, Poles as robust pigs, Americans as friendly dogs, and Swedes as antlered reindeer—all with human bodies and astonishingly expressive animal faces—the book just had to be make-believe. Or so it seemed to the *Times* editors. It was not to last,

however. Following a passionate letter from the author that unequivocally identified his nonfictional intentions, this Pulitzer Prize–winning
biography was moved to nonfiction. Spiegelman wrote:

> If your list was divided into literature and nonliterature I
> could gracefully accept the compliment as intended, but to
> the extent that "fiction" indicates that a work isn't factual, I
> feel a bit queasy. As an author I believe I might have lopped
> several years off the thirteen I devoted to my two-volume
> project if I could only have taken a novelist's license while
> searching for a novelistic structure. The borderland between
> fiction and nonfiction has been fertile territory for some
> of the most potent contemporary writing . . . It's just that
> I shudder to think how David Duke—if he could read—
> would respond to seeing a carefully researched work based
> closely on my father's memories of life in Hitler's Europe
> and in the death camps classified as fiction. I know that by
> delineating people with animal heads I've raised problems
> of taxonomy for you. Could you consider adding a special
> "nonfiction/mice" category to your list?[9]

Sure enough, just like its predecessor, *Maus* (1986), *Maus II* was
a narrative *tour de force,* designed to play havoc with established categories. Still, the editors' decision about its fictionality—and then
nonfictionality—was made on the basis of *some* criteria, and the nature of
such criteria is worth examining in detail. Even though in Spiegelman's
case the initial assumption of fictionality was made on the basis of textual attributes, the factor that ultimately trumped all others was the author's explicit testimony about his executive intentions. Such, however,
need not always be the case.

A point in question is Forrest Carter's *The Education of Little Tree,*
published in 1976 (and in 1997 turned into a made-for-television Canadian film), which inaugurated a notorious scandal in postwar American
literary history. Set in the Smoky Mountains of Tennessee, the story is
purported to be the autobiography of a Cherokee boy who, orphaned
at the age of five, is raised by his grandparents. In the course of events,
Little Tree becomes a witness to and even co-conspirator in their resis-
tance to dispossession by white culture and Big Business.

This moving Depression-era story initially spent nineteen weeks on
the *New York Times* list of bestselling nonfiction. Cashing in on the brisk

sales, the author repeatedly asserted it to be a true account of his childhood and his victimization at the hands of white neocolonialists. The ardor of his declarations were matched only by the vagueness about the details of his life before 1973, the year in which he burst onto the literary scene with a western, *Gone to Texas* (in 1976 filmed as *The Outlaw Josey Wales* with Clint Eastwood directing and starring). Soon, however, the whole story began to unravel.

Evidence, later confirmed in a *New York Times* exposé, began to accrue that unambiguously identified Asa Earl Carter as a white supremacist who used to work both for the Ku Klux Klan and the White Citizens' Council and who had been a speechwriter for the notoriously racist Alabama governor George Wallace. The disparity between these facts and the image that the author projected in the book—that of an ill-educated, part-Indian itinerant—led to further inquiries, which determined that the story was no more than a sophisticated fabulation of events that had never taken place.

When all was said and done, there was no doubt about the fictitious nature of this "autobiography." Here, interestingly, the circumstances proved the reverse of Spiegelman and *Maus II*. Despite the author's remonstrations about authenticity, *The Education of Little Tree* was bumped to the fiction list, where it continued to sell well and attract critical acclaim. Carter died in 1979 still claiming Cherokee ancestry, leaving open the possibility that he may have been genuinely delusional about it. Such charitable interpretation is not, however, an option in another notorious literary deception: Alex Haley's *Roots* (1976).

Depicting the life of an American slave born in The Gambia—of whom the author claimed to be a descendant—this modern American epic was publicized as bona fide nonfiction (at the end of the saga the writer even travels to The Gambia to unite in spirit with Kunta Kinte). Initially accepted as such on the strength of the author's claims, the story was subsequently proven to be fraudulent. In an out-of-court settlement Haley had to pay $650,000 to Harold Courlander after admitting that extensive passages and even the central plot line were lifted from Courlander's novel *The African,* plagiarism Haley blamed on his research assistant.

The moral of these stories is straightforward. *Contra* constructivism, it does matter whether what we read is fiction or not. We do care whether we are hoaxed into believing that what we read is truth or make-believe. As readers, editors, and critics we habitually make decisions about the nature of what we read, and we are prepared to reevaluate those decisions as better evidence becomes available. An essential—though not always decisive—source of that evidence is the author's testimony about his intentions. And, as such, it does make a difference whether the author genuinely reports on his executive intentions or merely purports to do so.

Furthermore, decisions about fictionality are made on the basis of public criteria and thus are far from arbitrary. Inasmuch as their accuracy depends on the quantity and quality of available evidence, like every epistemic enterprise directed at knowing the world, ascription of fictionality is a potentially fallible but corrigible process. When they judge a work to be fiction or not, readers can get it wrong, especially when authors cunningly set out to trip them. From this, however, it does not follow that the distinction between fiction and nonfiction is arbitrary, that it is of little significance, or even that it does not exist at all.

Lastly, as the depictions of the Holocaust in *Maus II* and of the present-day plight of Indian tribes in *Little Tree* make clear, inquiries into the nature of fiction have wide repercussions for inquiries into ethical values, historical accuracy, and literature's function as an instrument of knowledge and social justice. The critical project of deconstructing the difference between fiction and nonfiction plays into the hands of those who would doubt the autobiographical veracity of Holocaust memoirs, the historical enormity of Stalinist genocide, the scientific accuracy of linking human evolution to primates, or (fill in the blank).[10]

Naturally, in most real-life contexts the category of a book is known before it is opened. Miscellaneous social, publishing, and advertising conventions settle the matter in advance of the act of reading, creating the impression that everyday reality and authorial intentions cannot be that complicated. But unexamined impressions can sometimes lead us astray, and counterexamples to any simplistically intentionalist account of the nature of fiction abound. A closer look at the publishing histories of Edgar Allan Poe and Stanislaw Lem reveals how complex such intentions can be.

As Poe's biographers chronicle, the publication of his philosophical treatise *Eureka* in 1848 did not occur without the playful ambiguity that so often marked his attitude toward his audience. Poe was fond of hailing *Eureka* as his magnum opus and as his undying contribution to philosophy and science. He considered its epistemological and epistemic implications so profound that, to his mind at least, they simply had to be accurate. Upon its completion, he confided to Maria Clemm with a typical touch of melodrama: "I have no desire to live since I have done 'Eureka.' I could accomplish nothing more."[11]

Whether sincere or affected, this Romantic pose must be squared, however, with evidence of pragmatic games and hoaxes that the writer almost compulsively played with his contemporaries. As David Ketterer reminds us in *The Rationale of Deception in Poe,* the author of *Eureka* was routinely "a much more complicated, duplicitous, and conscious artist than was previously supposed" (1979, xii). We must thus allow that Poe's intentions in composing this philosophical essay may have, in fact, been quite heterogeneous, involving a complex mix of artistic and pragmatic goals.

Poe's frequent assertions of the truth of *Eureka* testify to his strong belief in the theory of knowledge and the cosmological model developed therein. On other occasions, however, he would glorify his treatise's literary and metaphysical vision, forsaking the assertive tone and asking that it be judged as a poem. This inconsistency makes it hard to separate his genuine intentions from apparent ones. Was *Eureka* intended as poetry or as philosophy, as philosophical fiction or perhaps even as a nonfictional prose poem? Did Poe perhaps create both fiction and nonfiction at once? Is such a state of affairs, as a matter of fact, possible? Or, granting that it is, what does it entail?

If Poe's career forces us to reconsider any simple notions of fictionality and authorial intentions, it is nowhere more so than in his twin mesmeric tales. Both "Mesmeric Revelation" and "The Facts in the Case of M. Valdemar" appear to be peculiar mixtures of fiction and nonfiction.[12] For starters, following the stories' appearance in print, Poe explicitly identified them on at least two occasions as straightforward fiction. Yet, at the same time, he took pains in various editorials to argue quite persuasively for their factuality.

It bears remembering that in the 1840s the educated American public avidly consumed accounts of new scientific discoveries, not least from such electrifying new "disciplines" as mesmerism or phrenology. Not surprisingly, therefore, both stories are styled after factual case histories, stenographing with quasi-empirical detachment the bizarre circumstances behind the mesmeric revelations supposedly observed by the narrator. These "facts" turned out to be sufficiently credible to prompt a vast number of reprints, the *Popular Record of Modern Science* among them, to tout these accounts as true and factual.[13]

At this point a functionalist like Wilder might be tempted to rest his case: Poe did not assert anything, and only his writerly cunning misled some (though not all) zealous editors into crediting his accounts as true. Such a conclusion does not, however, square with other facts of the case.

Shortly after "Mesmeric Revelation" appeared in print, Poe contacted the faculty at New York University, eagerly seeking to corroborate and substantiate his metaphysical speculations. Bolstered by a favorable reply, he proceeded to promote his *article*—no longer a story—as "the vehicle of the author's views . . . which he apparently believes to be true, in which belief he is joined by Professor BUSH."[14]

## THE INTENTIONS OF WRITING FICTION

*At most, recognizing that our history has been shaped by many stories that we now regard as false must make us cautious, and always ready to call into question the very stories that we now hold as true.*
UMBERTO ECO, *ON LITERATURE*

It would appear that Poe was motivated in different degrees by the intentions of writing fiction and advancing original nonfictional ideas as well as doing so in a clever enough way to permit both alternatives. Any credible theory of fiction must be able to capture the complexity of his intentions, which seem considerably less straightforward or homogeneous than often is assumed. This is far from claiming that Poe's tactics erase the boundary between fiction and nonfiction. To position oneself on a boundary, and for the readers to recognize such a move, one needs the boundary in the first place.

Another instructive example of heterogeneous intentions at work is recounted by Greetham in *Textual Scholarship:*

> When Steinbeck handed over the text of *The Grapes of Wrath* to his publisher in 1940, he was concerned that his attack on the agricultural growers in California and on the banking practices in the United States not be misinterpreted as a foreign-inspired piece of radical agitation. (He had already written and then destroyed an earlier draft which was much more overt in its criticisms.) Accordingly, he insisted that the book have in its end-papers the text and music of that patriotic song, *The Battle Hymn of the Republic,* and when the publisher initially included only the text, he responded by demanding that the whole thing be there—

music as well. Thus the socially conscious book almost literally wrapped itself in the flag to protect itself against misconstrual of its meaning—except for one thing. While *The Battle Hymn of the Republic* might have been taken by most readers as a bibliographical defense against a charge of sedition (then and now), the fact was that in the Thirties, the *Hymn* had regularly been sung at meetings of the Communist Party in the United States—as Steinbeck was well aware—so that he might have been disingenuous in claiming that his new end-papers brought only one meaning: maybe there were two, one for each audience. (1994, 293)

But what of Lem? That truth can be stranger than fiction is evinced by the circumstances surrounding one of his later works, *Prowokacja* (*Provocation*, 1984).[15] In real life we know how to approach fictional flights of fancy as opposed to nonfictional reviews, recognizing beforehand the category to which they belong. Yet, just like *Maus* two years later, *Prowokacja* defies easy categorization. After all, this short work is not just a fictional review but a fictional review of a fictively nonfictional study by a fictitious German scholar—that is, a study and a scholar who simply do not exist. Or is it? And how would we know?

First of all, there is nothing in Lem's text to suggest that it is anything but a nonfiction. Stylistically it is indistinguishable from a regular review—so much so that professional historians and anthropologists spent a great deal of time trying to get their hands on the original. Still, like Cinderella the author leaves a clue that suggests otherwise.[16] The publication date of the review is one year ahead of the reviewed work, and since one cannot review a book that has not been written yet, *Prowokacja* must be fiction. Or must it? Reviewers frequently obtain advance galleys from the press, and if Lem really wanted to disambiguate things, he could have placed it twenty years in the future.

The book advances explicit theses regarding the role of *thanatos* in today's world. Lem argues that the ethics of evil and aesthetics of kitsch that paved the way for the mass murders of the Nazi era return in modern incarnations such as terrorism, ritualized violence in art and the media, the increased sanctioning of death in national doctrines, political and social extremism, and a resurgence of neofascism on the electoral far right. There is no uncertainty, in other words, about the earnestness of the author's political and sociocultural theses in this work. Do his cognitive ambitions make it, however, any less fictional?

Fictional narratives and nonfictional reviews pose no interpretive problems as long as we are sure which is which. Only when we run afoul of easy category ascription do we turn to theory for succor. In the intentionalist theory of fiction, in which the key factor is the speech act of its author, the case is unproblematic. Notwithstanding the ambiguities of reception, Lem's work is fiction because it was created (reflexively intended) as such. On the competing theory exemplified by Wilder, fictionality is determined by the work's function in a community—that is, by its history of reception.

These days functionalism is defined in terms of a (dominant) community of readers who ask not "What is fiction?"—which would imply that there is an objective, reader-independent state of affairs—but "When is fiction?"—implying that the work's status is reader-dependent and contingent.[17] Interestingly enough, much as with the Martian broadcasts, Poe's mesmeric "articles," Miller's *Tropics,* Kosinski's *Painted Bird,* or Hildesheimer's *Marbot,* some aspects of the reception of Lem's made-up review would seem to suggest that it is anything but fiction.

To begin, some scholars took the publication to be a genuine nonfictional review of a genuine historical study. How genuine it appeared can be inferred from the attempts some made to actually order it from the purported publisher! Other enterprising researchers, cognizant that during the politically turbulent 1980s Lem resided in West Berlin and Austria (where he wrote *Prowokacja*), repeatedly tried to request it through interlibrary loan systems. Truth being stranger than fiction, there was, however, an even more bizarre twist to the story.

In a 1984 interview with Peter Engel, Lem recalled a meeting between an acquaintance of his, a historian and then director of the Central Commission for the Investigation of Nazi Crimes in Poland, and a member of the Polish Academy of Sciences. The encounter took place in West Berlin in the immediate aftermath of the publication of *Prowokacja.* Upon hearing that the study made a profound impression on the academician, the historian remarked: "I believe that Lem wrote a review of that book," to which the other replied, "I don't know if Lem wrote anything, but I've got the book at home!"—in reference to a book that never existed.

At this point a functionalist might simply shrug and conclude that this sort of response classifies *Prowokacja* as nonfiction. However, the reception of Lem's work as a genuine review of a genuine study is anything but the norm. The majority of readers who correctly read the book as fiction put functionalism in a quandary, since the same work is now fiction for some and nonfiction for others or else fiction today, nonfiction tomorrow, and then back and forth again, depending on how it is perceived. Such a radical dichotomy of reception is less improbable than it may seem: a similar kind of ambiguity also surrounds Lem's *Golem XIV.*

The disparity between the functionalist and intentionalist accounts of Lem's work is striking. The former stipulates that there is no reader-independent fact of the matter and hence that *Prowokacja* is nonfiction for some readers and fiction for most, as attested by its reception. According to the intentionalists there is a reader-independent fact of the matter established by the author's fiction-making intentions. For that reason, notwithstanding the playfully assertive text and the scattershot reception, *Prowokacja* is a brilliant and provocative fiction.

The intentionalists stand on firm ground since, in interview after interview, Lem unequivocally identified his fiction-making intentions, apparently tetchy that anyone could think otherwise. During our meetings in the 1990s he reiterated this intention of providing a serious analysis of a crucial aspect of modern civilization in a work of fiction disguised as a serious review. Together with the deliberate discrepancy between the dates of publication and the playfulness with which he rewrote literary categories throughout his career, all this offers a consistent body of evidence that *Prowokacja* was reflexively intended as a work of fiction.

We have thus two competing approaches to the nature of fiction, complete with two results of their applications that for obvious reasons are incompatible with each other. If functionalism appears intuitively untenable, it is because it is almost solipsistic, allowing the same work to flip from being fiction to nonfiction in accordance with the readers' fancy. On the other hand, it is not immediately obvious that we should side with intentionalism. As evident from my case studies, no simple "atomic" account of authorial intentions could capture the gamut of attitudes that went into the creation of these works—and many others.

Take Matthew Rossi's *Things That Never Were* (2003). The dust jacket advertises it as "speculative nonfiction, or crypto-journalism, or historico-literary ranting, or guided daydreaming, or collective-unconscious channeling, or edutainment disinformation, or fabulaic mimesis, or polymorphously perverse media-jamming, or any other semi-oxymoronic term you care to employ." That same jacket classifies it as *both* science fiction and nonfiction. Whatever this state of affairs may entail, it is clear that no idealistically coherent and homogeneous account of fiction-making intentions will be adequate vis-à-vis complex and untidy reality.

Writers love to transgress and confound, and it is no accident that so many are drawn to testing the boundaries between the most important categories for any novelist and reader. Thus, in the opening sentence of an unheaded preface to *Un día de cólera,* Arturo Pérez-Reverte claims that the book "is neither fiction nor a work of history." At the start of *No Laughing Matter,* Joseph Heller and Speed Vogel forewarn: "What follows is essentially a true account that is accurate in every detail but those in which it is not." Michael Crichton's thriller *Next* is preceded by a similar disclaimer: "This novel is fiction, except for the parts that aren't." The only thing the writers do not tell us is *which* parts are fiction and which are not. For that we need to turn to theorists.

## DOES FICTIONALITY RESIDE IN THE TEXT?

*A book is made up of signs that speak of other signs, which in their turn speak of things.*
UMBERTO ECO, *POSTSCRIPT TO THE NAME OF THE ROSE*

Let us look at the nature of fiction more systematically. Does fictionality reside in the text? The answer, going back to Aristotle, is negative since the text of a chronicle and that of a historical novel can be identical. Lem hammers this point home in *Prowokacja,* a fiction indistinguishable in its verbal structure from a nonfictional review. Naturally, often enough the text itself is a good guide to the nature of the work. But while textual factors such as diction or narrative form may count as evidence, one must not confuse evidentiary issues with categorical ones.

A different tactic, in the tradition of Russian formalism and Prague School structuralism, is to look for fictionality in nonliteral, "poetic" language use. Since novels and poems are replete with metaphors and other tropes, perhaps those can be used to determine fictionality. Since the straightforward variant of this thesis is a nonstarter—nonfictions are rife with metaphors too—in the quantitative variant fiction is only said to be denser in verbal texture. But just like fever is not itself a disease, this again confuses evidence for a state of the matter with the state of the matter. Density of nonliteral language use might be a part of the evidence for the nature of a work, but it does not by itself establish the nature of a work.

After all, although novels are packed with figurative language, it would be hard to find nonfictions that are not. Wrought to compete with fiction, some of the best New Journalism of Tom Wolfe, Gay Talese, and Joan Didion is replete with dialogue, figurative language, and every other rhetorical armament from a fiction writer's arsenal. Much for the same reasons, attempts to locate fictionality in the membership of various literary genres also are doomed from the get-go, especially given such ready counterexamples as Lem's innovative fiction or Spiegelman's innovative nonfiction.

In general, there is nothing in any genre to make it inherently fictional. A political tract may be dressed up as a flamboyant burlesque, and a fictional satire may be fashioned to resemble a sober political pamphlet. To boost sales, real-crime bestsellers employ all the stock devices of the mystery genre—Mailer's *The Executioner's Song* and Wambaugh's nonfiction classics from *The Onion Field* to *Fire Lover* are sterling candidates for this category—yet remain nonfiction. Genre membership is thus both an insufficient condition and an unnecessary one.

A more promising approach takes fictionality to be a relational property, that is, not one contained in the text but rather enjoyed vis-à-vis entities outside it. One such evident relational property arises from the relation of works to their readers. Can fictionality be assessed along functional lines, in terms of readers' attitudes? An obvious objection that readers can be mistaken about the nature of a work does not persuade at this stage, insofar as it is circular. It would be valid if criteria other than functionalist ones were already in place to settle the matter, which begs the question of the need for the inquiry in the first place.

Still, there are persuasive reasons for rejecting the functionalist approach to the nature of fiction. Here is one: functionalism must at some point resort to some form of consensus building, whether institution- or community-based, which opens it to the charge of incoherence when such consensus is lacking. Making one and the same work flip from being fiction to nonfiction in keeping with the perceptions of its readers is as hard to accept as the idea that, in the functionalist view, there would be no untrue nonfiction.

Science can, after all, on occasion get things wrong, but is the geocentric cosmology of Claudius Ptolemy fiction just because it gets its facts wrong? Or, in other versions of functionalism, is it nonfiction merely by dint of some vaguely defined tradition? In functionalist terms, if a sufficient number of readers (and how many exactly?) believed that the geocentric system was fiction, it would indeed become one. By that token the theory of evolution *is* fiction in the United States, although not in the rest of the world, given that the majority of Americans reportedly believe it is. Not all functionalists might be sanguine about this upshot of their theory.

Another class of relational properties is formed by truth and reference, both indexed by literature's semantic relation to the world. Some critics have actually proposed that fictions are distinguishable from nonfictions by virtue of lacking any referential properties. Some of the direct consequences of the view that fiction does not refer to anything outside itself are, however, less than plausible. One of them is that it is meaningless to claim that Poe's sleuth Augustus Dupin or Simenon's inspector Jules Maigret plod about their cases in the streets of, respectively, nineteenth- and twentieth-century Paris.

The claim seems baffling at best, wrongheaded at worst. Readers are clearly meant to discern, and have no difficulty discerning, that Poe and Simenon want us to think of the capital of France. The historical fact that Paris was never the home of the ratiocinating Dupin or the methodical Maigret proves only that some details the authors wrote are not true in our world, and nothing else. It certainly does not logically establish that literary fiction has no referential properties. Were that true, Heinrich Schliemann's discovery of the historical Troy with a copy of *Iliad* in hand would rate as a miracle.

Similarly, the putative semantic gulf between fiction and nonfiction begs the question of how readers know that Maigret and Dupin were, in fact, residents of the City of Lights and not the Windy City. In sum, it makes little sense to claim that fictions do not have referential properties (truth values) just because they are not asserted. We have, after all, no trouble recognizing something to be false in our world—for instance, that there is no such thing as the Library of Babel or the Lottery of Babylon—but true in the story, as in Borges's eponymous tales.

At any rate, the semantic distinction does not have the desired upshot since truth and reference are attributable to nonfiction *and* fiction. Most literary fictions are literally false, but scientific theories, historical reconstructions, and philosophical systems can be false as well. At the same time fictions are often true in part, and some—for example, Thomas Keneally's *Schindler's Ark* (*Schindler's List* in American editions)—may even be true in their entirety. Bearing all this mind, it is unlikely that the fictionality of a piece of writing can be decided by reference to its truth value, even though truth of reference can be a source of evidence in the matter.

More generally, this type of confusion stems from a failure to pry apart the meaning of a proposition from its contextual, speech-act meaning. Two identical texts can have the same literal meaning yet differ on the level of the speech act. One and the same text can, for example, be a question and a request—as in "Will you stop that?" Or, as Aristotle noted, one text can be fiction and not fiction. Since in the next chapter I take the speech-act route to the nature of fiction, it will help us to rehearse a few of the theory's salient points.

The key to the theory is contained in the title of J. L. Austin's *How to Do Things with Words* (1962).[18] Far from being mere passive units of language imbued with dictionary meaning and grammatical function, words can do things, affect reality, provoke actions, and even become actions themselves. "I do" in response to "Do you like sorbet?" plays a different role (constative) than the same words uttered in the presence of a justice of the peace. When you say "I do" in the latter case, you indeed "do" something: you perform a speech act by means of which you form a binding pact with your spouse, the witnesses, and society's legislative apparatus.

In the first approximation, the things we do with words fall into one of two categories. *Constatives* are statements characterized in terms of truth or falsehood. The constative "I like sorbet" is true of me, Pete Swirski, but "I am the author of *Odyssey*" is not (it is true of Homer and of Nicos Kazantzakis). The status (truth) of a constative depends, in other words, on the fit between the statement and what the statement refers to. Not so with a *performative*, which necessarily produces the state to which it refers. "I do" in city hall at once performs and produces a marriage vow. Performatives enact all kinds of communicative conventions—declarations, requests, threats, thanks, promises, and baptisms, to name a few. Those can be explicit, as in "I sentence you to ten years," or implicit and even nonverbal (assent to a bet can be communicated by a nod).[19]

Obviously, performatives can go wrong, and for them to work as intended, certain felicity conditions must obtain between the parties involved.[20] Unlike structuralist or transformational linguistics, speech-act theory is thus necessarily enmeshed in the context of the interaction. It is concerned with how utterance in a context relates to what it means outside a context. In Austin's words, "To explain what can go wrong with statements we cannot just concentrate on the proposition involved (whatever that is) as has been done traditionally. We must consider the total situation in which the utterance is issued—the total speech act" (1962, 52).

This is brought out by the part of his theory directly relevant to us: the types of force (meaning) associated with speech acts. The three types are:

- locutionary force—the referential value of a statement, or its *semantic meaning;*[21]
- illocutionary force—the performative value of a statement, or the *speech-act meaning* implied by the speaker/author;
- perlocutionary force—the perceived value of a statement, or its *inferred meaning* by the listener/reader.

Crucially, the speech act of a statement is *not* entailed by its "surface" semantic meaning. That is, the illocutionary meaning of a statement is not entailed by its locutionary meaning. The difference here is between speech and speech act—or between dictionary meaning and contextual meaning. The rhetorical trope of *occupatio*, for example, works by stating the exact opposite of what is to be conveyed. If all this sounds complicated, it should not be; it is the way all of us make words do things for us in daily interpersonal commerce (and unlike Humpty Dumpty, we do not even pay them extra).

Austin's crucial insight was that language always states *and* performs.[22] Here is an illustration of the difference between locutionary and illocutionary meaning. Entering a room where a window has been left open in wintertime, I can express the fact that the room is cold with a simple statement: "It's freezing." In this case the locutionary force of the sentence and its illocutionary force match perfectly: the sentence says what I literally say. But when, on entering the room, I bark at you, "It's freezing," the sentence retains its normal meaning, but now it performs the role of an order to close that goddamn window!

The locutionary aspect has not changed. The second sentence still means what it means—that the room is cold. But the illocutionary meaning has changed. I am now doing something with words—namely ordering you to perform an action—rather than simply stating the fact of the matter. Analogously, if you answer, "I hear ya," the locution comes from the normal meaning of the words "I hear ya." The illocutionary force comes from your reflexive intention to communicate that you will close the window. The perlocutionary force comes from my recognition of your reflexive intention and acceptance of your promise.

In short, when you say "I promise to close the window" or just "I hear ya" (locution), you promise me something (illocution), and recognizing the promise, I accept it (perlocution). Real life rarely is so schematic, though. Intentions can be ill expressed, complexly layered, or even deceptive. Illocutionary status can be ambiguous, obscure, or idiosyncratic, and the whole process can run afoul of a number of communicative pitfalls. But, as in real life, intentions can be clarified, meanings disambiguated, and communication fine-tuned on the basis of past performance, both successful and not. When you think about it, for the most part we experience little difficulty understanding other people or making ourselves understood.

It is worth reiterating that performative language necessarily involves more than one person. Speech acts derive their meaning from the collective recognition of a given sociocommunicative convention. Utterances may be uttered *in vacuo,* but performatives are not unilateral, nor do they involve tape recorders, parrots, and other utterance-producing entities. When we employ language to perform a speech act, we are always embedded in social intersubjective communication. And the reason communication, this almost automatic recognition of intended linguistic and nonlinguistic expression, is so effortless, efficient, and effective is because of humans' innate ability to project intentional states—in short, because of an evolutionary adaptation known as theory of mind.

*Five*  THE NATURE OF FICTION

*While a work is in progress, the dialogue is double: there is the dialogue between that text and all other previously written texts (books are made only from other books and around other books), and there is the dialogue between the author and his model reader.*

UMBERTO ECO, *POSTSCRIPT TO THE NAME OF THE ROSE*

# THE REFLEXIVE INTENTIONS
# OF A WRITER

*Writing a novel is a cosmological matter, like the story told*
*by Genesis (we all have to choose our role models, as Woody*
*Allen puts it).*
UMBERTO ECO, *POSTSCRIPT TO THE NAME*
*OF THE ROSE*

Fictionality resides neither in the text nor in the text's relational properties, be they referential or functional. Instead, the nature
of fiction is determined by the reflexive intentions of a writer during
the work's creation. In the lexicon of speech–act theory, fictionality is a
matter of performance. Style, diction, genre, rhetorical tropes, the degree of veracity (mimesis) are all sources of evidence about the fact of
the matter. But the fact of the matter lies in the illocutionary force of the
work in question.

Indeed, different approaches to the nature of fiction can be contrasted
in terms of speech–act terminology. Textualists, who take the inherent
linguistic features of a discourse to be determinant of its fictionality,
focus on locution. Functionalists, who relate fictionality to the reception of a discourse, focus on perlocution. Both stand apart from the illocutionary approach, the essence of which is epigramatized by Sandy
Petrey in *Speech Acts and Literary Theory:* "Like saying and doing, writing
performs" (1990, 56).

It must be quickly pointed out that the earlier speech–act analyses
of the nature of fiction have not been particularly successful. Among
those one must count the efforts of the founder of speech–act theory
himself. Insofar as Austin was an ordinary language philosopher, he did

not regard fiction making as an "ordinary," that is, a natural way to use language. As such, he did not regard fiction making as a speech act, no matter how ubiquitous, transcultural, and natural—in the sense of being evolutionarily adaptive—it has been throughout the ages.

Austin's suspicion of the manner in which language behaves when put to making fiction influenced other philosophers. Notable among them was John Searle, who also attempted to theorize make-believe by setting it apart from the things we normally do with words. Furthermore, in *How to Do Things with Words* Austin inclined to assign speech-act values to individual propositions in a play or a story rather than to see fiction making as a distinct speech act in its own right. In his opinion:

> A performative utterance will, for example, be *in a peculiar way* hollow or void if said by an actor on the stage, or if introduced in a poem, or spoken in soliloquy. . . . Language in such circumstances is in special ways—intelligibly—used not seriously, but in ways *parasitic* upon its normal use. (1962, 22)

Harriet Beecher Stowe, Upton Sinclair, Thomas Keneally, and myriad other fiction writers might have something to say about not using language parasitically. Worse, Austin's embargo runs counter to his own theory. Insofar as a felicitous speech act is enabled by social conventions, it is hard to see how such a universal and transcultural convention as fiction making is not a speech act but an act of linguistic parasitism. Granted, readers do not react (perlocute) to fiction as they would to real-life assertions or threats. But Austin never considers an alternative, namely that a distinct speech act of "fiction making" leads readers to adopt a distinct "fiction reading" attitude.[1]

Yet the evidence for the latter is incontrovertible. Take any fiction—say, John Donne's poem "Go and Catch a Falling Star." As Petrey spells it out, the literary convention attendant on fiction making invites readers

> to *interpret* Donne's imperative [i.e., "go catch a falling star"] rather than *execute* it through social processes identical in kind to those that invite an infantryman to execute a sergeant's imperative rather than interpret it. (1990, 52)

Indeed, in the *Distinction of Fiction* Dorrit Cohn maps out the whole spectrum of narratological conventions employed to signal that readers are to "read as fiction." These conventions run the gamut from content-based through plot or genre conventions down to explicit disclaimers of any correspondence to real events or people, dead or alive.

Every installment of Ed McBain's 87th Precinct series is, for example, prefaced with: "The city in these pages is imaginary. The people, the places, are all fictitious. Only the police routine is based on established investigatory technique." Clues of this order, inserted with a reflexive intention of signaling the nature of the story, trigger an automatic recognition that one is reading fiction. It is only when we run into difficulties that we start paying heed to the manner in which such clues are put forth to be recognized as having been intended to be recognized.

Searle's chapter "The Logical Status of Fictional Discourse" (1979) is another attempt to explain what makes fiction fiction in terms of speech-act theory. Proceeding via the *via negativa,* the philosopher lays the foundations for his own "pretense theory" by first discounting a number of rival approaches. Since they provide a helpful recap of what we have covered so far, here they are together with my annotations.

1.     *Fiction is not coterminous with literature.* This is uncontentious: *The Electric Kool-Aid Acid Test* and *Armies of the Night* are literature but not fiction. On the other hand, jokes are fiction, but some at least are not quite literary.

2.     *Fiction is not a matter of figurative language (tropes).* This is just as uncontentious: since metaphors *et alia* are found in history, philosophy, and science, they are clearly not fiction-specific.

3.     *Fiction is not a matter of frivolity.* Like Austin, one can label fiction "unserious" in the sense of being unasserted, but when it comes to social commitment or emotional gravitas, *Uncle Tom's Cabin* and *The Jungle* are very serious indeed.

4.     *Fiction is not a matter of lying or, conversely, assertion.* Not intended to deceive, fictions do not lie, but neither are they meant as gospel truth. Still, Searle overlooks fictions such as *Schindler's Ark* that may be true in their entirety.

5.     *Fiction is not a matter of textual or stylistic properties.* Once again, this is uncontentious (as described in Chapter 4).

6.     *Fiction is not equivalent to works of fiction.* Searle separates fictional discourse, which according to him is by definition a matter of pretense, from works of fiction, which are not necessarily a matter of pretense insofar as literature does tell the truth—or at the very least refers to real people, places, and events. Thus, for some narratives, Searle suspends his

criterion of fictionality without, however, telling us when
literary works renounce pretense in order to tell the truth. For
example, the philosopher takes the opening sentence of *Anna
Karenina* to be "not a fictional but a serious utterance" (74).
He is right: literary fictions can and do assert. But he gives
no explanation of how to sieve make-believe from assertion.
Alas, without it his theory is little more than just a new label
(pretense) for something we already knew was there (fiction).[2]

Searle's troubles begin in earnest when he contends that fiction is not
a matter of an illocutionary act of fiction making—precisely the theory
I defend below. Usually a paradigm of clarity, the philosopher becomes
curiously hazy and laconic when it comes to defending this contention.
Even as he declares that the illocutionary approach is incorrect, he states:
"I shall not devote a great deal of space to demonstrating that it is incorrect" (64). But it is Searle's own argument that is incorrect, and it does
not take a great deal of space to demonstrate it.[3]

In defense of his contention the philosopher asserts that "the illocutionary act performed in the utterance of a sentence is a function of the
meaning of the sentence" (64). That is, he claims that the illocution of a
sentence is a function of the locution of that sentence—in other words,
semantic meaning fixes contextual meaning. And on the basis of this er-
roneous premise, Searle states that if fiction performed a different speech
act than that determined by its normal meaning—for example, a speech
act of fiction making—its meaning would be different from its normal
meaning. He concludes:

> Anyone therefore who wishes to claim that fiction contains
> different illocutionary acts from nonfiction is committed to
> the view that words do not have their normal meaning in
> works of fiction. (64)

However, knowing what we do of speech-act theory from Chapter 4,
it is clear that, as stated, Searle's functionality principle is unequivocally
wrong. Words do retain their normal meaning in fiction because normal locutionary meaning does *not* fix their illocutionary meaning. The
functionality principle may be operative for constatives, where the locutionary (dictionary) meaning of "It's freezing" corresponds to its illocutionary (contextual) meaning. But, as we know, this is not true for other
types of illocution.

The same sentence, meaning the same thing, can initiate quite disparate illocutionary acts. "It's freezing" can be an assertion or an order. "Will you stop that?" can express a request or an inquiry. Even Searle's own example—"Can John run a mile?"—does not function exclusively as interrogative. A sardonic repetition of the question, using the same words with the same meaning, can become a contextual assertion of "Yes, c'mon, of course he can!"[4] The locutionary force of *Maus II* and *Prowokacja* is perfectly compatible with their being fiction or nonfiction—with no textual clues as to which is which.

So much for Searle's attempted refutation. Now let us take a closer look at his alternative. The philosopher proposes that fiction *is* a matter of a distinct illocutionary act performed by the writer or speaker—the act of "nondeceptive pseudoperformance which constitutes pretending to recount to us a series of events" (65). Note right from the start that even if the pretense theory worked as prescribed, it would still be incomplete. *Contra* Searle, one might, after all, engage in pretended recounting without necessarily producing fiction, as in verbal parody (the late George Carlin doing the John Byner Ed Sullivan?).

Searle's pretense theory suffers from other shortcomings, the most obvious of which is that it is at odds with critical experience. It stipulates, for example, that insofar as they are pretended, fictions cannot satirize—which hangs a big question mark on what exactly it is that *Animal Farm* does. Also, on Searle's account, plays are merely recipes for fictions, making it impossible to classify Thornton Wilder's *The Skin of Our Teeth*—in which dinosaurs warm themselves in the house of a twentieth-century Antrobus family—as fiction.

These and other drawbacks of Searle's approach—his so-called vertical rules do not work as prescribed, while the horizontal ones are not prescribed—must not blind us, however, to the fact that in crucial respects it marks an important step forward. First, departing from Austin's piecemeal approach to individual textual propositions, Searle clearly appreciates that fictionality is a matter of a distinct illocutionary act (or a meta-act over sundry propositions and attitudes expressed in the story). In his view fictionality is a result of such a global, temporarily extensive speech act.

Second, fully aware of the conventional and reciprocal nature of fiction making, Searle identifies the author as the key player who initiates the literary communicative game. It is the author who determines the nature of the speech act and consequently the nature of fiction. It is *his* intention that the utterance be reflexively recognized as fiction that in-

vites readers to adopt an appropriate fiction-reading response: the "identifying criterion for whether or not a text is a work of fiction, must of
necessity lie in the illocutionary intentions of the author" (65).

Unhappy with Searle's contention that literary fiction suspends normal communication, Petrey goes on to interpret this appeal to authorial intentions as meaning that illocutionary conventions—which must
involve more than one person—are also suspended. In fact, it is just the
opposite. The authorial speech act of fiction making necessarily invokes
and takes advantage of the conventions that govern the functioning of
fiction in society. Without such conventions in place, one's intentions to
create fiction—an important part of which is that what is written should
be read as fiction—would be stillborn.

Are Searle's reliance on authorial intentions and Petrey's functionalism—whereby fiction is said to become fiction by communal
ratification—irreconcilable? I do not think so. The fact that an utterance
becomes fiction by dint of its author's speech act is perfectly compatible
with the need for these intentions to conform to the conventions already
in place in society. Petrey himself appears to acknowledge as much by
citing Brown and Steinman: "A discourse *is* fictional because its speaker
or writer intends it so. But it is *taken as* fictional only because its hearer
or reader *decides* to take it so."[5]

## NONDECEPTIVE SPEECH ACT
## OF FICTION MAKING

*There are people who have based their entire reading of Poe's*
*"Purloined Letter" on the position of the letter with regard to*
*the mantelpiece.*
UMBERTO ECO, *ON LITERATURE*

On the theory articulated by Currie in *The Nature of Fiction*
(1990), writers do not pretend anything but engage in a genuine, nondeceptive speech act of fiction making. Far from an immanent property of
the text, fictionality is therefore an intentional property of the work. In
what follows I analyze Currie's theory with a view to the necessary and
sufficient conditions for a literary work to be a work of fiction. Although
I am much indebted to Currie's theses, there are critical differences between us, as will become apparent in the last section of this chapter.

The linchpin of the speech-act approach to the nature of fiction is the reflexive interdependence of the author and the reader. The author wants the reader to adopt a certain stance toward the work—a stance of make-believe, to invoke Kendall Walton's terminology from *Mimesis as Make-Believe* (1990).[6] The term means simply that readers ought to adopt the attitude of "fiction reading" to works such as *Tarzan* or *Harry Potter*. More generally, audiences are asked to espouse a different attitude to fiction and nonfiction by recognizing the creator's intention that they do so: make-believe and belief, respectively.

In this elegant way the theory captures what is at stake. Fictionality is a matter of the author's speech-act intentions, one part of which is that readers read the work as fiction rather than as nonfiction (the difference is enormous). Reflexively recognizing this intention, readers will make believe rather than believe a story. Recognizing intentions is, I must stress, part of a broader cognitive adaptation for making sense of the world by dint of making sense of people's behavior. Being an adaptation, recognizing people's intentions is an instinctive ability, as shown by research in imitative learning.

Michael Tomasello, a leading expert in the field and a leading exponent of theory of mind as a cognitive adaptation, leaves no doubt about it in "Understanding and Sharing Intentions." Imitation in children is not a case of blind repetition and unthinking mirroring of adults. Research shows that it is "only if a young child understands other persons as intentional agents that she can acquire and use linguistic symbols" (2005, 675). Intentionality, in short, is the bedrock of agency and of interpersonal communication. It underpins the cognitive faculties and social interactions that depend on collective beliefs, or what Tomasello and the co-authors call skills of cultural cognition.

How exactly do reflexive intentions work in a literary context? Here is how Currie breaks down the reflexive "loop" by means of which writers communicate—and readers interpret—fiction-making intentions.

> I want you to make believe some proposition P; I utter a sentence that means P, intending that you shall recognize this is what the sentence means, and to recognize that I intend to produce a sentence that means P; and I intend you to infer from this that I intend you to make believe that P; and, finally, I intend that you shall, partly as a result of this recognition, come to make believe that P. (1990, 31)

For a colorful illustration of this process we can turn to one of Poe's best-liked fictions. "The Purloined Letter" provides brilliant examples of two-person interactions characterized by each person's reflexive awareness of the other party. One reason the tale merits closer examination is that it foregrounds the analytical structure of the underlying conflicts at the expense of the social and psychological background. Far from a realistic narrative with the proper depth and veracity of its psychosocial "framing," "The Purloined Letter" is a model of reflexive intentions in action, stripped down to narrative essentials.[7]

Acclaimed for his portrayals of the darker niches of the human psyche, here Poe illustrates the essence of a reflexive guessing game. His emphasis on the deep structure of the conflict—first between the queen and the scoundrel, then between the detective and the scoundrel—endows the story with analytic flavor. One would look in vain in "The Purloined Letter" for a pathological complexity of a Roderick Usher, the satirical impishness of "How to Write a Blackwood Article," or the exotic adventure of *Arthur Gordon Pym*. Instead, we are rewarded with a parsimonious, logical structure of a reflexive game of cops and robbers.

Far from presenting a cross-section of Parisian society, the principal cast is limited to four types that have since become the staple of the genre: the archvillain, the assiduous but inept officer of the law, the master sleuth, and the faithful sidekick. Equally unrealistically, the central event is a result of a chain of credulity-defying coincidences. Not only is the queen reading an incriminating letter at the very moment when the king pays a surprise visit; not only is she unable to conceal it; not only does the king fail to see anything amiss; not only does the malefactor, Minister D—, drop by the royal boudoir at this opportune instance; not only does he instantly size up the envelope and recognize the handwriting; not only does he happen to be in possession of a look-alike letter; but, improvising his Machiavellian scheme on the spot, he executes it without a hitch by switching the letters.

It is remarkable how even this brief scene underscores the degree to which the interests and strategies of the players are interrelated and mutually anticipatory. In order to steal the letter from under the queen's very nose, D— must be relatively sure that he will not be caught in the act. This confidence can only be a result of his clever reasoning *about the queen's point of view*. It involves an analysis of her choices and their respective outcomes: (1) stop the thief but reveal the contents of the fateful letter, and (2) consent to the theft but preserve the anonymity of the contents.

Having weighed the queen's likely preferences about these outcomes, the minister makes his brazen move. However, perhaps he is not risking that much, since the similarity of the letters effectively limits the queen's options. Were she to cry foul, punishing the minister at the cost of compromising herself, the diabolical D— could ascribe his behavior to a guileless error. The queen's range of replies to D—'s opening move in this game of perfect (and possibly complete) information is thus severely restricted.

In game-theory terms, perfect information means that players know the moves of all other players at each stage in the game. In games of complete information players know each other's preferences as well as the rules of play. In Poe's artful scenario the queen and D— know exactly what is going on and can effectively reason what course of action (or in the queen's case, inaction) is open to the other. The lady dares not call attention to the theft, anticipating humiliation at no cost to D—. The minister, reproducing the queen's train of thought, anticipates her passivity and, thus emboldened, proceeds to exploit it.

What makes the story so illuminating in terms of game theory and of literary pragmatics is the reflexive interdependence of both players' behavior. By this I mean the need not only to consider the other player's moves but also to anticipate the opponent's anticipation of one's own moves. In other words, reflexive interdependence turns the tables not just on the other player but on oneself as well. In "The Purloined Letter" Poe captures it in terms of "the robber's knowledge of the loser's knowledge of the robber" (977).

Poe's awareness of the importance of this formula is evident: first it is stated by his narrator, only to be restated verbatim two paragraphs later by Dupin. Later in the story, when the Prefect G. describes the ease with which he gains access to the malefactor's house and person, one begins to suspect that D— must have anticipated G.'s moves and was in fact playing into his hands. Dupin, who by dint of his position in the detective game needs to anticipate the minister's moves, understands this at once. He calls D— "not altogether a fool" who "must have anticipated these waylayings, as a matter of course" (979).

This summation confirms the reciprocity of D—'s and Dupin's actions, symbolically highlighted by the similarity of their D-splaying names (echoing "William Wilson"). To outwit his opponent the detective must preempt his moves by staying ahead of the anticipated anticipation of his own, although the minister almost until the end mistakes his adversary for the *gendarmerie*. Thus Dupin correctly interprets the prefect's apparent success. D— "could not have failed to anticipate—and events have proved that he did not fail to anticipate—the waylayings to which he was subjected," just as he "must have foreseen . . . the secret investigations of his premises" (988).

Modeling a series of strategic situations, Poe unerringly focuses on the key elements of their underlying structure. After all, besides the "letter" game of perfect information between the queen and Minister D—, "The Purloined Letter" also develops the detective game between D— and his august adversary, Dupin. Interestingly, this detective game is not one of perfect or complete information. Just like in the game of literary interpretation, the rules of the interaction are not known to the same degree by both participants.

Dupin's concluding remarks, which reveal that the minister is not even aware of the detective being his nemesis, reveal Poe's grasp of the strategic nuance of literary interpretation. Analyzing the contents of the note that the detective leaves for the villain, Poe is aware that this final communication is of a special, reflexive nature. Although in the text the change is almost imperceptible, there is nothing subtle about the contrast between the strictly antagonistic "letter" game and this final "game of literary interpretation."

What kind of process does the author, Dupin, undergo while deciding what to write in the message for D—? The detective clearly desires for D— to "get the message," as it were. The process of choosing the text—analogous to the process writers undergo when creating a work of fiction—is thus the result of a reflexive anticipation of the other's interpretation of what is written. The detective *qua* writer must anticipate how his intentions will be interpreted in light of the fact that the minister will recognize them as having been intended to be recognized.

Dupin's intentions, besides being reflexive, are quite complex at this stage. For one, even though he does not wish to disclose his identity outright, he wants to communicate enough of it for the minister to surmise it. At the same time, despite demurs that it would not be "altogether right to leave the interior blank—that would have been insulting" (993), Dupin does long to communicate his superiority to the enemy whom he assumes to be as astute an interpreter as he is himself.

Last but not least, Dupin wants to achieve all this while making an oblique reference to an evil turn that D— had done him at some undisclosed point in the past in Vienna. Composing his message, Dupin clearly takes into account its anticipated interpretation by the minister. Thus, depicting his detective's train of thought for settling on a specific text, Poe depicts intentions intended to be recognized as having been intended to be recognized. It is this communicative loop that endows "The Purloined Letter" with such remarkable strategic and pragmatic acuity.

## REFLEXIVE COMMUNICATIVE EXCHANGE

*There is only one thing you write for yourself, and that is a shopping list. . . . Every other thing that you write, you write to say something to someone.*
UMBERTO ECO, *ON LITERATURE*

Poe formulates a number of insights into the interaction between individuals in a detective game in which the behavior of one is inflected by the anticipated behavior of the other. I will now systematize his intuitions by grafting them onto a broader context of reflexive communicative exchange. Here I follow the account developed by Kent Bach and Robert M. Harnish in *Linguistic Communication and Speech Acts* (1979), which incorporates the findings of several other linguists and philosophers and which remarkably dovetails with the research into TOM.[8]

To begin, fiction making involves a reflexive intention. First described by Paul Grice in "Meaning" (1957) and refined in successive papers, it is essentially of the type we encountered in "The Purloined Letter."[9] In brief, a reflexive intention is one intended to be recognized as having been intended to be recognized (recall Currie's blow-by-blow description of such a loop). Recently some philosophers have argued for a "thinner" version of communicative intentions. Still, the Gricean table-turning loop remains the linchpin of speech–act analysis, not least because the TOM it presupposes seems to be a *necessary* condition for social understanding and communication.[10]

Speech-actwise, linguistic and thus literary communication is taken to be successful if, as Bach and Harnish put it, the "attitude the speaker expresses is identified by the hearer by means of recognizing the reflexive intention to express it" (1979, xv). This formulation mirrors not only the fiction-making process and the reading process in general but also the results of the booming research into theory of mind. TOM, if you recall, refers to our ability to attribute mental states to others in the process of making sense of their behavior, be they humans or animals (which we tend to anthropomorphize with a telling regularity).

Today, investigations of the neural basis for theory of mind—the ability to think about other people's thoughts and reflexively of other people's thoughts about our thoughts about theirs—are the leading edge in evolutionary psychology. An alphabet soup of clinical techniques (fMRI, EEG, TMS, et al.) and developmental and cognitive studies of children, twins, and patients with chronic or acquired neural damage gradually reveal the cognitive and neural structure of theory of mind. Studies with infants and autistic individuals are especially important since they conclusively indicate that TOM is an innate rather than in-cultured faculty. This response is so widespread and instinctive, in fact, that TOM is regarded not merely as an adaptive mechanism but as an actual domain-specific biological adaptation, that is, one dedicated to a specific task.

Research into TOM focuses on several central topics, one of which is the relation of theory of mind and interpersonal cognitive processes such as empathy. Another is the relationship between TOM and other domain-general modules such as language. Finally, there is the question of what role theory of mind plays in social exchange, a crucial instan-tiation of which is the exchange between writers and readers. In this last communicative context, interpreters are aided by the so-called Mu-tual Contextual Beliefs (MCBs). In the literary context these can range widely, from sundry genre conventions and publicly recognized symbols to fundamental conventions such as information disclosure within the story or linguistic and/or modeling uniformity.

Mutual contextual beliefs—mutual contextual conventions, if you will—are critical constituents of the reflexive inferences made by both the author and the reader. Bach and Harnish explain:

> We call such items of information "beliefs" rather than
> "knowledge" because they need not be true in order to
> figure in the speaker's intention and the hearer's inference.
> We call them "contextual" because they are both relevant
> to and activated by the context of the utterance (or by the
> utterance itself). And we call them "mutual" because $S$ and
> $H$ not only both have them, they believe they both have
> them and believe the other to believe they both have them.
> (1979, 5)

In and of itself, the recognition of a reflexive intention does not suffice to accept a proposition, that is, to instill a belief commensurate with the locutionary and illocutionary meaning of the utterance. Beliefs or attitudes are not generated merely by dint of recognizing intentions meant to generate these beliefs or attitudes. I can recognize that you intend for me to interpret your novel in a certain way and recognize that I am meant to recognize your intention, but I can refuse to comply all the same, out of spite, playfulness, transgression, ignorance, or even aesthetic refinement in the face of kitsch.

The reflexive inferences between authors and readers in fiction making and fiction reading are among varieties of communicative acts governed by mutual contextual beliefs. For our purposes, the important aspects of interpretation considered as a communicative exchange are three:

- the reflexive (though not necessarily fully deliberate) recognition of interpretive interdependence by the participants
- the presence and activation of mutually shared beliefs about various literary categories, from figurative meanings through genres down to fictionality
- the readers' assumption of reflexive intentionality on the part of the author in approaching this exchange

The assumption of reflexive intentionality does not entail that every tactical move on the writer's part, be it word choice or even placement of a punctuation mark, is explicitly intentional. But given the very structure of the reading process—its interdependence, reflexive nature, and the presence of explicit and implicit conventions—the assumption of shared intentionality, in itself deeply implicated in theory of mind, is the only one to make sense of the situation. Bach and Harnish concur: "Awareness of the situation invokes the rules; recognition of the rules activates the expectations" (1979, 95).

Naturally in fiction, much as in our daily lives, we do not always speak literally. In fact, we habitually take advantage of rhetorical tropes, narrative conventions, and symbolism across the private/public spectrum. In such cases, communicators again fall back on reflexive intentionality (the third aspect above). This is to say that the interpretation of a literary work is guided as much by the text as by the reflexive recognition of the contextual role a given "prop" plays in the literary game. In short, readers compute figurative or symbolic meanings in the story on the basis of the text and the context as delineated by the MCBs.

Literary interpretation is readily expressed as a variant on the Gricean loop. A good confirmation that our model depicts the situation correctly comes from the remarkable parallels between speech-act theory, theory of mind, and the kind of strategic reflexivity investigated by game theorists. Here is how Tomasello describes the empirically tested reflexive interdependence implicit in TOM: "while she is speaking, the speaker is constantly monitoring the listener's attentional status (and vice versa)."[11] Now compare this to how the Nobel Prize–winning game theorist Thomas Schelling characterizes the "mind reading" in a tacit coordinative process, here involving two people who lost each other in a busy store:

> One does not simply predict where the other will go, since the other will go where he predicts the first to go, which is wherever the first predicts the second to predict the first to go, and so on ad infinitum. What is necessary is to coordinate prediction, to read the same message in the common situation, to identify the one course of action that the expectations of each can converge on. (1960, 54)

The same principle of reflexively turning the tables on the other party lies behind bibliographic reconstructions. In fact, prompts Greetham, being a textuist "means being sensitive to another person's quirks and peculiarities; it means that the critic must, by an almost phenomenological leap, 'become' that other person while preparing the text for publication" (1993, 296). Like so much else in life, of course, category ascription is a process of theory formation on the basis of evidence available at a given stage of inquiry. And like so much else in life, intentions—whether accessible directly or circumstantially—are a big part of the picture.

Time to return to our theory of fiction. Currie's proposal goes through a number of refinements before it is delineated in *The Nature of Fiction* (1990, 33).[12] In this final version, the theory is comprehensive enough to account for literary works that come about as a result of a complex set of creative goals. If our theory is to reflect reality, it must allow for heterogeneous intentions. Indeed, notwithstanding Sidney-type red herrings that the poet nothing affirmeth, it must allow that the speech act of fiction making can sometimes be coupled with assertion.

Whether cast in the form of naturalistic mimeticism or out-of-this-world fantasy, fiction affirms sundry truths about life. Recognizing this, Currie allows that fiction making and assertion may be combined. Under these circumstances writers may rely on conditional intentions to convey the heterogeneous nature of their prose to the public. For example, if some readers display a trait not shared by others—say, knowledge that the story is an inside joke—they will make believe rather than believe the story. In this way, the theory copes with the hard cases in which the author performs two speech acts at once: asserting for some members of the public, fiction making for others.

In "Fiction, Fiction-Making, and Styles of Fictionality" (1983), Kendall Walton raises two objections to any theory of fiction that recognizes a distinct speech act of fiction making—precisely the type of theory I defend. Walton disallows that fiction-making intentions are necessary to the production of fiction. His argument rests on the fact that there can be entirely asserted fictions and fictions without any intention behind them whatsoever.

The first objection misses the mark altogether, insofar as Currie allows for entirely asserted works of fiction. Although the scenario is uncommon, there is nothing illogical about intending to create fiction without forsaking claims to the truth of the narrative. Keneally's novel *Schindler's Ark* may be one notable example of such a globally asserted fiction. Winner of the Booker McConnell Prize for fiction, it is a historical recreation based on the oral testimony of Holocaust survivors and their families. Thus Keneally writes in the author's note, "The novelist's craft is the only one I can lay claim to . . . I have attempted, however, to avoid all fiction" (1990, 10).

Walton's second objection dishes out the tired functionalist scenario of natural rock erosion that just happens to spell out "Once upon a time, there was . . ." and so on. This is supposed to prove that fiction can arise even in the absence of fiction-making intentions. Instead of reflogging the dead monkey of entropic implausibility, let me note that no such conclusion follows. All that Walton's counterfactual proves is that one can respond to such a rock-face text as if it were fiction—which is a far cry from proving that it *is* one. Because almost everything can be read as fiction, as the avatars of Derrida delight in showing, it does not follow that everything is fiction.

Naturally, even explicit testimonials do not always provide the best accounts of authorial intentions. Although writers frequently communicate their goals by means of interviews, prefaces, letters to editors, and so forth, the core of interpretive evidence is provided by the text

Globally asserted fiction? The scene at the end of the film in which Schindler breaks down is not in the book. *Keneally writes in the author's note, "The novelist's craft is the only one I can lay claim to . . . I have attempted, however, to avoid all fiction."*

itself. After all, intentions can evolve or even change entirely during the genesis of a work. Recollections can be inaccurate owing to opportunism, forgetfulness, or even lack of explicit awareness. Moreover, complex goals are difficult to articulate concisely, and the finished work may already be the best expression of its author's design.

## CONTROVERSIAL ABOUT–FACE

*We all know that if we listened to philosophers everything would be contested, and we would never get anywhere.*
UMBERTO ECO, *ON LITERATURE*

I come at last to the controversial about-face in Currie's philosophy where he recruits an ad hoc clause to forestall objections to the sufficiency of his theory. The clause stipulates that fiction, if true, can be no more than accidentally true. This abandonment of the intentionalist approach to fiction for the sake of the referential one—by reference to story contents and its relation to the world—is especially baffling in view of compelling speech-act reasons against it. At the very least it proves the aesthetician to be inconsistent: in *The Nature of Fiction* (23) he declares that reflexive intentions are necessary *and* sufficient to produce fiction.

But there are more consequential reasons for doubting this move. Currie concocts several scenarios to uncover a hole in his own intentionalist account, none of which, as I will show, is up to the job. The first involves a speaker who recites a fictional story created by somebody else. The speaker intends his listeners to make believe it, and this intention is recognized as such and acted upon. For Currie the utterance is not fictive since it is not productive of fiction. I beg to differ, since the whole issue arises simply out of conflation of two terms: "fictive" and "productive of fiction."

As soon as we distinguish the production of fiction from its *re*production, the apparent quandary disappears. The answer to the question that baffled Currie, namely what speech act is performed during a recitation of a work of fiction, is quite straightforward. It *is* a speech act of fiction making, although it is not productive of fiction. Anyway, this is not an argument against Currie's theory. To prove the incompleteness of his own theses, the philosopher must furnish a case in which reflexive intentions of a fiction-making kind fail to produce fiction. Let us examine his case.

One scenario involves a plagiarist who, badly lacking in imagination but genuinely intending to make fiction, rewrites a newspaper article in his own words and style without materially affecting the facts of the matter. The story in question is of such nature that the rewriter can reasonably presume that others will make believe it (read it as fiction). What is Currie's verdict? Oddly enough, he maintains that such a work is nonfiction, even though it is the product of the right kind of intention. His evidence, however, is skimpy—an appeal to his intuitions.

As it happens, the intuitions of the numerous students and colleagues I have canvassed flatly contradict Currie's. Most respondents countenance that if the rewriting is substantial enough, the rewriter will indeed produce a work of fiction. Even more to the point, Currie's proposal would make it impossible to create fiction based on real life. A case in point is a recent bestseller turned Hollywood blockbuster. Lacking in imagination, as evident from his entire output, Dan Brown rewrote the nonfictional if speculative *The Holy Blood and the Holy Grail* (1982) into *The Da Vinci Code* (2003) and weathered the charges of plagiarism in a court of law.[13]

Another of Currie's scenarios involves a fiction writer who grounds the novel in real-life events that are, however, of such unlikely nature that they can easily be taken to be made up. Yet another involves a person who intends to write fiction and indeed does so, although unbeknown to him, his story is a true account of events that happened to him in real life (his lack of memory could be variously attributed to amnesia, trauma, repression, senility, and the like). Again the right kind of reflexive intention produces a story that, Currie insists, is nonfiction—against the precepts of his own theory.

A consistent intentionalist account seems perfectly capable of handling all of the above scenarios. Since all three hypothetical authors genuinely intend to create fiction and can reasonably expect the public to reflexively recognize it as such, they do in fact all compose fictions, notwithstanding the nonaccidental truth of their efforts. After all, if it were to be accepted, Currie's clause would deny an everyday phenomenon in the publishing world—fiction based on fact.

Currie multiplies increasingly contrived counterexamples in an effort to cast doubt on his own theory, which resolutely resists these efforts. Instead of dealing with them piecemeal, let me rehearse a more general argument against accidental truth in fiction. Thomas Disch's futuristic novel *334* prognosticates the devolution of the American welfare state at home and a perpetual state of postcolonial militarism abroad. According to Currie's addendum, we would have to withhold judgment on whether *334* is fiction until its prognoses could be verified as (accidentally) true or not!

This odd result comes bundled with another. In Currie's addendum, fictions could not make cognitive assertions because whatever is true in them is only accidentally true. This counterintuitive and counterfactual upshot casts even more doubt on the addendum—quite apart from the problem of deciding the degree of accidentality of Disch's prognoses or, conversely, the degree to which they are truthful. However, all these difficulties can be put to rest by embracing a consistently intentionalist speech-act–based approach to the nature of fiction.

Fiction is, of course, a much broader concept than literature. Not all that meets the criteria of fictionality is literary fiction. To be a literary fiction, the item in question must also be a literary work, which entails some minimal conditions—such as originality of the created text—that rule out mere copycats as fiction makers. The author must have a genuine intention of making fiction and must have reasonable grounds for believing that his audience will read (make believe) it as such. As long as these conditions are met, whether accidentally true or not, the result is fiction.

Livingston argues (2005) that as with other types of intentions (for example, to make a soufflé or be nice to the in-laws), fiction-making intentions can fail. While I take his general point, I am not quite sure how that can come about in this case. If the artist *genuinely* intends to make fiction, then irrespective of the "uptake" (he may leave no textual clues while consistently claiming to have written nonfiction), he creates fiction. Livingston's scenario presumably would involve an artist with *non*genuine intentions to write fiction, in which case we have deception, or one whose genuine fiction-making intentions change in the course of composition, in which case we end up with nonfiction or, if the vacillation persists, a collection of alternatingly fictional and nonfictional passages.

In addition, Currie's theory could benefit from some fine-tuning. During his discussion of textual identity and the intentional fallacy, the philosopher anchors interpretation first in the fictional author, then in the real author—either way with barely a sketch of how one relates to the other. One thing, however, is clear. The heuristic entity such as the fictional author is not an independent agent but the result of the real author's executive strategy. After all, the only agent capable of having—and acting on—artistic intentions is the real author, no matter what narrative guises he may assume.

Next, Currie sensibly states that a fictional story is not "a set of distinct propositions but one big proposition" (101). However, he insists on the atomic account of fiction making in which the writer adopts the relevant attitude not toward the work but separately toward each individual proposition. In other words, the philosopher applies the concept of fictionality only derivatively to fiction as a whole from the analysis of isolated sentences. This both undercuts his own claim above and goes against the grain of critical theory and practice in which we approach literary fictions wholistically (not to say holistically).

Another instance where the philosopher parts with psychological and aesthetic plausibility is his insistence that readers make believe the story only after having reached the end.[14] Does it mean that readers believe the story until then? Or that they suspend belief and disbelief till the last page? What about works issued serially that do not have a clear end until the last installment? What about narratives that await prequels or sequels? What about Kafka, McBain, and hundreds of other writers who die without finishing works in progress? What if I read Harry Potter minus the last paragraph—does it really inhibit me from recognizing the story as flagrant make-believe?

Currie's prescription does not seem to match what people do. Reading as fiction, that is, forming a relevant attitude toward the story, seems hardly a matter of the single instant that coincides with scanning the final period after the words "The End." The make-believe attitude emerges as a working hypothesis either prior to or in the very early stages of reading, even though it is subject to revision. At the same time, the further into the story, the more unlikely the shift becomes, even though it may be subject to revision even after the reading is over—as it was in Spiegelman, Carter, and Lem.

In sum, make-believing a story is not an act that follows reading but a process concurrent with it, subject to interpretive inertia of the once-adopted view as well as to potential update and revision. This and other refinements should not obscure the systematic and successful framework that the main body of Currie's theory provides for analyzing the nature of fiction. As such, it answers the demurs raised by Hugh Wilder about the status of what he calls pseudo-fictions, of which the Bible is the most famous exemplar.

According to the brand of historicism professed by Wilder, fictionality is determined by historical precedent; hence, when it comes to the Bible, the critic pronounces it fiction. To his credit, Wilder acknowledges the checkered history of this foundational anthology of early Judean and Christian writings. He allows, for example, that at some unspecified earlier time (that of the Catholic Church's founding fathers? the Nicean Council? medieval monastic orders?) the Bible was read as nonfiction. Hence, according to his theory, it was then nonfiction. However, as a consequence of the twentieth-century preference to read the Bible as fiction—Wilder conveniently overlooks hundreds of millions who do not conform to this picture—the Bible is fiction.

Should this change, the Good Book may yet revert to being nonfiction, then possibly back again to fiction and again nonfiction, like a literary ping-pong ball. Clearly, Wilder's historicism is just another brand of functionalism. Thus, it has little to add to the debate, even in terms of speech-act theory, given that perlocutionary uptake does not affect illocution. What readers do does not overturn the speech acts of the authors. Historical context and precedent are, of course, vital to the overall pragmatic picture. Following the original recognition of fiction-making intentions, a way of interpretation may ossify that later may foster an illusion of being *the* motive for such interpretation, since the original motive is now obscured by time.

I thus fully agree with Wilder on the importance of historical tradition in interpreting a given work. Traditions, however, do not originate *ex nihilo* but out of concrete decisions made on the basis of the critical evaluation of available evidence about authorial intentions. There is no denying that, outside orthodox religious circles, many twentieth-century readers approach the Bible as a magnificent fiction. However, the fact that nowadays this heterogeneous collection of scriptures from many sources and many centuries is interpreted by some as fiction and by others as fact does not necessarily make it one or the other.

A two-thousand-year-long tradition of nonfictional interpretation of the biblical narratives may be, as a matter of fact, an index of the actual rather than historically contingent state of affairs. The operative factors here are the intentions of the authors of the biblical tales and whether they could have reasonably expected others to read the described events as nonfiction. This is because fiction becomes fiction not through the actions of the reader but through the action of the writer who generates the book. One could say that even as the Bible begins with the Book of Genesis, fiction or nonfiction begins with the genesis of the book.

Whether what the Bible says is true and accurate is another story.

Six        FICTIONAL TRUTH

*There is a dangerous critical heresy, typical of our time,
according to which we can do anything we like with a work
of literature, reading into it whatever our most uncontrolled
impulses dictate to us. This is not true. Literary works encourage freedom of interpretation, because they offer us a discourse
that has many layers of reading and place before us the ambiguities of language and of real life. But in order to play this
game, which allows every generation to read literary works in
a different way, we must be moved by a profound respect for
what I have called elsewhere the intention of the text.*

UMBERTO ECO, *ON LITERATURE*

# IMPLICIT STORY CONTENT

*What remains unsaid in Stendhal's* Armance *regarding the protagonist's potential impotence pushes the reader towards frenetic hypotheses in order to complete what the story does not tell us explicitly.*
UMBERTO ECO, *ON LITERATURE*

The author-reader model of reflexive interdependence continues to be of value when it comes to the problem of implicit story content—a *sine qua non* of all interpretation. Known in analytic aesthetics as the problem of fictional truth (or, sometimes, truth in fiction), it is a matter of literary competence that allows readers to "flesh out" the implied contents of narratives. After all, when making sense of stories, readers do not limit themselves to what is on the page. Sometimes readers even justifiably disregard what *is* printed on the page.

Using an array of inferential tactics to make sense of the story, readers automatically fill in what in *The Act of Reading* (1978) Wolfgang Iser calls "textual gaps."[1] Who would doubt that when smoking a pipe in "The Purloined Letter," Dupin inhales through the mouth and not a hole in his forehead? Or in Lisa Zunshine's example (2006) that Peter Walsh in *Mrs. Dalloway* trembles uncontrollably on encountering his old love out of excitement and not because he has Parkinson's disease? Yet one would look in vain for any statement in the text to that effect. On the other hand, we do not assume that Walsh is a humanoid space alien, even though nothing in the text explicitly contradicts it.

Figuring out what happens in the story—which is to say, what is true in it—is the first step in contact with any work of fiction. After all, we must first know what the story is in order to interpret it. An account of

fictional truth is thus a prerequisite for any theory of interpretation, insofar as it precedes the symbolic or sociocultural level of analysis in which
critics typically engage. Which backgrounds readers use in retrieving
the implicit contents of fiction and what role authorial intentions play in
this process are the questions I try to answer in this chapter.

Once again I turn to Poe to illustrate the issues at stake. "The
Thousand-and-Second Tale of Scheherazade" adroitly forefronts the role
of pragmatic considerations in our contacts with fiction. Poe is keenly
aware of what the interpretation of fictional truth entails—so much so
that he constructs the entire story around different types of background
assumptions needed to flesh out implicit story content. It would be an
exaggeration to claim that "Scheherazade" delineates a solution to the
problem of fictional truth, but Poe's astute manipulation of the conventions of realism and fantasy points us in the right direction.

Mockingly embedded in a narrative framework of the *Arabian Nights,*
"Scheherazade" is a metafictional account of Sinbad's marvelous expedi-
tion through the natural and scientific wonders of nineteenth-century
"Cockneigh" land. This is, in turn, embedded in an even larger frame
in which the narrator recounts the results of his research into an obscure
Oriental text, *Tellmenow Isitsöornot* (Tell-me-now Is-it-so-or-not). It is
there that he allegedly finds the true, if apocryphal, account of what had
happened to Scheherazade on the thousand-and-second night.

Thus, in a series of concentrically nested narratives, the narrator retells the story of a queen who in turn retells the story within a story
within a story of Sinbad, the intrepid wayfarer of antiquity who embarks
on the mother of all voyages. His trip is estranged both geographically
and temporally, for it becomes an anachronistic romp through the wonders of Poe's world. Picked up by a passing steamship and befriended by
one of the men-animals who run it, this early Gulliver quickly masters
their language and joins them on a round-the-world cruise.

On the way Sinbad records with a keen but innocent eye the marvels
of Western science and technology. Poe stuns and amuses his contemporaries by filtering these facts through the sensibility of an anachronistic
observer, estranging banal industrial reality into a tale of mind-boggling
wonder. From time to time, however, the story is punctured with reports of fantastic (from our point of view) objects, such as a continent
supported by a giant sky-blue cow. These self-reflexive "asides" display
a nuanced grasp of the principles guiding the interpretation of fictional
truth.

The scarce critical commentary tends to pigeonhole "Scheherazade" as a minor satire of the materialism of nineteenth-century industrial America or a parody of sensational pop journalism.[2] For our purposes, however, the story is more important as a perceptive illustration of the pragmatic dimension behind the literary conventions of realism and fantasy. Befitting a tale that inverts what is true and what is fantastic, Poe veils a caution in the motto "Truth is stranger than fiction" (1151),[3] the first of several cues to the interpretive background the author can reflexively expect readers to adopt to make sense of the story.

Put simply, what is true and fantastic in each layer of Poe's story turns out to be relevant to a given layer of the fiction. Thus, in the middle layer, Scheherazade entertains her husband with tales of wonder, from the giant cow to a blue rat to a pink clockwork horse with green wings wound up with an indigo key. Peculiar and incredible as all these are, the sultan accepts them as real and true. Clearly the criteria that determine plausibility for the fairy-tale monarch are at odds with those we would employ for that purpose. In fact, they are symmetrically reversed: what is fantastic for us, creatures of the real world, is real to denizens of fairy tales, and vice versa.

By means of this symmetry, Poe estranges the wonders of nature and technology into fairy-tale miracles. The mutual beliefs of the teller and listener of the story are thus the determinant factor of what would, *prima facie,* seem an empirical question. To amplify the effect, instead of a straightforward and unambiguous narration, Poe goes for the sensational, hyping up the fantastic appearance of his subjects *both* to the sultan and to the contemporary reader. He carefully selects facts and artifacts with singular properties and employs a number of rhetorical tropes to increase the impression of futuristic novelty.

In one hyperbole, for example, he describes ash ejected by a volcanic explosion to be so dense that at one hundred fifty miles away it is "impossible to see the whitest object" (1161) however closely held to the eye. Then, with no warning, the next passage adopts the viewpoint of a Lilliputian, describing "monstrous animals with horns resembling scythes" that inhabit "vast caverns in the soil" (1162). It takes the unsuspecting reader a while to realize the relative size shift in the description and recognize in the rapacious giant a tiny ant lion.

Poe's oblique allusions to facts of science have lost none of their grip today. At one point Sinbad describes the local atmosphere as being "so dense as to sustain iron or steel, just as our own does feathers" (1161). Poe refers in this roundabout way to powdered steel, which, indeed, can float in atmospheric air. Without knowledge of this fact, readers who contemplate this seemingly outrageous lie in light of something like the Reality Principle (described below), are bound to deny its truth. The narrative ruse jolts readers into a new perspective on the familiar, as estrangement is supposed to do.

The effectiveness of Poe's technique is magnified by his tone. Far from surprised or enthralled, the narrator is thoroughly at home with all manner of exotic formations of nature and science. That is why she reports them with patient nonchalance, so at variance with her husband's excitable incredulity. But then, without forewarning, Scheherazade inserts into this prosaic brave new world a report of yet another miracle. This time it is an entire continent supported on the back of a sky-blue cow that has no fewer than four hundred horns.

What is the sultan's reaction to this apparent fact? Consistent with his previous acceptance of blue rats and pink horses, Scheherazade's husband finds the imaginary cow entirely more believable than the empirical reality of Poe's times. While scientific accomplishments and natural discoveries of the nineteenth century left him incredulous, the sultan accepts the fantastic cow as a known fact. Evidently, writes Jerome D. Denuccio, the interpretation of the facts described by the queen hinges "not upon their inherent truth or falsity, but upon their credibility" (1990, 367).

By means of such clever transpositions, Poe alerts the reader to some important interpretive principles of fictional truth. For one, he shows that the knowledge of conventional beliefs *relevant to a given fiction* is indispensable to the understanding of its contents. Second, he suggests that such background knowledge may take precedence over nominal facts of science. By illustrating that we cannot read fictions without taking the pragmatic stance, Poe points to some important aspects of readers' expertise in story content retrieval. In what follows I refine these insights in a systematic account of fictional truth.

To begin with, much like in nonfiction, the grasp of story content must obey the same basic causal constraints that obtain in reality. Notwithstanding the idea highlighted by Baudelaire and Borges that writers do create their own predecessors, any claims about the influence of Sherlock Holmes (first edition 1892) on Poe's Dupin are patently anachronistic and unacceptable. Naturally, this imposes only the broadest restriction on admissible story entailments. Our theory must specify the right kind of background knowledge for fleshing out any and all varieties of fiction.

After all, depending on the choice of background, inferences about the contents of fiction may differ dramatically. They also differ between fiction and nonfiction. Given that all nonfictions are perforce embedded in reality, readers fill in contents using something like a Reality Principle, that is, their everyday empirical and psychosocial assumptions about the real world. We do not need to be told, for example, that people inhale pipe smoke through the mouth, that when hungry they eat food, or that lovers miss each other when apart. In nonfiction all of those are givens.

Not so in fiction. Propositions can be true in the story but not true *simpliciter* (not true in our world, or simply not true). Outside of 100 percent mimetic narratives like *Schindler's Ark,* the background relevant to understanding a work of fiction may differ—more or less dramatically— from the background relevant for nonfiction. The whole point of "Scheherazade" is that the natural and scientific wonders described by Poe really exist. But it is equally the case that we cannot employ the Reality Principle to interpret what happens elsewhere in the story.

It is true in Poe's fiction and true in our world that (in the Mammoth Cave of Kentucky) there are "immense rivers as black as ebony, swarming with fish that had no eyes" (1161) or that one can engineer "a deep darkness out of two brilliant lights" (1168) using light-wave superposition. But at the same time, while it is true in "Scheherazade" that the queen recounts Sinbad's adventures, it is not true that either character ever existed in reality. Truth is thus one thing and fictional truth another. They can, but need not, correspond to each other.

## TRUTH AND FICTIONAL TRUTH

*The Library described by Pavel, which naturally is also made up of works by Borges, including his story about the Library, seems curiously to resemble Don Quixote's library, which was a library of impossible stories that took place in possible worlds.*

UMBERTO ECO, *ON LITERATURE*

Distinct though they are, there has been no shortage of attempts to relate truth and fictional truth to each other. Typically it is assumed that fictional "worlds"—heuristic projections of the semantic "space" in which stories unfold—map onto possible worlds, those coherently complete and completely coherent projections of states as understood in possible worlds semantics.[4] If fictional propositions are not true in our world, perhaps they are true in some possible world associated with the "world" of a literary fiction?

Although not implausible at first glance, the correspondence between storyworlds and possible worlds fails for several reasons:

1.      In contradistinction to storyworlds, possible worlds are in principle determinate with respect to truth. In a possible world the answer to a question may not be known, but it by definition exists. Not so in fiction. Take the number of crewmen on Sinbad's ship. Although it must be determinate, neither the text nor any form of background knowledge can determine the exact value of "a vast number" (1157).

2.      Because of reason 1 above, possible worlds and storyworlds do not exactly map onto one another. A literary fiction, in other words, does not affix itself to a unique possible world. In fact, any storyworld is consistent with an infinity of possible worlds. The entire contents of "Scheherazade," for instance, are compatible with the possible worlds in which Sinbad owned a flying carpet at the age of five and those in which he did not, in which Martians invaded the earth the day after Orson Welles's broadcast and did not, in which Frank Zappa released *Sheik Yerbouti* in 1979 and did not, and so on *ad infinitum*.

3.      Like our own reality, possible worlds are, as a matter of principle always consistent. Nothing logically impossible can be true in them. Not so in fiction. To take one illustration, Lem invokes a constellation of time-travel paradoxes in "The Seventh Voyage," and chronomotion entails all manner of logical inconsistencies.

4.      Logic aside, it is psychologically and epistemically impossible that readers do, or even could, reconstruct complete possible worlds from works of fiction. Because so much in fiction remains indeterminate, no person (or even supercomputer) could hope to reconstruct an entire and complete possible world from a story. Borges's "Tlön, Uqbar, Orbis Tertius," in which a corpus of encyclopedists labors to invent another world down to the last detail, vividly narratizes the infinitude of detail needed to accomplish such a supertask. Mapping out a possible world in totality is a psychological and empirical dead end.

We must scratch the idea that fictional truth can be analyzed in terms of what is true in one possible world. But what about truth in various possible worlds, all consistent with a single fiction? David Lewis approached fictional truth in terms of such a counterfactual setup. He proposed that what is true in fiction can be treated *as if it were uttered in the world of the story as known fact* (1983). In other words, Lewis wants us to think of propositions relating to a story as prefixed by the operator: "It is fictional in the work X that . . . ." For example, it is fictional in *The Godfather* that Don Corleone is a mafia boss.

This is nothing new, of course. When interpreting what is true in the story, we implicitly apply this fictional modifier. Notice, however, that inferences about a story are legitimate only if preceded by the same modifier. Nothing follows from a mix of modified (prefixed) statements and unmodified ones. Sherlock Holmes lived in London (fictionally true), and Conan Doyle lived in London at the same time (true *simpliciter*), but it does not follow that the detective could run into his creator.

To get to what is true in the storyworld, Lewis considers a plurality of possible worlds (which he calls S-worlds) associated with it. Though different from one another, they all have a common core consisting of all that is made explicit in the text. In other words, the intersection of all possible worlds associated with any story corresponds to what is in the text. Why is this so important? Because, as a consequence, it makes no sense to equate fictional truth with what is true in all possible worlds since that would make it identical with the text.

This is a crucial point, worth reiterating for the sake of those literary theorists who are still inclined to think that what we can legitimately say about the contents of a story is determined solely by the text. This is emphatically not so. Is it true in "Scheherazade" that Sinbad is a keen observer of natural and scientific wonders? The proposition is so obvious as to be almost truistic, yet there is nothing in the text that explicitly states so. If the text determines fictional truth, however, it should not be true in the story.

Clearly, we can understand (retrieve) much more from the story than is stated on the page. This knowledge is also symmetrical. Just as we can infer some extratextual propositions to be true, we can judge others to be false—even when there is nothing in the text to contradict them. Ask yourself this: Is Poe's Sinbad a black comedian and occasional Hollywood movie actor? Ridiculous as the proposition is, there is nothing in the text of "Scheherazade" to say that he is not. Is the proposition true, however? Decidedly not.

The same reasoning applies to what we can legitimately say about Agamemnon, Lear, Yossarian, and other fictional characters, events, or environments. We know much more about the stories we read than what is explicitly enunciated in the text. The upshot is clear: we must abandon the idea that fictional truth is limited to what is on the page (we can call it Analysis 0). Clearly, fictional truth is determined by the text interpreted in accordance with an appropriate background. Which background is appropriate is, however, the mother of all questions.

In a seminal paper, "Truth in Fiction" (1983), Lewis submits two alternatives for selecting the relevant background to retrieve implicit story contents. Even though they look rather forbidding, I reproduce them to give readers a flavor of his analyses.

> Analysis 1: A sentence of the form "In the fiction $f$, $\Phi$" is non-vacuously true iff some world where $f$ is told as known fact and $\Phi$ is true differs less from our actual world, on balance, than does any world where $f$ is told as known fact and $f$ is not true. It is vacuously true iff there are no possible worlds where $f$ is told as known fact. (270)
>
> Analysis 2: A sentence of the form "In the fiction $f$, $\Phi$" is non-vacuously true iff, whenever $w$ is one of the collective belief worlds of the community of origin of $f$, then some world where $f$ is told as known fact and $\Phi$ is true differs less from the world $w$, on balance, than does any world where $f$ is told as known fact and $f$ is not true. It is vacuously true iff there are no possible worlds where $f$ is told as known fact. (273)

In *Mimesis as Make-Believe* (1990) Walton christens Analysis 1 the Reality Principle. The name fits, for it highlights that what is true in the story is *as close as the text allows to the real world of the reader*. In other words, what is true in the story is the text augmented by what is known or believed in the reader's real world. On first blush it might look like a sound general rule for generating inferences about fictional truth. It works, after all, for all historical, realistic, or naturalistic novels, where things not explicitly stated can be imported whole-hog from the world as we know it.

Perhaps motivated by such considerations, a number of literary critics have succumbed to the illusion that the Reality Principle is the master key to all fiction. One of them is Eco, who explicitly endorses the Reality Principle in *Six Walks in the Fictional Woods* with the following dictum:

> [E]verything that the text doesn't name or describe explicitly as different from what exists in the real world must be understood as corresponding to the laws and conditions of the real world. (1994b, 83)

An earlier backing for the Reality Principle comes from Jonathan Culler when he speaks of hermeneutics that leads us to the truth of the work "based on our expectations about the text and the world" (1973, 157). Even Lisa Zunshine, who is so perceptive about why the fictional Peter Walsh is atremble, extends the Reality Principle to all stories by calling it the "default interpretation of behavior" (2006, 4).

However, this is not so for two elementary reasons. First, Analysis 1 generates inappropriate inferences outside realistic fiction. In *Aladdin,* magic carpets rise by dint of magic and not magnetic levitation. Second, the Reality Principle is too indiscriminate, for it generates an infinity of irrelevant truths in fiction. When we think about what happens in a story, we do not invoke *all* the inferences warranted by the Reality Principle. Is it true in Poe's "Scheherazade" that Homer Simpson of *The Simpsons* "mooned for rebuttal" in his high school debating class? Nothing in the text disputes it, and the proposition is as close as the text allows to the world of the reader. Yet it is starkly anachronistic and aesthetically irrelevant.

Given these evident and unfixable drawbacks, let us turn to Lewis's Analysis 2—the Mutual Belief Principle. Here the appropriate background for fleshing out textual gaps is the *conventional beliefs in the author's community.* The immediate advantage of the Mutual Belief Principle is that it rules out the Homer Simpson example. Nothing about Homer Simpson was believed in Poe's community, hence such anachronistic inferences can be correctly ruled out. Similarly, Analysis 2 is sensitive to various beliefs that may not be part of our reality but that were the intellectual coin of the writer's times. Geocentrism, theory of humors, or phrenology are not true but were believed at one point or another and thus may be indispensable to understand certain stories.

But while clearing the hurdles that tripped the Reality Principle, the Mutual Belief Principle runs into its own brick wall. The background needed to make sense of certain fictions may be idiosyncratic rather than a part of a network of communal beliefs. In Poe's vignette "The Oval Portrait," we are to assume that the protagonist's undertaking to transfer his wife's lively beauty onto the canvas drains her life spirit until, upon the completion of the work, she dies. The doctrine of mimetic art depleting life from people was not commonly believed in Poe's times, nor is it part of the modern reader's world knowledge, yet it is necessary to make sense of this story.[5]

In general, what is distinctive about Lewis's account—that is, his treatment of truth in fiction along the lines of truth in possible worlds—is also the source of his problems. Among others, it forces him to assume that "Truth in a given fiction is closed under implication" (1983, 264). This means roughly that *all possible* implications are true in a given story. Yet, as we noted in the discussion of possible worlds, one of their most unlikely features was the need for readers to make all inferences that could be made. In psychological terms, it is doubtful that anything resembling such a total inferential process could ever take place.

Even if we could, we would not want to generate all implications of a story anyway, since most would be aesthetically irrelevant (recall Homer's rebuttal). Moreover, Lewis's theses are helpless vis-à-vis inconsistent fictions that, by definition, cannot be mapped onto any (logically) possible world. Still, galvanizing research into fictional truth, Lewis laid down the rules of engagement. What is in the text is fictionally true almost by default. But given that we can assert much more than what is printed on the page, fictional truth is delimited by the text plus the appropriate "inferential grammar."

## THE INFERENTIAL GRAMMAR

*On the other hand, as far as the world of books is concerned, propositions like "Sherlock Holmes was a bachelor," "Little Red Riding-Hood is eaten by the wolf and then freed by the woodcutter," or "Anna Karenina commits suicide" will remain true for eternity, and no one will ever be able to refute them.*
UMBERTO ECO, *ON LITERATURE*

While on the subject of the inferential grammar, we need to say a few more words about the text. As already mentioned, the reflex assumption is that the text is inviolable: what is on the page must be true in a given fiction. Thus if Mario Puzo says that Don Corleone had three sons and one daughter, this is what is true in *The Godfather.* Most of the time, as with Newtonian mechanics, this is indeed a good approximation of how things work. But just as Newtonian mechanics can sometimes give inaccurate results, so can the assumption that what is in the text is necessarily true in a given fiction.

Since most people are more familiar with the film than the novel, let us take a closer look at the cinematic text of Coppola's *Godfather.* The film is set for the most part in the 1940s. However, in the scene when Don Corleone shops for fruit just before he is gunned down, boxes of Sunkist oranges in the upper part of the frame clearly display graphics from the 1970s. Is it true in *The Godfather* that during the 1940s time-travel devices were available to local grocers? No. The anachronism is an error, and even though it features in the text, it must not guide any inferences about the story.

When Sonny is gunned down at the toll booth, the windshield of his automobile is utterly shattered by machine-gun fire but almost intact a camera cut later. When the police Captain McCluskey readies to strike Michael at the hospital, the latter's coat is wide open at his chest, but after the camera cut, it is closed and straight when the punch lands. What happened? Did Michael ask for time out to neaten up? Was Sonny's windshield partially replaced by a repair crew who happened to pass by? No. Once again, even though they are in the text, neither of these unintended textual elements is fictionally true.

Recall (from Chapter 3) that "text" is but a convenient shorthand for "intentionally configured text." The restoration of the text in accordance with authorial intentions will correct such lapses. Thus, in the scene in Las Vegas when Michael is getting out of the automobile in the hotel driveway, a hirsute, bearded, unmistakably 1970s hippy can be seen inside the lobby. Confessing on the DVD to acute embarrassment about the oversight, director Coppola effectively excises that part of the text. Not part of his executive intentions, this textual element does not thus validate the inference that, like Rip Van Winkle, the story skips twenty years in chronology.

Bearing all this in mind, let us return to our formula for determining fictional truth. It is the joint product of the intentionally configured text *plus* the relevant background (in the discarded Analysis 0, ß = 0):

$$\Phi = T + ß$$

While it may not be immediately clear how to pick the right ß for each and every story, it is clear that to retrieve what is fictionally true—and

Fictionally true or untrue? The windshield miraculously repairs itself in *The Godfather*. When Sonny is gunned down at the toll booth, the windshield of his automobile is utterly shattered by machine-gun fire but almost intact a camera cut later.

thereby to execute the opening gambit in any literary interpretation—we must look beyond Lewis's analyses. What we need is a rule that will derive *only true and only relevant inferences* about the story.

Before I present my own recommendation, let me review one more proposal intended to do just that. In *The Nature of Fiction* Currie grounds fictional truth in the persona of the fictional author, defined as "that fictional character whom we take to be telling us the story as known fact" (1990, 76). Fictional truth is thus offered as the text plus inferences from the belief system of the fictional author. However, the linchpin of this innovative approach—the concept of the fictional author—is demonstrably circular, insufficient, and unnecessary, not to mention its several lesser drawbacks.

For instance, according to Currie, readers cull the belief system of the fictional author from the text: "as we read we learn more about his beliefs" (76). In other words, we interpret the story to get to the fictional author's beliefs so that we can use his beliefs to interpret the story, in a vicious circle that offers no point at which to jump-start the interpretation of fictional truth. Also, as Alex Byrne points out (1993), the postulate fails in the face of "mindless" fictions—stories without an apparent narrator—from which it is impossible to reconstruct the belief system of the fictional author and, consequently, what is fictionally true.[6]

What with textual underdetermination and finite cognitive resources, it is also impossible that readers could reconstruct a complete belief system of the fictional author no matter how interminable the work. Neither can Currie's treatment of inconsistent fictions handle the tough cases I describe in the last section below. Finally, as a consequence of his recourse to the fictional author, he pays inadequate attention to genre as one of the relevant background beliefs that reflexively regulate interpretation. Fictions, after all, "belong" to genres only because authors intend for readers to recognize that genre conventions are being employed in order to be recognized as such.

Considerations of genre can, after all, deeply affect interpretation. The canons of verisimilitude and coherence in James's "Turn of the Screw"—or, in the contemporary reworking of James, in Disch's *The M.D.: A Horror Story*—dramatically alter the perception of what is true in their fictions. In accordance with a realistic or supernatural interpretation, the ambiguities in the plot cast a shadow over the remainder of the story. The point is, knowledge of genres belongs to the creative tactics of the real author, from which the heuristic construct such as the fictional author is entirely cut off.

Curiously, although in other aspects of interpretation Currie is a realist about intentional attitudes, he embraces hypothetical intentionalism when it comes to story content (in this he mirrors a few other aestheticians).[7] After all, there are few narratives in which real authors could tell their stories as known fact, as Currie's treatment of fictional truth demands. On the other hand, Currie finds that he cannot simply dispense with the fictional author altogether. Consider the interpretive puzzle of "The Flash Stockman," first brought up by Lewis. In this traditional Australian folk song the narrator brags,

> I'm a stockman to me trade and they call me Ugly Dave,
> I'm old and grey and I only got one eye.
> In the yard I'm good, of course, but just put me on a horse
> And I'll go where lots of young 'uns daren't try. . . .

> Just watch me use the whip, I can give the dawdlers gyp,
> I can make the bloody echoes roar and ring.
> With a branding-iron, well, I'm a perfect flamin' swell,
> In fact I'm duke of every blasted thing.

It is true in the poem that the narrator is a braggart who is not to be taken at his word. Even though the stockman may believe every boast he makes, there is little doubt that things are just the opposite of his verbal antics. But the latter point of view is clearly not the narrator's, leading Currie—who, remember, wants no truck with the real author—to fall back on the fictional author, with all the problems that follow.[8] Nor is this the end of them. One more instance in which Currie's theory breaks down is when the beliefs of the real author's community, the beliefs of the fictional author, and the fictional events of the story are all temporally distinct.

Suppose I, a contemporary author, endeavor to portray a pre-Christian Viking community but from the point of view of an enlightened late-medieval cleric (thus automatically ruling out both the Reality Principle and the Mutual Belief Principle). As long as the beliefs of the medieval narrator coincide with those of his Viking subjects, we can indeed rely on the belief system of the fictional author to make appropriate inferences about the story. But as soon as those beliefs begin to diverge—as they certainly do in this example—Currie's proposal yields anachronistic inferences that could not satisfy any competent reader.

Leaving the problems with the fictional author aside, we still need the inferential grammar for competent inferences about story content. With this in mind, Currie contemplates a proposal operationally similar to Lewis's Analysis 2: the background for a correct interpretation of what is true in a given story is the mutual beliefs in the author's community, so long as they are not explicitly contravened by the text. In this view, retrieving what is true in fiction, readers should follow what was conventionally (in another remix, only predominantly) believed in the real author's times and deviate only when the text explicitly contradicts these beliefs.

Although superficially alike, Lewis's and Currie's proposals are categorically distinct. While the former involves possible worlds, the latter relies on a fallible, incomplete, and potentially inconsistent *system of beliefs*.[9] This is in itself an important improvement, inasmuch as it replaces the dubious demands of inferential completeness, which plagued Lewis's account, with a much more realistic view of actual readers' actual reading strategies. In one move, replacing a set of possible worlds by a set of beliefs solves the problem of generating irrelevant truths about fiction.

Still, apart from the drawbacks discussed heretofore, there are other reasons to reject this refurbished Mutual Belief Principle. Currie himself, for one, admits that the deviation from conventional beliefs may be subject to an inferential domino effect. When a sky-blue cow is explicitly introduced in "Scheherazade," it may be reasonable to conclude that other fantastic entities, such as unicorns, inhabit the storyworld, even though the text has no mention of them. I believe, however, that there is an even more compelling reason for rejecting this particular heuristic.

W. W. Jacobs's story "Monkey's Paw" (1902) puts a new spin on the folk tradition of magical objects granting wishes. An aging couple comes into possession of a magic amulet said to grant three wishes. Immediately they wish for two hundred pounds, which they indeed get the next day, but in the form of compensation for their son who dies in a work accident. Bereaved, they wish for his return, and in the dead of night someone starts breaking into their house. Petrified with terror, the old man uses the third wish to send the intruder away.

What is remarkable about Jacobs's story is that, *prima facie,* there is not a single supernatural event in it. People do get killed while on the job, and strangers do knock on doors at night, only to desist when no one answers. The Mutual Belief Principle, which in this case agrees with the Reality Principle, follows the conventional beliefs of the author's community and would thus have us conclude that there are no ghosts, no resurrections, no magic. But such an interpretation contradicts the purpose of the story, which derives its power and coherence precisely from the implication that the monkey's paw may after all work.

Having advanced the Mutual Belief Principle, Currie is well aware that it may not make the grade. Admitting that he has "no rules to substitute for this one," the philosopher closes the matter with a wishful remark: "I take it there would be considerable agreement in practice about how such inferences as this ought to proceed" (1990, 80). But this misses the point. No one has ever doubted that readers are capable of making appropriate inferences about the fictions they read. The whole purpose of the analysis was to fashion a workable model of this process.

## THE PROBLEMS THAT DOGGED LEWIS

*Naturally, as far as maxims and aphorisms are concerned, the concept of truth is relative to the intentions of its author: saying that an aphorism expresses a truth means saying that it is meant to express what the author intends as a truth and which he wants to convince his readers of.*
UMBERTO ECO, *ON LITERATURE*

Currie's abandonment of possible worlds resolves the problems that dogged Lewis. It makes good sense to treat a story not as an intersection of logically complete and necessarily consistent worlds but as a set of propositions that are incomplete and sometimes openly contradictory. The source of Currie's own problems, however, is his source of relevant propositions—the heuristic device of the fictional author. I submit that a shift from the hypothetical author to the real author and from hypothetical intentions to real intentions can resolve the outstanding problems.[10] More formally, I submit that what is true in fiction follows from

> (T), what is enunciated or directly warranted by the text, and
> (ß), a reflexive recognition of the *real* author's successfully executed goals and intentional attitudes *relevant to a given fiction*.

Being a realist about intentions entails that, much as in other aspects of everyday life, one can sometimes fall short of the intended goal. A theory of fictional truth based on real intentions allows, therefore, for failed intentions when the evidence, textual or otherwise, shows that the author tried to express a proposition P, but the end result means not-P. Real intentionalism does not mean that we interpret the meaning as P. But it makes it possible to distinguish between P and not-P, which is crucial when assaying—as we will do in Chapter 7—writerly skill and artistry.

Here is how, in "Intention and Literature," Livingston and Mele depict the reflexive correlation of the author's creative—and the reader's retrieval—strategies for determining what is true in a story. The author had a reasonable and effective communicative intention for a given proposition if he "had the intention and had good and sufficient reason to believe that the proposition would be imagined and accepted for the purpose of the fiction, on the basis of available evidence, by members of the target audience" (1992, 10).[11]

The appeal to actual intentions does not settle all interpretive questions insofar as literature can contain inadvertent meanings—allusions, ambiguities, puns, ironies—that did not figure in the authors' intentions. To deal with such unintended meanings, Stecker argues that apart from successfully realized authorial intentions, interpreters must take into account the linguistic, cultural, and artistic conventions in place at the time the work is created.

> It is very plausible that much unintended meaning can be accounted for by the working of such conventions. For example, it is plausible that it is part of the meaning of a work that it puns on a certain word in virtue of linguistic conventions about word meaning and artistic conventions that puns are artistically significant features of works in the genre in question. (1993, 485–486)

Assaying the merits of hypothetical intentionalism, Stecker considers two of the most representative proposals in that category: Tolhurst's intended reader and Levinson's ideal reader. He disposes of both summarily. First of all, intended readers—and thus literary meanings attributed to them—can be idiosyncratic, arbitrary, and accidental, leading interpreters astray. Moreover, it is doubtful that meaning varies *merely* as a result of variance in the target audience. Also, relevant interpretations can arise outside the target readership. Levinson's ideal reader, on the other hand, leads to interpretive relativism on top of being a normative rather than a descriptive notion.

Most interestingly, concludes Stecker, so long as we do not artificially rule out certain kinds of evidence about authorial intentions, hypothetical and real intentionalism yield identical interpretations. In practice, in other words, both approaches are for the most part indistinguishable. That being the case, Occam's razor dictates that we not multiply entities beyond necessity. Grounding the interpretation of implicit story content in real authors' intentions removes the stumbling blocks encountered by Currie and other hypothetical intentionalists.

Let me highlight the advantages of real intentionalism with regard to retrieving fictional truth:

- The circular concept of the fictional author yields to a determinate reality of the real writer with real goals and designs, while the focus on the author's executive intentions—those that actually went into the work's execution—rules out true but irrelevant inferences.

- Since we are now dealing with a real-life person, there is no need to generate complete belief systems. The relevant background beliefs are now limited to those associated with the author's executive reflexive intentions for the fiction in question.

- A significant part of the real creator's and the real reader's Mutual Contextual Beliefs is the knowledge of genres, used reflexively by the former to signal the relevant context for interpretation.

- In instances of explicit incoherence, we can interpret the entailments that follow from contradictions only to the extent warranted by the author's intentions.

The last point is crucial. The challenge for any account of fictional truth is how to interpret logically inconsistent fictions, such as time-travel stories. In classical logic anything follows from internal incoherence (a condition expressed as *ex contradictio quodlibet* or *ex falso quodlibet*), rendering a story meaningless. For example, in Lem's "Seventh Voyage" the protagonist tries to repair his spaceship on Tuesday and does not try to repair his spaceship on Tuesday. From this apparent discrepancy it logically follows that you and I do not exist, that cabbage is a flammable mineral, and that anything at all is true in the story.

Needless to say, such entailments are utterly irrelevant to the aesthetic interpretation of the story. Since this issue is the litmus test for any account of fictional truth, we need to look at it in more detail. Let us return for a moment to Currie. In his view the reader would adopt any interpretation, no matter how implausible, rather than conclude that the author actually meant what he said when composing an inconsistent fiction. Naturally, the issue here is logical incoherence, such as in time travel, rather than a less troublesome inconsistency that may arise out of simple forgetfulness. An example of the latter is provided by the placement of Watson's war wound in the Sherlock Holmes stories, sometimes said to be in the shoulder, other times in the leg.

Real intentionalism, grounded in the real, fallible author, provides a sensible and universally practiced solution to such inadvertent inconsistencies. All else being equal, if most of the evidence suggests that the wound is in one place rather than the other, we should go with the greater number, one mistake being more likely than many. If, on the other hand, the numbers are roughly equal and the matter cannot be settled by an appeal to authorial intentions, there is no determinate answer. It is true, then, that the wound is in *either* place but not true that it is in one or the other. One way or another, however, unintended contradictions are not to be considered fictionally true.[12]

The more thorny problem arises in stories like "The Seventh Voyage," where Lem is far from equivocating, metaphorizing, or misunderstanding his words. On the contrary, his evocation of time-travel paradoxes could hardly be more explicit. In the story, Ion Tichy embarks on a cosmic voyage only to be thwarted by the breakdown of his rocket in a region of space plagued by gravitational vortices. Fittingly enough for a comic caper in which our space-age Crusoe fries a steak on the overheating atomic pile, Tichy becomes chrono-duplicated in all stages of his life. With the spaceship full of appearing and disappearing Tichys, the protagonist is forced to interact in all kinds of loopy ways with his own multiple selves, trying to sort out the causal and temporal entanglements of his (their?) chrono-multiplication.

Although logical incoherence in a possible world entails that world's complete collapse, this clearly need not be so in fiction. Lem deals with inconsistencies by narrating individual scenes in a logically consistent way but avoiding their self-contradictory entailments. For example, although the Tuesday Tichy knows by virtue of being his own older chrono-twin that the Monday Tichy will not help him repair the rocket, he still tries to persuade the other to change his mind as if it were indeed possible.

The above pattern is common to most time-travel fiction, from Wells's prototypical *Time Machine* to later blockbusters like *The Termina-*

*tor*. Although at a deeper level all such stories are irredeemably incoherent, the audience is implicitly asked to suspend judgment with regard to what follows from such incoherence. This is psychologically plausible, since readers could not trace all implications of all textual propositions anyway. Even when we try our best, we fall prey to deductive corruption, memory lapses, or mental partitioning.

Thus from explicit inconsistencies it does not follow that any arbitrary proposition is true in a given fiction. If Lem's story is anything to go by, in fact, the correct interpretive strategy is to follow standard logic within the text but, as you might anticipate, only to the extent warranted by the author's reflexive intentions. When the contradictory narrative "bubbles" overlap, the reader must acknowledge the global incoherence of the story, without necessarily transferring it to the individual propositions—all the more so, that narrative illogic can be employed with a serious purpose in mind.

Chronomotion can, after all, be harnessed to artistic goals that can outweigh the price levied by the logic department. Time travel can model the sociocultural or psychological effects of a future shock—or conversely the effects of repeatedly undergoing a controlled experience, as in Alain Resnais's *Je t-aime, je t'aime*. Such cognitive and artistic goals are, in fact, a good guide to the extent of inferential entailments relevant to the story. I thus fully agree with David Davies that "'truth *in* fiction' and 'truth *through* fiction' are *not* as distinct as some would have us believe" (1996, 53).[13]

Since some of my conclusions echo Lewis's postscripts to "Truth in Fiction," let me close by reviewing the objections that Currie raises against Lewis's account. Clearly the second and third objections are solved by the transfer of relevant interpretive strategy from a complete and coherent possible world per Lewis to a fallible and not necessarily coherent set of beliefs of the actual author. We are left, then, with the first argument: "It is not clear that every inconsistent story will have consistent segments from which we could obtain a recognizable narrative."[14]

Real intentionalism offers a clear way forward: the range of valid implications is determined by the real author's executive intentions, which are independent of the feasibility of segmentation. There is nothing amiss per se with segmentation, and in many contexts the appropriate strategy may indeed involve partition of the text into self-contained sections that will follow the standard logic of entailment. Theory aside, what does all this tell us about the logical calisthenics in "The Seventh Voyage"?

It is true in the story that time travel is possible but not true that any arbitrary proposition follows. It is true that the past is fixed and determined and that the characters are aware of that. Indeed, some of them invoke it as an argument not to repair the rocket (If I fix it today, how come the Tomorrow Me asks me to fix it today?). But this is not the focus in understanding the characters' behaviors and beliefs. Instead, these are approached by the author as standardly consistent. The hilarity and finesse of Lem's spoof stems, in fact, from the murderous logic with which he tracks some, but not all, of the implications of this illogical setup.

*Seven*  INTENTION AND
INTERPRETATION

*Whenever someone tries to tell us that D'Artagnan was moti-
vated by a homosexual passion for Porthos, that Manzoni's
Innominato was driven to evil by an overwhelming Oedipus
complex, that the nun of Monza was corrupted by Com-
munism, as certain politicians today might wish to suggest,
or that Panurge acts the way he does out of hatred of nascent
capitalism, we can always reply that it is not possible to find
in the texts referred to any statement, suggestion, or insinua-
tion that allows us to go along with such interpretative drift.*
UMBERTO ECO, *ON LITERATURE*

# IS THERE A SINGLE RIGHT
# INTERPRETATION?

*The world of literature is a universe in which it is possible to establish whether a reader has a sense of reality or is the victim of his own hallucinations.*

UMBERTO ECO, *ON LITERATURE*

Featuring some of the best-known names in contemporary analytic aesthetics, Gary Iseminger's and Michael Krausz's respective anthologies, *Interpretation and Intention* and *Is There a Single Right Interpretation?*, represent efforts to make sense of the historical divisions of opinion regarding intentions and interpretations. The main fault line runs between the radical anti-intentionalists and the equally radical intentionalists. Over the decades the two stances have become practically synonymous with the names of Monroe Beardsley and E. D. Hirsch Jr., who with remarkable lucidity staked out a variety of arguments in their defense.

Insofar as meaning is activated only in the presence of consciousness, Hirsch sensibly concludes that intentions are indispensable to communication. The cardinal question is whether the intentions that channel literary meanings—and hence interpretations—are the author's, the reader's, or both. Although Hirsch does not dwell on this point, his tone strongly implies that he takes these alternatives to be mutually exclusive. And since he abjures the reader, in the central part of argument he asserts that "*the* meaning of the text" is identical, or logically equivalent, to the author's meaning (1992, 14).

Although it may not be immediately apparent, in this single statement Hirsch commits himself to three distinct, though not entirely unrelated, errors. One, he identifies texts with works. Two, he posits that there is the best or the correct meaning of a literary work. Three, he reifies the author's meaning for any and all literary scenarios. There is nothing in the moderate variety of intentionalism I espouse to warrant any of these claims. All the same, it will be instructive to look at them in turn in order to calibrate the difference.

To begin, for reasons belabored in Chapters 2 and 3, literary works are ontologically and aesthetically not equivalent to their texts. Rather than reiterate what has been established before, let me move straight to Hirsch's second proposition. Is there *the* best or *the* correct meaning of a literary work? Intransigent as this "singularist" stance sounds, over the years it has attracted a few adherents. In *Interpretation,* Peter D. Juhl insists, for example, that a "literary work has one and only one correct interpretation" (1980, 198). Are there coherent reasons for skepticism about such uncompromising claims? I think so.

To begin with the simplest of these, critical praxis across the ages is uniform in belying it. Has anyone ever managed to resolve to everyone else's satisfaction the one correct interpretation of Iago's cruelty to Othello? Or of Huck Finn's vexingly deceptive attitude to Jim—playing cruel practical jokes one moment, humbling himself to the "nigger" the next, only to abandon his friend to Tom's elaborate theatrics of escape? And what about *the* meaning of Jim's deceptive attitude to Huck—mothering the boy like a substitute father while keeping mum about the fact that Huck's real father is dead, which would obviate the need for the boy's escape?

The skeptic may demur that this does not necessarily prove that radical intentionalism should be abandoned once and for all. To establish that authorial intentions do not uniquely determine interpretations one needs a methodological rather than a historical argument. Here is one: texts are finite in how much they determine (that is why every text is compatible with an infinity of possible worlds). Interpretations, on the other hand, can be refined without end. If we identify each possible world with a different possible interpretation, the number of the latter must also be infinite instead of one—the best one.

Take Bernard Malamud's last novel, *God's Grace*.[1] The climactic scene depicts the last man on earth, a nuclear holocaust survivor, being dragged by a sentient chimpanzee toward sacrificial death. Calvin Cohn's demise has been intimated to him by God, for whose forgiveness he had long prayed. Now, about to die, the protagonist—and with him the reader—is made to ponder the nature of God's grace. Is this sacrificial death a symbol of divine forgiveness or a judgment on human sin and hubris? Is it an epiphany of reconciliation or an agony of abandonment? Is Malamud's God grace-full and compassionate or grace-less and cruel? There are no grounds to believe that the author intended either of these interpretations—or their conjunction—as *the* correct one, and no appeal to the text can decide the issue.

Interpretive indeterminacy occurs at one point or another in virtually all narratives of any complexity. Does Hemingway's *To Have and Have Not* exalt rugged individualism or rather trace the limitations of such individualism in the continental corporation known as the United States of America? The whole issue comes to a head in Harry Morgan's famous last words, when the fatally wounded man skewers the myth of individualism in the era of mass bureaucracy: "No matter how a man alone ain't got no bloody fucking chance" (1987, 225). Asks Wirt Williams in *The Tragic Art of Ernest Hemingway:* "Is this a primitive, intuitive revolutionary declaration? Or a postulation of a primitive, intuitive tragic sense of life? Or both?" (1981, 114). Because there is no answer, it makes no sense to speak of *the* meaning of this line and this novel.

Historically, Hirsch's uncompromising intentionalism was a response to I. A. Richards, who in *Principles of Literary Criticism* famously argued that two readers reading one and the same sonnet by Wordsworth were "reading quite different poems" (2001, 208). Anti-intentionalist from the beginning to the end, Richards and his impressionist theory of interpretation claimed that literature is an experience in the reader's mind—hence different interpretations had to entail different experiences, which in turn entailed different poems. Swinging the pendulum the other way to the end, Hirsch's third error stems directly from his assault on Richards's subjectivism.

For assistance in this matter I turn to one of the staunchest opponents of intentionalism. Beardsley mounts a forceful challenge, echoed since in endless variations, to Hirsch's claim that the meaning of a literary work is identical with the author's—or to Brian Vickers's more recent claim that "a novelist's control over his materials is total" (1993, 139). Beardsley's counterarguments are simple and direct:

> There can be authorless texts that are meaningful and interpretable.
> Interpretations can change after the author's death.
> Works can have meanings unintended by the author.

Demonstrating the nonequivalence of the work's and the author's meaning, each demonstrates radical intentionalism to be a fallacy. Crucially—in what is often unappreciated—it leaves *moderate* intentionalism wholly unaffected.

To appreciate the limits of Beardsley's counterarguments vis-à-vis moderate intentionalism, we need to pry them apart into two strands already familiar from earlier discussion—ontological and aesthetic. Let us begin with Beardsley's ontological argument. According to the critic, even though in real life people perform any number of acts with language, such as satirizing or asserting, literary fictions specialize only in representing these acts. Literature, in other words, parasitizes ordinary language: instead of engaging in speech acts, it merely represents them.

Significantly, the critic concedes that in life the communicative goal of interpretation demands attention to the speaker's intentions. Literary language, however, is said to be the exception to the rule. Beardsley's entire ontological argument rests, therefore, on this alleged segregation of fictional discourse from real-life discourse. Since language in literature is said to merely represent speech acts—rather than instantiate a speech act of fiction making—the critic feels justified in dismissing authorial intentions. If this sounds like *déjà vu*, it is: Beardsley's tenets are a rehash of the tenets discredited in Chapter 5.

Needless to say, the alleged ghettoization of language in fiction makes little sense. Few readers fail to recognize that Philip Roth's 1971 satire *Our Gang (Starring Trick E. Dixon and His Friends)* conveys a great deal about the real-life "Tricky Dicky" Nixon. The crusading tone of the piece as well as all available contextual evidence make it clear that Roth speaks at least in part in his own voice, instead of merely representing the speech act of satirizing. In fact, a large part of the book's piquancy owes to the recognition that it is the real author, rather than his narrative alter ego, who lampoons the president of the United States.[2]

If language in fiction were indeed divorced from the way it functions in real life, something else would have to explain Abraham Lincoln's quip that Harriet Beecher Stowe's little fiction started the Civil War and the blacklisting of *Animal Farm* and *1984* by Big Brother censors around the globe. Of course, fiction is one thing, nonfiction another. But as I have demonstrated elsewhere, if there is something puzzling about milking real knowledge from unreal cows, placing literary fictions on the level of thought experiments comes close to disentangling the riddle.[3]

So much for Beardsley's ontological argument against intentionalism. Since language in literary fiction does not merely represent illocutionary acts, it demands the same communicative attention to the speaker's intentions as ordinary language does. This basic point about intentions in action is again corroborated by research in cognitive psychology that targets human biological adaptations for culture. The results of developmental studies that explore the complexities of our adaptation for mind reading (theory of mind) are unequivocal on this point. A persuasive argument can be made, in fact, that "children can only understand a symbolic convention in the first place if they understand the communicative partner as an intentional agent."[4]

Now, let us move on to Beardsley's aesthetic argument against attributing intention. In essence it poses the following question: Must aesthetic interpretations be informed by authorial intentions? The theorist himself shows why the answer is affirmative. In *The Possibility of Criticism,* arguing that aesthetic attributes arise out of the ingredients of the text itself, Beardsley concludes that originality (or novelty or uniqueness) is a feature of the text (1970, 34). His equation of texts with works has, however, grave consequences for his anti-intentionalist theses. Originality, as we have seen, is an attribute of works, not texts. If a narrative exhibits the aesthetic quality of being original, detecting this quality entails going beyond the text to the context, of which authorial intentions form a proper subset.

Simply put, texts are not original—works are. And since artworks are aesthetic structures created in specific art-historical contexts, attributions of aesthetic qualities such as originality are compatible only with intentionalism—albeit one appreciably different from Hirsch's. After all, far from taking the singularist line (that there is only one best interpretation fixed by the author's intentions), moderate intentionalism allows that some of the work's meanings may not be fixed by the author. As a corollary it makes no sense to speak of *the* most correct interpretation, even though some interpretations may be more competent—and can be demonstrated to be more competent—than others.

In "Incompatible Interpretations of Art" (1982), Susan Feagin tries a similar tack to Beardsley's with a similar degree of success. The philosopher argues that since fictional events and characters have no referents, critics cannot attach any truth values to statements about them. If correct, this argument would invalidate not only talk of true or untrue interpretations but also talk of authorial intentions. Feagin's objection can be repealed, however, by recasting statements about events and characters into statements about works; for example, work (W) depicts event (E) or character (C) as having attribute (A). The disappearance of the reference problem voids the argument.

## MODERATE INTENTIONALISM

*But there are rules governing interpretation: that our planet is,
as Dante says, "the threshing floor that makes us all so fierce"
(Par. 22.151) might suggest thousands of poetic inferences,
but it will not convince anyone, so long as there are cultural
conventions we all agree on, that it is a place where peace and
benevolence flourish.*

UMBERTO ECO, *ON LITERATURE*

Moderate intentionalism has as little to do with the intentionalist fallacy as with the anti-intentionalist fallacy. All it conveys
is that the executive intentions that guide writers during composition
may not be *a priori* ruled out by interpreters. Tellingly, even advocates of
hypothetical intentionalism concede that, at the bottom, their heuristic
constructs necessarily correlate with the actual intentions of actual artists. Thus Currie writes in *The Nature of Fiction:* "The kind of person
the fictional author is will depend in some way or other on the kind of
person the real author is" (78).[5]

Unremarkable in itself, moderate intentionalism runs, however,
counter to the current critical orthodoxy, which by default decouples
interpretations from authors and intentions.[6] A standard argument offered in defense of this move is that interpreting literature in the light of
what is known of the author's intentions would be tantamount to crediting all of the writer's pronouncements as gospel truth. This, however, is
a complete misconception of moderate intentionalism. Although artists
indeed frequently elucidate their intentions postpartum, in most cases
the main body of interpretive evidence is provided by the work itself.

There are a number of reasons for that. For one, intentions can evolve
or even change entirely during composition. In *Flawed Texts and Verbal
Icons* (1984), Hershel Parker details, for example, how in the case of Melville's *Pierre,* Crane's *Red Badge of Courage,* Twain's *Pudd'nhead Wilson,*
and Mailer's *The American Dream,* the writers' intentions were in a flux
right until their galleys went to print. Another reason the work may on
occasion trump its author is that complex intentions are often difficult
to articulate concisely. The published novel may already be the best expression of its author's design, irrespective of later elucidations.

Also, the finiteness of our cognitive resources often enough mani-
fests itself in forgetfulness, inability to think through all implications, or
simply a lack of explicit awareness of the kind that makes many writers

report surprise at the behavior of their own creations. Even under the best circumstances—that is, when precisely enunciated and not misinterpreted by the audience—authorial introspections can also be inaccurate owing to marketing opportunism, taking credit for happenstance, or reporting intentions that never were. Indeed, the following counterfactual wittily shows the perils of taking such revelations at face value.

Suppose, muses Gary Taylor, that one day we unearth Shakespeare's own testimony about his habits of composition. It could be an autograph letter, such as: "Dear Anne, I'll be home next week, as soon as I finish revising that old play of mine, *King Lear*. Your loving Willy. London. 1 April 1610." A stunning critical coup? Not necessarily. Artists may be an invaluable source of information about their creations but not always a reliable one. "For all we know," cautions Taylor, "'revising *King Lear*' might have been Shakespeare's alibi, to cover an adulterous weekend" (1987, 297).

Finally, there is the familiar difficulty in intention attribution of an evidentiary nature. One need not be confronted with an anonymous medieval palimpsest or a coverless Club Med paperback to recognize that in the messy world we inhabit, in many contexts authorial intentions may be inaccessible to the reader outside the evidence offered by the text itself.[7] Readers with no extratextual account of authorial intentions, i.e., most of us, normally have to read the intentions off the works themselves. Once again, however, the potential empirical difficulties of elucidating the fact of the matter—the executive intentions of the creator—do not negate that there *is* a fact of the matter.

It is for no other reason that Fitzgerald's biographer Matthew J. Bruccoli could insist that many of the writer's intentions are recoverable from the study of his manuscripts, galleys, and even the marked copy of *The Great Gatsby*. Another scholar put the matter this way: "We may legitimately not care whether they accurately reflect the author's, or anyone else's, intention; but if that is our position, it must be made clear."[8] Whether disregarding authorial intentions is even possible in practice is doubtful. Even the most ardent anti-intentionalists are, after all, inconsistent in their exegetical travails, referring to aims, authors, contexts, or aesthetic attributes as a matter of course—as they should, given that their theories bear little resemblance to what their contacts with literature are about.

Naturally, as in everyday life, we are not after the complete account of anyone's intentions, only the best account of the intentions relevant to a given fiction. There is nothing in moderate intentionalism to imply that authorial intentions are invariably accessible, free of contradiction, or conducive to critical interpretation. It is certainly not true that for every work of literature one can pinpoint its creator's goals with incontestable accuracy. However, to exclude such knowledge *a priori* from aesthetic considerations is not to interpret a literary work but merely to engage in reading the text.

To reiterate, the epistemic truism that intentions may not always be knowable provides no grounds for epistemological doubts about moderate intentionalism. Like all epistemic domains, intention attribution relies on the process of forming hypotheses based on evidence available at the given stage of research. This process, while certainly fallible, is also self-correcting, as demonstrated by the successful reconstructions of historians, archeologists, cryptographers, or indeed literary scholars—all of whom rely at least in part on attributions of intentions.

Clearly, no monolithic account of intentions can capture the complex, dynamic, and heterogeneous nature of human beings' goals and actions. But, conversely, it seems inconceivable that authors consistently and utterly fail to implement any part of their intended design. Granted that sundry stages of creation may not be fully deliberate—in the sense that an array of options often is dished out by subconscious processes. These options are then evaluated with a view to leaving them as is, rewriting them, or discarding them altogether. Such appraisal is where deliberate, intentional decisions come into play.

In his introduction to the classic study of theory of mind, *Understanding Other Minds: Perspectives from Developmental and Cognitive Neuroscience,* Simon Baron-Cohen concludes flatly that "attributing mental states to a complex system (such as human being) is by far the easiest way of understanding it" (2000, 21). From understanding human beings it is not far to understanding human art. Given how much time and effort—at times many years and many thousands of draft pages—go into the composition of literary works, it is unconscionable to reject out of hand an aesthetic appreciation of these works as intentional artifacts.

This principle is captured in the words of one textuist: "If we respect our authors we should have a passionate concern to see that their words are recovered and currently transmitted in as close a form to their intentions as we can contrive."[9] Textual variants can, after all, be at odds with one another, sometimes to a remarkable degree. This leaves anti-intentionalists no leg to stand on because if any discriminations are to be made between defective and authoritative texts, they are presumably to be made in line with authorial intentions.

One might ask which is the text of T. S. Eliot's *The Rock.* Is it the

1934 Harcourt Brace edition, which through a splicing error in the photo offset lost an entire line, or the version intended by Eliot and his collaborators for the benefit of the London Diocese? Which text of *This Side of Paradise* is Fitzgerald's text—the one from the first three prints or the one from later editions that integrate authorial revisions? Which is the text of Vidal's *The City and the Pillar*—the original 1948 edition or the 1994 version in which description and dialogue are altered on almost every page and a previously dead character is brought to life?

This is not to even mention egregious cases such as *The Jungle*, which, unbeknownst to generations of readers of the book's eight hundred editions worldwide, was eviscerated by Sinclair between its publication in *The Appeal to Reason* and the book edition. Quantitatively, the authoritative text shrank from thirty-six to thirty-one chapters, nearly 30 percent overall. Passages on socialism, critiques of big business, the robber barons, and the press trust—even the telltale alliteration of the Packingtown moguls (Armour-Anderson, Swift-Smith, Morris-Morton)—all got cut. Which is the authorial text—and why?[10]

In "An Essay on Criticism," which in many ways embodies the spirit of moderate intentionalism, Alexander Pope counseled that a good critic will read each work of wit with the same spirit that its author writ. This sensible proposal yields no ground to intentionalist fallacy whereby authorial intentions are said to determine *the* meaning and thus the best or correct interpretation. A moderate intentionalist's contention—albeit one fraught with repercussions for critics inclined to level all interpretations in the name of textual *jouissance*—is that authorial intentions must inform (rather than determine) any interpretation of a literary work *qua* an artwork.

Interestingly enough, the appeal to the artist's intentions may need to be made in order to establish the very authorship. So it was, for instance, in the recent process of authenticating some of Pollock's drip paintings—and, conversely, proving that other canvases of unknown provenance held by their owners to be genuine were not. The experts in this case were not art historians or aestheticians but scientists. Using fractal analysis, Richard Taylor and his team proved that Pollock's drips were fractal to a high degree both on small and large scales—a quality that other drips lacked. From work to intention to the authentication of authorship, the causal chain in this scientific-cum-artistic reconstruction is clear.

Although moderate intentionalism is frequently and unjustly confused with the most strident and unsustainable intentionalist claims, critical attitudes may be slowly a-changing. One reason for guarded optimism in this respect is that, long pronounced dead, the biographical author is slowly reemerging as "a major player in the economy of current critical writing."[11] It must be made clear, however, that such guarded optimism is not the first symptom of relapse into biographical fallacy whereby—to repeat the words with which Proust denigrated the *méthode* of its foremost nineteenth-century practitioner, Charles-Augustin Sainte-Beuve—critics should talk to the writers' friends rather than read their books.

Moderate intentionalism is not about turning literature into a graveyard to be excavated for traces of psychological, to say nothing of psychoanalytic, profiles of their authors.[12] Moderate intentionalism is about approaching data on agency, intentions, and the overall economy of the art-historical context *critically* with a view to their relevance to aesthetic interpretation. One crucial reason moderate intentionalism is distinct from—and superior to—the position embraced by Hirsch or Vickers is that it allows for failed intentions. The conceptual difference and interpretive consequences could hardly be greater.

Moderate intentionalism does not mean we must always interpret stories in accordance with the author's intentions. This central tenet frequently eludes anti-intentionalist critics who typically lump all intentionalist theories into one bag, weigh it down with concrete, and drop it off a bridge. In fact, moderate intentionalism is as distinct from all-or-nothing anti-intentionalism as from all-or-nothing intentionalism. In contrast to either of these two extremes, moderate intentionalism allows critics to distinguish between the intended and obviously unintended—since failed—results. The distinction is enormous, and a recent literary example highlights the matters at stake.

## A BRILLIANT REWORKING
## OF *THE TURN OF THE SCREW*

*Reading works of literature forces on us an exercise of fidelity and respect, albeit within a certain freedom of interpretation.*
UMBERTO ECO, *ON LITERATURE*

Thomas M. Disch's bestselling novel, *The M.D.: A Horror Story* (1991), is in many ways a brilliant reworking of *The Turn of the*

*Screw*. As in James's novella, Disch's genre-buster poises itself on the cusp of a ghost or horror story and psychological dementia. As a young boy, the protagonist, Billy Michaels, appears to succumb to the temptations of Mercury, a malevolent deity. Armed with Mercury's supernatural powers, the boy grows up into a preeminent medical researcher and a business tycoon, even as he methodically inflicts evil on his family, acquaintances, and countless victims of ARVIDS, a worse-than-AIDS epidemic he unleashes on America.[13]

Far from tipping his hand, however, the author is at pains to develop Billy's supernatural acts in equivocal light, leaving the door open to their nonfantastic interpretation. For example, when Billy curses his brother, Ned, with paralysis, the symptoms of Ned's affliction are indistinguishable from that of Bubby Corning, a minor character in the novel who is in a vegetative state owing to natural causes. When Billy apparently smites his grandmother with baldness, she loses her hair in a salon, thus allowing for an innocuous interpretation (perhaps a super-allergic reaction to shampoo chemicals).

When people see faces in ice and when neighbors rapidly lose teeth, some trees fail to succumb to an otherwise ubiquitous blight, when a baby is born monstrously disfigured, and when the country is ravaged by an incurable epidemic of unknown etiology, all these and other events could, in principle, be attributed to natural causation. In fact, at least on one approach to the story, they *ought* to be. Halfway through the novel, while talking to Mercury, Billy himself wonders: "Of course, there was Ned, and grandma O. going bald, and the rest, but all those things could have happened naturally" (1991, 234).

Disch's equivocal design is reinforced by his choice of genre. His self-styled horror story is developed on the narrative level as a *Bildungsroman,* in manner and tone perfectly conforming to its mimetic conventions. Another clue is the author's penchant for aesthetic playfulness and syncretism, both of which characterize so many of his novels (e.g., *White Fang Goes Dingo, Camp Concentration, 334, Black Alice, On Wings of Song, The Priest*). Given that all are carefully positioned on the brink of disparate narrative conventions and genres, Disch's *oeuvre* primes interpreters for the intricate game played out in *The M.D.: A Horror Story.*

Considered in isolation, each instance of magic in the story could be explained by coincidence, accident, hallucination, or genetic or psychological aberration—consistent with the author's design not to close the door on nonfantastic interpretations. It is only when considered as a series that their joint likelihood far exceeds the realm of probability, shifting the denominator from natural to the supernatural. Thus, in the course of the novel, the readers are asked to ponder the following questions, among others (the complete list would be substantially longer).

> Grandma O. commands the alarm to stop, which it instantly does: is it magic or coincidence? (8)
>
> Described on the preceding page as having "a different way of seeing," Billy has a fateful conversation with a magical being who manifests himself as Santa. Is Santa a ghost equipped with supernatural powers, or is he just a figment of Billy's peculiar "way of seeing"? (14)
>
> Billy's mother, Madge, sees Santa's face in the ice: is it magic or just overwrought imagination? (18)
>
> How does Billy know where to look for the snake-entwined magical wand, the caduceus—by magic or intuition? (43)
>
> Is grandma O.'s headache the result of Billy's wrongdoing or a natural migraine? (54)
>
> Is grandma O.'s hair loss in the salon due to natural or supernatural circumstances? (85)
>
> Is the strange answer Henry gets from the *I Ching* a coincidence or magic? (85)
>
> Whatever happens to Billy's stone? (119–120)
>
> Not one person in the household gets ill: magic or coincidence? (130)
>
> What is the cause of Henry's violent death: an accident or evil magic? (136)
>
> Is the visitation by Mercury just a pot-induced vision or a supernatural manifestation? (171)
>
> Is Henry's visitation just a dream, or is he a ghost who visits his son (as in *Hamlet*)? (207)
>
> Is Deeter's death caused naturally by apnea or by Billy's supernatural curse? (219)
>
> Does Billy's wife, Sondra, botch the strangling of their baby because of supernatural magic or because of her inability to kill her own child? (288)
>
> Is the quarter sitting conveniently in the coin slot a coincidence or magic? (298)

> Is the interlinked series of events that lead to William/Billy's downfall (roadblock, shooting, confinement in quarantine, etc.) coincidental or is it the result of Mercury's revenge on the apostate? (368)

The clearest textual sign of Disch's desire that his story be interpreted in light of this parallel design—at once natural and supernatural—occurs in the denouement. Judith, the sole survivor of the family massacre, discovers a letter left by Billy's long-deceased father that reveals that the boy (and his offspring) may have suffered from Huntington's chorea, a genetic malady marked by acute dementia and superviolent behavior. Inserting this *deus ex machina* a few pages before the end, the writer is at pains to devise a natural explanation for visitations by Mercury to Billy and his son, Judge, for their belief in supernatural powers, and for their pathological tendencies.

In view of such copious and consistent evidence, the author's intentions can be reconstructed as follows. The novel is meant to be read *both* as a horror story, with Mercury's magic behind Billy's supernatural acts, and as a realistic tale of psychopathological dementia, with Mercury as a mere figment of Billy's diseased mind and a series of coincidences in lieu of supernatural causality. Naturally, this ambiguity—whereby the author walks the tightrope between horror story and alternate reality—does not exhaust the interpretive possibilities. The complete set of interpretative possibilities includes:

- a horror story (H) containing supernatural elements such as ghosts, malevolent deities, magic curses, and supernatural causation
- an alternate-reality science fiction (SF) in which all events can be explained rationally—no ghosts, malevolent deities, magic curses, or supernatural causation
- an ambiguous story (A) that deliberately suspends interpretation between (H) and (SF) by providing no conclusive evidence for deciding between these alternatives

In each case, the result can be either a success or failure; and in the event of failure, the result is either of the other two interpretive possibilities. The complete set of authorial decisions (first tier) and outcomes (second and third tiers) is represented by the following diagram:

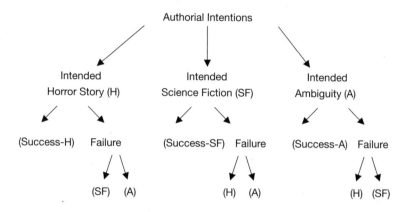

Going, as Hirsch would, by authorial intentions, one would have to read *The M.D.* as a consistently ambiguous tale, an interpretation delineated in the diagram as Success-A. But here is where things get complicated. About a third of the way into the novel (on page 164), three family members hear a bell tinkling upstairs—the manner in which Mercury usually summons Billy—even though nobody is there. Since three people experience this event independently, there is no clear-cut way to explain it as a result of natural causes.

The same type of inconsistency involves Bubby Corning. The text offers no evidence to support the belief that he is crippled because of magic. As a matter of fact, since his affliction precedes Billy's first encounter with Mercury, it strongly implies natural causation. But if that is the case, Bubby's condition should not improve when Billy's evil powers begin to unravel—yet it does, much as those of Billy's other victims do. Try as one might, neither episode can be explained rationally, forcing, through a domino effect, a consistently *fantastic* interpretation of the entire narrative.[14]

In terms of our executive tree, notwithstanding the author's definite intention to create an ambiguous story (Success-A), the incidents that refuse to fit into the rational framework peg *The M.D.* as a horror story (H) instead. Yet the novel seems obviously conceived and executed as a double entendre and loses much in the appreciation of aesthetic and artistic complexity, not to mention the appreciation of the writer's imagination and plot design, if the ambiguous interpretation is discarded. So what did the author himself—who took his own life in July 2008—have to say about all this?

When I put the question to him directly, his first reaction was: "What a devious fellow I am! and/or what a crafty god Mercury!" When it

Horror or dementia? Thomas M. Disch (photographed by Ariel Hameon) and the cover of *The M.D.: A Horror Story.* *"Certainly it was my intention to 'have it both ways.' Natural/supernatural."*

came to the crux of the matter, his confirmation of my reconstruction was unequivocal: "Certainly it was my intention to 'have it both ways'. Natural/supernatural. The same can be said for *The Priest*—but not for either *The Businessman* or *The Sub,* where the balance tips toward the supernatural right from the start, and is there in the auctorial voice." In short, Disch endorsed the interpretation as "apt and correct."[15]

It ought to be clear by now why moderate intentionalism wins the day when it comes to rendering interpretive justice. Being able to triangulate both for the authorial intentions and the actual result, this type of intentionalism is aesthetically and analytically superior both to radical anti-intentionalism and to radical intentionalism. *The M.D.* is a textbook example of a story in which it is imperative to determine the author's intentions in order to appreciate his artistic design and aesthetic appeal. But it is equally imperative to distinguish those intentions from the published novel with which, in some respects, they are inconsistent. It is only the analysis of the author's intentions that permits a full account of this disparity and, as such, an aesthetically apt interpretation.

## WHAT LITERARY INTERPRETATION IS ABOUT

*I'm not saying that the author may not find a discovered reading perverse; but even if he does, he must remain silent, allow others to challenge it, text in hand.*
UMBERTO ECO, *POSTSCRIPT TO THE NAME OF THE ROSE*

On the strength of what we have said so far, we can put together a picture of what literary interpretation is about. Broadly speaking, my theses are anchored in the contrast between art interpretations of literary works and textual readings. Neither the terms nor the concepts are entirely new. To cite but one example, in "Incompatible Interpretations" (1992, 291), Stecker also differentiates between aesthetic interpretations and textual readings.[16] I also find an unlikely confederate in Barthes, who in "De l'oeuvre au texte" thrashes out (although for entirely different reasons) interpretations of works from readings of texts.

It ought to be obvious by now that in aesthetic interpretation, a significant part of interacting with literary works lies in determining what their authors intended to accomplish. This is a *sine qua non* if our goal is to appreciate literature in aesthetic and artistic terms—terms such as complexity and originality or indeed the degree of success in realizing aesthetic goals. Apart from this crucial concession, there is no way to establish the best interpretation, even on the basis of the author's explicit avowals. Art criticism is intrinsically open-ended, and no appeal to anyone's intentions can ever close a literary work in the single best exegesis.

But neither does this open-endedness validate free-for-all relativism. The presence of some art interpretations between which no rational choice is possible does not mean that no rational choice is possible between all and any. Just as countless propositions are true for all interpretations of a given story, countless other propositions are not true once and for all. It is true that at the end of *One Flew Over the Cuckoo's Nest* Chief Bromden uses a ward pillow to smother to death the lobotomized maverick Irishman, R. P. McMurphy. It is false that Chief is an extraterrestrial from Aldebaran raised like a cuckoo by an American Indian family.

In short, to dispense with intention attribution altogether is to dispense with aesthetic interpretation for a different set of interpretive goals. To be sure, work-oriented interpretations do not exhaust the range of strategies open to literary critics. The plurality of critical aims underwrites a plurality of critical approaches, not all focused on determining what aesthetic goals the artists sought to achieve—and succeeded or failed in achieving—in their works. The evidence is abundant, in fact, that some critical strategies depart radically from this goal. Programmatically chary of intentionalism, they aim instead to stimulate critical debate by means of complex textual readings.

In general, it may not be unfair to compare textual readings to music sampling. The sampler adapts someone else's artistic creation for his own purpose by amputating it from its original art-historical context. As before, however, I must point out that textualist theory and practice are not the same. As we saw earlier, even critics like de Man, Bloom, and Derrida inevitably use statements freeloading on authorial intentions or art-historical context.[17] This alone raises methodological questions about the legitimacy of their textualist theories of interpretation.

What types of critical inquiries can be supported by textual readings? The answer can easily be culled from contemporary professional publications. In no particular order those seem to be: enhancing the value of the textualist critical enterprise, presenting a personal or just an interesting way of reading, recasting the text in a socially or ideologically novel context, illustrating the tenets of a particular school of criticism, transgressing canonical boundaries, or even, as Andrew Field appears to attempt in *Nabokov—His Life in Art: a Critical Narrative,* producing an artwork of one's own.

Evidently, textual readings can support a wide variety of critical aims and strategies and stimulate discussion as effectively as aesthetic interpretations. The evidence is overwhelming in that respect. But, one is compelled to ask, why bother with art at all when one's interests lie demonstrably elsewhere? Given the determination with which many critics disregard authorial intentions embedded in literary works—those texts in contexts—it would make as much sense to generate discourse *ab ovo.* Since textual readings can never render aesthetic and thus interpretive justice to the works they are purported to analyze, why not dispense with them altogether?

The answer, I think, should be obvious. To bypass literature in critical discourse would be to ignore a source of aesthetically gratifying, emotionally enriching, and cognitively valuable scenarios of marvelous subtlety, diversity, and complexity. On the other hand, if literature is to remain the linchpin of critical labors, we must not lose sight of the fact that it is bequeathed to us by creators who intend to communicate with their audiences. "When we read . . . we enter into a relationship with its creator that is roughly analogous to conversation," prompts Nöel Carroll in "Art, Intention, Conversation" (1992, 117). "Just as an ordinary conversation gives us a stake in understanding our interlocutor, so does interaction with an artwork."

This is why so many readers and critics of literature find it rewarding—not to say essential—to ponder authorial intentions as guides to the aesthetic attributes, the artistry, and the intellectual content of what they read. This is also why I agree with Levinson that textual readings, "often bounded by only the loosest requirements of plausibility, intelligibility, or interest in the work in question" (1996, 177), have little to do with aesthetic appreciation and interpretation. Instead of promulgating the myth that they enhance our understanding of art *qua* art, textual readings should be owned for what they are: aesthetic tangents at best, dead ends at worst.

Let me give a quintessential example of such an aesthetic dead end. In her canonical study, *The Life and Works of Edgar Allan Poe, a Psycho-Analytic Interpretation,* Marie Bonaparte would have us believe that she is interpreting Poe's "The Murders in the Rue Morgue." Her starting fiat is that children of about one year old are inevitably exposed to a *scène initiale* of lovemaking of their parental figures. Although the children cannot, we are told, grasp the meaning of the event, it cannot but leave ineradicable traces in the psyche. But because education represses children's so-called primal sexual instinct, it must find other venues through sublimation.

According to this self-fulfilling prophecy, Poe—who, by this accounting, as a child must have caught his parents in the act—reenacts his repressed sexual fantasies in "The Murders in the Rue Morgue" by means of the orangutan. Indeed, for the French critic the entire import of the story hinges on the ape's decapitation of the victim—a symbol of "castration of a woman which is one of the central fantasies of little boys" (1949, 540). As such, nothing in Poe's detective story is what it appears to be. All the characters are only playthings of little Edgar's real-life "sadistic concept of coition" (*conception sadique du coït*).

In brief, Bonaparte shrugs off any value the story might have as a superb detective yarn, as one of the first modern American crime fictions, as a crucial stage in the development of the genre formula that will be plied on both sides of the Atlantic for decades to come, as a prototypical logical puzzle of the "locked room" variety, as an avatar of Poe's aesthetics aimed at what he called "a light artillery of the mind," as an experiment in artertainment, as a bridge in taste cultures, or indeed any other interpretation consistent with the writer's aesthetic and artistic goals.

Uninterested in Poe's work, the critic reads his text as a psychoanalytic *roman à clef* instead. The key here is the orangutan—at the risk of blowing the solution, the only creature that could escape from the scene of the crime—said to escape from the writer's allegedly repressed subconscious. Naturally, such a reading of Poe's text has precious little to do with the aesthetic and intellectual content of his work.[18] Looking solely for textual elements that can be pressed into the service of this outlandish reading, Bonaparte discards all kinds of negative evidence, that is, all kinds of narrative elements that fail to fit her formula.

In the end, everyone is free to say what they please in the critical game of who is the cleverest dude around this text.[19] In the current critical milieu nothing stands in the way of, for example, psychoanalytic deconstructions of *Alice in Wonderland* as Phallus in Wonderland. Such off-the-wall exegeses might even stimulate critical debate in ways I do not profess to know. No matter what, however, textual readings of this kind that ignore the aesthetic and historical context circumscribed by authorial intentions can hardly be said to contribute to our appreciation of the English mathematician's artwork.

Nor, it is as important to point out, can such readings be a viable research contribution, based as they are on an outdated and unsound body of work. The list of conclusive refutations of psychoanalysis's claims to the status of science is long, starting with classical biographical studies by Cioffi and Macmillan and ending with the more clinical but by no means less devastating research by Scharnberg and Grünbaum. Inevitably, this last point brings us to the question of literary interpretation in the service of literary research. How does what we have said so far bear on interpreting literature from a cognitive rather than aesthetic standpoint?

Looking for cognitive pay dirt, critics do approach literature selectively, sometimes at odds with the authors' intentions. Are cognitive readings therefore constrained only by a minimal dependence on the contents of the work? Not necessarily. Ethnographers or anthropologists who unrepentantly use literature to understand the society that produced it may conceivably do so without interpreting it in aesthetic terms. Yet they, too, make an inordinate effort to situate stories in their contexts, in the process developing hypotheses about the historical intentions of the authors and the socio-aesthetic interests of the audiences.

Similarly, whenever researchers set out to refine and evaluate cognitive models derived from works of fiction, authorial intentions can fruitfully guide the reader's response. This is because, to quote a leading literary Darwinist, the meaning of a literary representation "consists in the interaction among the points of view of author, characters, and implied audience. That interaction is largely controlled by one of those three distinct sets, the author."[20] Departing from the author's modeling strategy is an option, but at the price of departing from the cognitive range that the author's artistry (skill, experience, research, and so forth) went into making.

The author's modeling intentions function here as a salient equilibrium point reflexively guiding the interpretive moves of the critic. The process is analogous to aesthetic interpretations, especially when writers' cognitive (modeling) goals are part and parcel of their successfully realized artistic intentions. The crucial difference is that it is often possible and always desirable to determine the relative values of cognitive statements derived from the work. This Modeling Heuristic, to use Livingston's term, which assumes that authorial intentions can guide readers to cognitively apt interpretations, is no more than a working hypothesis to be validated or overturned by evidence.[21]

The above does not mean that the Modeling Heuristic will invariably yield the optimal cognitive reading of the work. Pursuing epistemically useful readings, researchers are at liberty to adopt any strategy that will maximize cognitive gain, including ones that depart from the hypotheses implied or even stated explicitly by the author. The decision to discard the Modeling Heuristic presupposes, however, that the researcher is confident it does not apply in a given case, which in turn presupposes its prior application. To rule out the author's modeling intentions, in other words, one needs first to rule them in.

The payoff from a cognitive engagement with a work of literary fiction depends exclusively on its knowledge content rather than on correlation with the modeling goals that (reflexively) guided the story's genesis.[22] But it is to be expected that, in many instances, models that correlate significantly with the creator's intentions will turn out to be more illuminating than others. This is one reason we continue to read fictions and continue to find in them not only aesthetic beauty but adaptive truth.

*Eight*   AESTHETICS
AND EVOLUTION

*I wrote a novel because I had a yen to do it. I believe this is sufficient reason to set out to tell a story. Man is a storytelling animal by nature.*
UMBERTO ECO, *POSTSCRIPT TO THE NAME OF THE ROSE*

# BEAUTY IS TRUTH, TRUTH BEAUTY

*Thus it is not so much that philosophers have given up
pursuing the truth as that art and literature have also taken on
that function.*

UMBERTO ECO, *ON LITERATURE*

"Beauty is truth, truth beauty, that is all / Ye know on
earth, and all ye need to know." Of John Keats's ekphrastic "Ode on a
Grecian Urn" most readers remember just this final couplet, perhaps not
even for its intrinsic beauty as for the sentiment it professes. It is, after
all, one that has reverberated in literature and literary studies ever since.
William Faulkner was only one of many who seized on Keats's mani-
festo as a bedrock for his own pronouncements on the artist's responsibility to his art. "If a writer has to rob his mother, he will not hesitate"
is how Faulkner notoriously put it to the *Paris Review* in 1956; "the 'Ode
on a Grecian Urn' is worth any number of old ladies."[1]

This archetypal equivocation, or at least intimation, of kinship between truth and beauty is, naturally, far from confined to literature.
Robert Adams, a photographer and theorist of the medium, inquires
at the outset of *Beauty in Photography*, "Is Truth Beauty and vice versa?"
before sensibly concluding: "The answer, as Keats knew, depends on the
truth about which we are talking" (1981, 31). *The Mathematical Gazette*
furnishes proof that even the proverbial queen of the sciences has not remained heedless of Keats's equation, beginning with Diogenes O'Rell's
mathematically mind-twisting verse titled, appropriately enough, "On
the Symmetries of a Grecian Urn" (1992).

The reason Keats's lines have resonated with so many is not because their sentiment is especially groundbreaking. On the contrary. Capping a long history of similar assertions, the poet only gave expression to what, in Pope's words from "Essay on Man," was "oft thought but ne'er so well expressed." Indeed, the tradition of pairing beauty and truth goes back at least to antiquity. While Plato was the first thinker we know by name to link truth to beauty, he has been echoed since by countless others, beginning with Plotinus (who threw good into the mix for good measure). This neo-Platonic lineage extends for more than two thousand years right down to the Romantics and the Transcendentalists' efforts to link innate aesthetics to moral knowledge.

Nor do theories positing some form of union between aesthetics and cognition stop with the nineteenth century. Walter de la Mare, for example, argued prominently that human beings are equipped with an innate faculty of imagination, which either atrophies with adulthood or else matures enough to face the world in the verses of the poet. Hence, de la Mare contends, the polarization of the human faculties: some are acquired and deductive, others intuitive and inductive (in the modern lexicon, we might describe the latter as innate adaptive evolutionary modules). Characteristically, the poet-critic again cast this distinction in Keats's terms: "The one knows that beauty is truth, the other reveals that truth is beauty."[2]

Neo-Platonism forms only one strand among philosophers, writers, and critics who throughout the ages grafted truth on beauty—or vice versa. "You may take sublimity in all its truth and beauty exists in such works as please all men at all times" (1965, 115), wrote Longinus in the first century AD.[3] Waxing on the nature of art, Shakespeare had no doubt in "Sonnet XIV" that "truth and beauty shall together thrive." By the time we come to Poe's *Eureka,* the bond between the two is as firm as rhetoric can make it. "I offer this Book of Truths," states Poe right at the outset, "not in its character of Truth-Teller, but for the Beauty that abounds in its Truth" (1997, 4).

A full twelve years earlier, of course, Emerson articulated in "Nature" much of what is found in *Eureka.* If possible, he was even more adamant, declaring that the "true philosopher and the true poet are one, and a beauty, which is truth, and a truth, which is beauty, is the aim of both" (1983, 917). Across the Atlantic, the same umbilical relationship was glorified by Schiller in his collection of essays *On the Aesthetic Education of Man.* "Beauty now gives laws to the social intercourse which was previously controlled by Truth," wrote the German philosopher (1954, 57–58). "There can, in a word, no longer be any question how he passes

O Attic shape! Fair attitude! with brede
Of marble men and maidens overwrought,
With forest branches and the trodden weed;
Thou, silent form, dost tease us out of thought
As doth eternity: Cold Pastoral!
When old age shall this generation waste,
Thou shalt remain, in midst of other woe
Than ours, a friend to man, to whom thou say'st,
"Beauty is truth, truth beauty," - that is all
Ye know on earth, and all ye need to know.

By John Keats

Truth and beauty. Keats's double-take on the Grecian urn. *"Beauty is truth, truth beauty, that is all / Ye know on earth, and all ye need to know."* Of John Keats's ekphrastic *"Ode on a Grecian Urn"* most readers remember just this final couplet, perhaps not even for its intrinsic beauty as for the sentiment it professes.

from Beauty to Truth, since the latter by its very nature lies within the former" (123).

Not surprisingly, by the twentieth century the rhapsodic tone of such assurances became considerably tempered. Philosophy of science, not to mention science itself, began to impress upon the age the degree to which concepts such as truth were far more complex than ever imagined by poets and scientists alike. Taking these developments into account, in 1925 philosopher Herbert Cory—who himself would go on to write *The Significance of Beauty in Nature and Art*—asserted: "Beauty is not truth nor truth beauty." Still, even he could not stop himself from adding: "The neglect of truth results in due time in the loss of beauty" (401).

Significantly, in the wake of the conceptual and empirical synthesis of Darwin's theory of evolution and modern genetics around World War II, a similar revolution took hold regarding the nature of beauty. Even as the nature of beauty became the subject of scrutiny by the bioscientific and social scientific disciplines, it quickly became apparent that many of our fundamental aesthetic percepts were transcultural. Artistic categories relating, for instance, to form, pattern, ratio, or symmetry were discovered to be highly invariable across disparate cultures, hinting at their evolutionary heritage.

From the perspective of more than a half-century, there is no denying that research into the evolutionary roots of our social conceptions and artistic traditions of beauty has undermined a number of myths (not to say paradigms) surrounding the relation between the nature of art and human nature. Still, as apparent from the statements cited above—and those below—the connection between the truth of representation and the beauty of aesthetic design endures. And, far from in literature or even art alone, it endures in rather unexpected quarters.

Mathematicians, as we saw already, take the correlation between truth and beauty quite seriously. In K. C. Cole's 1998 study *The University and the Teacup: Mathematics of Truth and Beauty* one finds, for example, the following conclusion: "The search for symmetry turns out to be a very effective tool for looking beneath superficial differences. . . . Symmetry therefore lends a satisfying concreteness to the vague sense that there is beauty in truth, and truth in beauty" (174). Pondering the startling correspondence between mathematical concepts and the nature of the physical world, another expert writes that even as no one can say "*why* beauty is truth, and truth beauty,"[4] all marvel at the intricacy of their partnership.

Theoretical physics, a domain not credited as a rule with too much deference to aesthetics, is not beyond the pale of Keats's ghost, either. Correlations between content (truth) and form (beauty) are regularly evoked in arbitrations between competing models of reality. Nor, it must be pointed out, are those a matter of obscure theories or obscure proponents. In a letter to Einstein about quantum mechanics—probably the best-tested and, at the same time, the most counterintuitive physical theory in existence—Heisenberg himself confessed: "You may object that by speaking of simplicity and beauty I am introducing aesthetic criteria of truth, and I frankly admit that I am."[5]

From the mathematical concepts of orderliness and symmetry, it would seem, it is not such a big step to the aesthetic concepts of simplicity, symmetry, and order. And the reason for this kinship can be summed up in one word: evolution. Evolution, as we now realize, has wormed itself into the very patterns of human thought, detectable from the patterns of art to the structures of classical logic. As Scully and Mulder might have put it, the roots of what pattern seekers—from mathematical physicists to logicians to visual artists to fiction writers—find beautiful and truthful are, indeed, out there.

"The basis of art is truth," stressed Flannery O'Connor in *Mystery and Manners* (1961, 65), and to the extent that her words can be cast in terms of adaptive behavioral economy, she was correct. Why, you may ask, bring in complex evolutionary theories to explain what appears to be a straightforward artistic tenet? Simple—aside from considerations of adaptive behavioral economy, the equation of truth and beauty is little more than an ill-defined, if not entirely misleading, metaphor. As Lily Tomlin quipped, if truth really is beauty, then how come no one has their hair done in the library?

More to the point, there are reasons for skepticism about equivocating these two terms when it comes to art—perhaps especially when it comes to art. For, if truth and beauty—or more formally, mimetic representation and aesthetic appreciation—converge often enough in artistic endeavors, it is far from necessarily so. Not to look too far, someone might appreciate a realistic painting of excrement for its truthful character, but I would wager a considerable amount of money that few of even the most ardent mimeticists would purchase one to adorn their living quarters.

In *S/Z* Roland Barthes notoriously critiqued the attachment of literary value to literary truth. On the basis of various readings of Balzac, the French critic maintained no less that the truth of representation—the realistic creed of sociohistorical, referential veracity—nauseates the reader! Literature, asserted Barthes, must not be ballasted with sociohistorical, referential duties, for then literature cannot be itself. Predictably, the critic did not elucidate what "itself" meant, perhaps because literature has been esteemed precisely for its sociohistorical and referential truth, as the enduring popularity of historical, or more generally, realistic fiction attests.

In a similar vein, in *Contexts of Criticism* Harry Levin wondered how it is possible for literature to be mimetically true when it is sustained by artifice. In "The Logical Status of Critical Discourse" John Searle went even further, deriding concepts such as mimesis as catchphrases employed to make it "easy to stop thinking" (1979, 60). Altogether, this seems too harsh. It may be that not much food for thought can be reaped from the academic distinctions between terms like "diegesis" (the telling of an action) and "mimesis" (the representation or enactment of action). But already in *Poetics* Aristotle proposes a more fecund way of approaching mimesis, appreciable in the light of contemporary literary-critical research in evolutionary theory:

> Poetry in general seems to have sprung from two causes, each of them lying deep in our nature. First, the instinct of imitation is implanted in man from childhood, one difference between him and other animals being that he is the most imitative of living creatures, and through imitation learns his earliest lessons; and no less universal is the pleasure felt in things imitated. (1961, 55)

It is worth noting that his key term, *mimesis*—routinely rendered in English as "imitation," sprang originally from Dionysian rites that, as they transformed into stage acting, retained the name "mime" for the actor whose role was to represent people and actions.[6] Yet mimesis is a far more versatile and encompassing concept than its etymology might suggest.

The approximately sixty references to mimesis in the preserved fragments of ancient Greek manuscripts derive not only from poets but also tragedians, historians, and philosophers. Reflecting this variety, the meaning of mimesis ranges from imitation to expression, to make-believe, to role playing, to game playing, and even to simulation. What unites all these divergent usages is the relation to the object of imitation. Although the ancients freely admit meta-level imitation of art by art, the paradigmatic object of imitation is an object or relation taken from life.

Across diverse forms of thought and expression, mimesis invariably refers to an accurate representation of reality. In fact, truth is frequently posited, or at least intimated, to be an arbiter of artistic value—even as the ancient thinkers remained keenly aware that the criteria of truth transcend the criteria of realism. Truth may, after all, be conveyed by means of a literary vehicle that *prima facie* involves any number of counterfactual conditions, from time travel and magic spells to unicorns and utopia. The truth of literary models is manifestly not a matter of adhering to reality or to conventions of literary realism.

## DEGREES OF NARRATIVE FREEDOM

*If telling stories is a biological function, Aristotle had already understood all that was needed from this biology of narrativity.*
UMBERTO ECO, *ON LITERATURE*

In one of my previous books I devoted a great deal of attention to the relation between narrative models and various degrees of narrative freedom.[7] Broadly speaking, one can distinguish three levels of mimeticism that permutate and recombine into the literary conventions of realism, fantasy, and anything else in between. In terms of their adherence to, or—which amounts to the same thing—divergence from reality, the three levels of mimeticism are (from the most general down): logical, empirical, and psychosocial. Permitting exactly four mutually exclusive types of modeling permutations, they thus subsume all types of literary narratives currently in existence and not.

Literary truth, in short, does not necessarily entail mimesis. One can model realistic relations using otherworldly means, for instance, evoking faster-than-light travel to examine real psychological or historical theses. More curiously still, truth does not necessarily bestow the greatest cognitive utility. To put it bluntly, it is sometimes advantageous to believe in a patent falsehood rather than in truth. In "Sevastopol in May" Leo Tolstoy insisted, "The hero of my tale—whom I love with all the power of my soul, whom I have tried to portray in all its beauty, who has been, is, and will be beautiful—is Truth" (1991, 43). But what the Russian realist failed to differentiate is the truth of representation and the utility of representation.

As far as human behavioral economy goes, not all that glitters is gold, and false beliefs can on occasion have more utility than truth. The morale of a shipwrecked crew may hinge, for instance, on a baseless belief in imminent rescue, which can nonetheless better their odds of survival. Religious beliefs may also be false *simpliciter* yet capable of instilling spiritual or psychological cohesion, offering solace, or eliciting self-sacrifice. The seventeen Saudi hijackers who on 11 September 2001 committed mass suicide by flying passenger airliners into American targets apparently believed, in accordance with their creed, that they would be amply rewarded in the afterlife.

In sum, the adaptive value of a belief cannot be measured by its strict veracity. But propositional and situational truth—including, notably, literary truth—*can* be measured relative to the behavioral economy of the believer. This, moreover, is irrespective of the contingent details of a story. Narratives may range from strictly mimetic (*Schindler's Ark*) to whimsically ahistorical (*Triste, solitario y final*). But the behavioral truth of all narrative creations, whether prehistorical (*The Inheritors*), postapocalyptic (*Earth Abides*), or even two-dimensional (*Flatland*), can be analyzed relative to human adaptive goals and strategies.[8]

The reason for reviewing the salient points about representational truth is that the hero of *my* tale is also truth, though in a more technical sense than Tolstoy's. In what follows I want to consider the evolutionary economies of behavior as a criterion for judging the veracity of literary characters and their actions—and, more generally, for judging the truth of literary representation. My central assumption is that our evolutionarily adaptive dispositions to love, fight, cheat, create, cooperate, seek resources, quest for power—in short, all that we do in the course of living and propagating—is the central source of our interest in literature as an adaptive modeling laboratory.

It ought to be clear by now that the truth of representation is a concept far more complex than a rote citation of "Ode on a Grecian Urn" might intimate. Philosophers, historians, aestheticians, and, not least, purveyors of art have for millennia rallied to the investigation of truth in art as an extension of inquiries into the nature of art itself. These days, however, at least among evolutionary and social scientists, the archetypal question "What is art?" has yielded to a different question: "What is art for?" Understandably enough, the answers to this latter query tend to cluster around human adaptive behavior.

Evolution excels in hardwiring minds and bodies to accurately respond to environmental constants. On the other hand, outside relatively short periods of rapid "punctuated" change—which, as we only recently began to recognize, can be extraordinarily rapid, indeed—evolution is a slow and lazy worker. As a result, it is often unable to quickly adjust the palette of established responses to radically novel stimuli. The uniquely human problem is that the unprecedented explosion of intelligence in our genus has multiplied novel environmental stimuli beyond measure. And that may be precisely where art comes in.

In *Consilience* Edward O. Wilson theorizes that artistic creativity helps fill the gap between our instinctive responses to the world and the infinity of possible responses latent in individual and societal intelligence. Art helps make sense of our environment by helping us navigate through what would otherwise remain a morass of forking paths opened up by our growing ability to grasp and instrumentally manipulate the world. Courting ire of disciplinary dualists (of whom more below), Wilson states, in fact, that art "might be understood fundamentally with knowledge of the biologically evolved epigenetic rules that guided them" (1998, 213).[9]

Some readers, critics, and artists may look askance at the proposition that their aesthetic likes and dislikes are underwritten by biology. We do not feel any evolutionary currents coursing through our veins when contemplating Rembrandt's *Homer Contemplating the Bust of Socrates* or when whiling the evening away with a Karl May western. So what? We do not feel the tug of our linguistic programming when composing birthday cards or haggling at a garage sale, yet there is no longer any doubt that a language module is implanted in each one of us by evolution. The proverbial wisecrack "I don't know much about art, but I know what I like" gives voice to the deep nature of some of our aesthetic preferences.

Are there really biological predispositons of aesthetics? Indeed, there are, and they run deeper than many of us realize. Furthermore, aesthetic and cultural traits are channeled not just by our biology but by the very physical attributes of the universe of which we are a product. When I explored both of these issues in *Of Literature and Knowledge*, I zeroed in on our innate propensity for thinking in stories and on how this propensity is cognitively adaptive in our contacts with the world. Here I would like to follow the obverse course and focus on what aesthetics can tell us about cognition and, through it, about the truth of literary representations.

A good place to start may be with the research into the duration of the present moment originally conducted by Frederick Turner and Ernst

Poppel. In a series of experiments, subjects were asked to reproduce the duration of a light signal or a sound or else to respond to the dilations of time intervals in the so-called metronome test (designed to measure the extent to which people subjectively group intervals). These early experiments have established what, since then, has been confirmed by a multitude of studies in developmental and adult psychobiology: the duration of the personal subjective "now."

It turns out that in most people the dimension of the present moment is about three seconds, although for some it can be about a half-second shorter or longer. Given the universality and constancy of this facet of our personhood—one that transcends biological factors such as sex, race, or age—it would seem that it opens a window onto the transcultural part of our nature. If so, however, the experimental results ought to be equally independent of *cultural* traits such as nationality, education, and various forms of artistic expression. In other words, if the duration of the present moment has indeed been chiseled out by evolution, it should be irrespective of the phenotypic factors in people's lives.

Does, for example, the duration of musical motifs or the typical pattern of poetic—perhaps even prosaic—recitation relate significantly to the duration of the present moment, as measured in the psychologist's lab? Startlingly, it does. Musicologists examining Mozart report that his musical motifs strongly group around the three-second base interval. The duration of this present-time frame is equally evident for poetry. Studies in Germany have shown that the reading of no less than 73 percent of all poetic lines—those natural units of the lyrical "here and now"—lasts about three seconds.

Even more to the point, the remaining 27 percent of lines that seem on the face of it to contravene the three-second base pattern in fact corroborate it. Longer lines, for instance, typically feature a caesura that splits them into two component units of approximately three-second durations. This pattern has been observed *in vivo* among readers, the majority of whom make a slight but perceptible pause in the middle. Conversely, lines of shorter length have been found to be dilated or else accompanied by a longer pause, so that the overall duration once again approaches the dimension of the present moment.[10]

Since then, researchers have moved further afield, studying Chinese, Japanese, English, French, Greek, and Latin poetry. Irrespective of the meter or language, all fit snugly into the basic time unit. Indeed, as the great scientist and poet Miroslav Holub surmised in *The Dimension of the Present Moment,* the three-second line "appears to be a 'carrier-wave' of traditional poetries in any language system" (1990, 3). Holub's own investigations suggest, moreover, that the three-second duration obtains also for free verse, while my own informal findings—replicated over a dozen subjects and texts—indicate that the carrier wave appears to be at work even in prose.

Naturally, none of the above should suggest a repetitive, monotonous, mechanical iteration. The three-second base unit is not a lyrical or narrative prison cell in which the artist-as-inmate takes three steps this way, three steps that way, and back again without respite or variation. Perfect repetition of formal rules of art rarely brings about the greatest aesthetic rewards. The mind—evolutionarily geared for swift pattern-recognition—can anticipate the conformist pattern all too easily. Self-similarity is not per se incompatible with art, but for most creators and consumers the trick is really about finding the right proportions of aesthetic convention and invention.

We can thus anticipate that strict symmetry, although guaranteed to draw attention to itself, will not sustain attention for as long as a seemingly perfect symmetry that breaks down at crucial moments. In the latter case, as in a musical fugue, the variations on the iterated theme will generate tension between the reader's expectation and the actual result. A brilliant exploitation of such tension is exemplified by William Blake's signature poem from *Songs of Experience,* "The Tyger." Its first, best-known stanza runs as follows:

> Tyger! Tyger! burning bright
> In the forests of the night,
> What immortal hand or eye
> Could frame thy fearful symmetry?

The first three lines of the quatrain are perfectly symmetrical, iterating the truncated trochaic tetrameter. In the final line, however, at the very instant the poet invokes symmetry, the rhythmic pattern self-reflexively falters. At the very same instant the rhyme scheme falters, too. Even as it preserves the symmetry of the "aabb" scheme, it changes a perfect masculine rhyme (bright/night) to a self-reflexive eye-rhyme (eye/symmetry). This deliberate break of a neat symmetric repetition creates an unmet expectation that calls attention not only to itself but to the broken fearful symmetry. The broken symmetry, in turn, demands reexamination of the aspects that conform to and transcend the base pattern of the poem's rhythm and rhyme.

## AESTHETIC VARIATION

*Biology strikes back: when literature refused to give us plots,*
*we went to look for them in films or newspaper reports.*
UMBERTO ECO, *ON LITERATURE*

None of this means that aesthetic variation is invariably preferable to conformity. Depending on the context, exact iteration may be exactly what is called for. Pinstripe patterns on business suits are perfectly symmetrical and perfectly boring and deliberately so, not to attract attention. Naturally no one would accuse suitmakers of producing art, the rules of which are often different from those in commerce. But in the case at hand, the three-second carrier wave easily accommodates variation of pattern within a pattern. Recall that longer units often come with a natural caesura, shorter lines, like musical lines, that come with their own crochet or quaver rests.

Contemplating the apparent presence of universal categories of thought and aesthetic experience, it is hard to escape a feeling of mystery and wonder. Given how subjective, not to say idiosyncratic, every human existence is, why should people share any categories of experience at all? The mystery, though perhaps not the sense of wonder, evaporates when inserted into the context of evolution. Independent of language, syntax, cultural formation, or historical epoch, these recurrent literary and melodic regularities are our evolutionary "carry-on" with which we travel three seconds at a time from the present moment into the future.

Human categories of experience—be they the three-second dimension of the present moment, the order in which all communities assemble their color palettes, the aesthetic predilection for bilateral symmetry, or any other such—are ultimately a product of natural selection. Minds, after all, evolved with and from brains. As a result, even today's art can be expected to bear evidence of the environmental pressures brought to bear over two million (lower value) to six million (highest value) years on the individuals whose genetic lineage we continue. And, as such, the truth of representation—whether considered in the direct context of struggle for survival or in the indirect behavioral context represented by art—should feature high in our categories of experience.

Though it need not be straightforwardly mimetic, the picture of the world that fosters a true understanding of how it works is, on the whole, more beneficial than one that does not. As the hapless recipients of the annual Darwin Awards would testify—if they did not languish in traction, in jail, or in a cemetery—it is decidedly advantageous, not to say biologically adaptive, to fashion a passably accurate picture of reality. Realism, in this sense, is the precondition for human existence and thus for the existence of art, insofar as a point-blank dismissal of, say, the distinction between fiction and nonfiction would quickly lead to the extinction of any such refusenik.[11]

It can be anticipated that the realistic impulse in art would thus be of great value to early societies. Not surprisingly, drawings on the cave walls of Lascaux and Altamira depict lifelike animals, people, and structures. In *What Is Art For?* Ellen Dissanayake makes, in fact, an explicit point of steering aestheticians clear of modern Western conceptions and traditions in art. Her reasoning is simple: Western modernity is anything but representative of the artistic impulses typical of the evolutionary past. The programmatic embrace of self-reflexive, autotelic, art-for-art's-sake aesthetics runs counter to the adaptive nature of pre/historic art, amplifying its nonfunctional aspects.

All that seems straightforward. But even as we focus our attention on artistic mimesis, we run into a quandary. There are so many degrees and hues of realism, so many ways in which realistic tenor can be hitched to a nonrealistic vehicle—so many ways in which our basic categories of experience impinge on even highly abstract and symbolic creations—that it is not easy to see what criteria could be employed to study and evaluate narrative realism. Fortunately, recent work in evolutionary studies on human nature, considered here as the species-typical behavioral economy, points the way forward.

One reason we easily identify with literary characters is that, just like us, they display goal-oriented behavior directed at understanding the world in which they are embedded (which for us forms the storyworld). These literary agents fashion interpretations, hypotheses, or half-baked guesses and proceed to test them in an elemental manner by adjusting their behavior. And so do we as readers and critics, forming hypotheses about the characters and about the behaviors they exhibit. In distinction from the literary agents, we have no means of testing the truth of our hypotheses. But what about *evaluating* them?

If literary-critical research is ever to amount to more than psychosocial impressionism, it needs an external yardstick to reliably thrash out behavioral truth from the chaff. Where to look for such a yardstick? The answer, as you probably guessed by now, lies in evolutionary behavioral economy. Think of the latter as a sum total of general and specific (modular) adaptations that form the biological bedrock for people's motives and actions. Assuming science can tell us what this bedrock is, this analytic yardstick can in turn be used to understand fictional characters' behavior as a function of their cognitive and emotional need to make sense of their storyworld.

Whatever else they are, works of literature are efforts to fashion order out of the contingent world. As such, the behavior of literary agents can be analyzed in terms of the almost infinite cultural variety in which they act out strategies aimed at securing resources, mates, and power—in short, strategies aimed at personal development and gratification. The evolutionary route to the analysis of characters' behavioral economy, and thus the veracity of their representation, has the additional advantage of correcting the modeling bias still evident in the social sciences. As research shows time and again, human motives and decisions often owe more to the adaptive needs of a biological organism than to the utility-maximizing calculations of neo/classical economic theory.

According to one of the most explicit campaigners on behalf of literary theory in the evolutionary vein, all elements of the reading process—including authorial intentions, readers' responses, characters' behavior, even the formal attributes of literary works—can be fruitfully analyzed within the evolutionary context. By adopting this framework, argues Joseph Carroll in "Adaptationist Criteria of Literary Value," literary studies can gradually merge with a body of interdisciplinary research aimed at unraveling patterns of human behavior and cognition. He concludes:

> We cannot claim that any of our own literary judgments
> are objectively correct in the sense that they are grounded
> in some system of values independent of personal feeling,
> but we can nonetheless identify the basis for our judgments;
> we can generalize the principles on which they are founded;
> and we can correlate these principles with the characteristics
> of our evolved psychology. We cannot justify our values,
> but we can explain them, and those explanations are part
> of the total body of knowledge relevant to literary criticism.
> (2004, 165)

None of this means that the motivational patterns displayed by literary characters are—or ought to be—exemplary of behavioral universals. While, tautologically, no culture operates independently from its species-typical evolutionary presets, individual conduct frequently deviates from these. Romeo and Juliet tragically commit suicide before they have a chance to have offspring, defying the regnant evolutionary theories of people as inclusive fitness maximizers or adaptation executors. That granted, using behavioral universals as yardsticks for behavioral particulars, literary critics can ground cognitive *and* aesthetic interpretations in a more comprehensive, systematic, and reliable frame of reference than heretofore.

The program of using evolutionary adaptive mechanisms as a matrix for analyzing the behavioral veracity of literary agents may not be as radical as it sounds. You may think of it as a more mature version of what we do anyway as part of our innate folk psychology. Perhaps for this very reason, it is echoed by a growing number of scholars in the field. One of them is Eco, who in his 2006 collection of reflections *On Literature* states flatly that "to tell and listen to stories is a biological function" (246). However, if any such program is to effect a paradigm shift rather than remain a perpetual rallying call, it must at some point entail a retraining of literary-critical disciplinarians into evolutionarily minded interdisciplinarians. Can this be done?

Much as with analytic aesthetics, mastering a new body of knowledge—especially one prospected by such a dizzying variety of natural scientific and social scientific disciplines as evolution—is fraught with pitfalls. From the pioneering studies of Hyppolyte Taine to the comparative endeavors of the Russian and Prague formalists, the history of literary studies has had its share of false starts and dead ends when it comes to bringing evolution into the picture. Naturally, the interdisciplinary difficulties cut both ways, for even experienced scientists can occasionally be led astray when approaching art from the evolutionary standpoint.

Here is one instructive illustration. Research suggests that very young children who have no experience of different habitats exhibit innate preference toward the savannah. In contrast, older children and adults—who may have been exposed to other environments such as the tundra, jungle, steppe—do not evidence this preference. From these slender data John Barrow, a thinker of the highest credentials, jumps to the following conclusion: the young children's innate predilection toward the savannah habitat, he declares, "creates a natural aesthetic disposition as a legacy of the adaptive success of our early ancestors" (2005, 113).

In one giant mental leap the author closes the gap between adaptive and aesthetic characteristics as if one necessarily entailed the other. Is this, however, a warranted inference? I do not think so. One persuasive argument against it is that not all adaptive traits are aesthetic in nature, and vice versa. Digestive responses to putrid food, which is rapidly voided, are clearly adaptive yet hardly indicative of any aesthetic disposition on the part of hominids. On the other hand, recordings of Keith Jarrett's Köln or Bremen performances are vastly pleasing aesthetically yet carry zero adaptive value.

While there certainly exist aesthetic attributes that are also adaptive—predilection for symmetry or generally for pattern recognition is one such—survival value does not neatly translate into aesthetic value. It may be true that the savannah landscape cues the eye with signs of safe and fruitful habitation. Yet the putative link between this particular aesthetic disposition and adaptive success remains to be proven. This is not to imply that other aspects of Barrow's exposition of the evolutionary dimension in visual arts lack in power or nuance. He writes, for example:

> The presence of trees, greenery, and water offers an instant evaluation of the suitability of a potential habitat. These primary indicators, together with the sense of the openness of the terrain, its prospects of shelter, and the furtive viewing of others, are valuable sensitivities that signal whether further exploration or settlement can safely ensue. If the environment is deemed safe for further exploration, then other features highlight the most attractive sites. The topography must allow us to navigate easily; landmarks, bends, and variations are welcome to the eye, so long as they do not create confusing complexities, or mask dangers.

This makes perfect sense, and I fully concur as far as the utilitarian and survival value of the savannah goes. But I cannot accept that this demonstrates an innate *aesthetic* predisposition for this type of terrain—in other words, one genetically transmitted in humans—not, at least, without an explicit chain of reasoning and experimental evidence as opposed to a general impression. This is all the more so because the research cited by Barrow seems, in fact, to disprove his contention. If youngsters indeed lose their preference for the savannah as soon as they grow up, this neo-Platonic loss casts doubt on whether the preference could be adaptive, insofar as it disappears before they begin to reproduce.

## LITERARY RESEARCH
## AND EVOLUTIONARY STUDIES

> *But these games cannot replace the true educational function of literature, an educational function that is not simply limited to the transmission of moral ideas, whether good or bad, or to the formation of an aesthetic sense.*
> UMBERTO ECO, *ON LITERATURE*

There remain scholars who perceive the putative alignment of literary research and evolutionary studies with less than unmitigated enthusiasm. One of the most outspoken among them is Eugene Goodheart, a self-styled gadfly on the body of literary-evolutionary scholarship. His 2007 *Darwinian Misadventures in the Humanities* is offered, in fact, as a corrective to the condescensions, mystifications, and plain errors allegedly perpetrated by evolutionary scholars—literary critics or not. Although there is little to be gained from going over its many rhetorical legerdemains and argumentative straw men, it cannot be dismissed altogether, inasmuch as one of its critiques hits the mark.

Before addressing this last point, I would like briefly to comment on a couple of matters raised by the critic that directly impinge on disciplinary methodology. For the record, no one, not even E. O. Wilson, has ever claimed that placing literature and literary studies in the context of empirical science could ever tap the full aesthetic nuance, artistry, or symbolic and interpretive contingency of literary works—the traditional provenance of literary criticism. The thesis that representational truth can be accurately analyzed in terms of human adaptive economy does not for a moment dispute that there are other important aspects of literary works worth talking about.

This last point is crucial—and amply demonstrated by the book in your hands. *Literature, Analytically Speaking* may be the missing link between the rigorous research orientation of evolutionary literary studies and the aesthetic-cultural criticism of traditional humanistic scholarship. It is for no other reason that I adopt the methodology of analytic philosophy in the service of getting to the bottom of aesthetic interpretation of literature. If anything, it vividly demonstrates that there is no enmity between analytically minded researchers and aesthetically minded interpreters.

Aesthetic interpretation is an indispensable part of literary-critical or, more broadly, sociocultural engagement with art. But this should not obscure the fact that literary criticism and literary research are far from the same types of professional activity. Subjective and adventitious responses to art cannot by default contribute to any ongoing, cumulative research paradigm. No matter how painstaking or voluminous, such critical interpretations do not amount to research in any proper interdisciplinary sense of the word.[12] The distinction is vital, not least because the confusion of research with aesthetic criticism is precisely what fuels Goodheart's denunciations of literary-evolutionary scholarship.

Second, even as he vociferates against reductionism in the humanities, the critic shows himself prone to a dismayingly reductionist view of literary research. While maintaining, somewhat self-defeatingly, that humanism "represents a view of life that resists systematic doctrinal definition" (119), Goodheart reduces the spectrum of research in literary studies to the tired bipolarity of postmodern skepticism and hardcore scientism. Needless to say, this simplistic bifurcation—which underpins his entire critique—is but a caricature of the gamut of contemporary critical responses to cognition and research.[13]

Goodheart's comments on the type of engagement between literary and evolutionary studies are, however, a different matter indeed. His concerns are fundamental and pressing, and his warning against impoverished translations of data from one field into another goes to the heart of any interdisciplinary research program. As the critic points out, even in its short history, literary-evolutionary studies has shown itself prone to cookie-cutter criticism whereby literature is used mainly as a dough from which the enterprising critic cuts out just the parts that confirm theories from other fields.

A similar warning rings from Frederick Crews's expostulations about the "monotonous preoccupation with the survival of Pleistocene psychology in modern works of art" (2005, xiii), which underwrites many literary-evolutionary studies.[14] This type of one-size-fits-all scholarship has to be warded off simply because art is much more than a cultural warehouse to be scoured for dramatic illustrations of already confirmed sociobiological theories. Even when studied in terms of its contribution to a research program, literature often transcends this illustrative role, inviting scholarship that will not merely exemplify but complexify research conducted in neighboring disciplines.

Within the type of research that concerns us the most here, the social sciences typically proceed by first identifying and then closely studying the various components of a universal suit of behavioral, emotive, and cognitive characteristics of intentional agents. At a minimum, therefore, literary scholars can ensure that this paradigm does not gloss over the adaptive function of human propensity for art, including literature. One crucial aspect of this propensity for art is our propensity for constructing imaginative projections of characters and events—in other words, for constructing literary fictions. Tellingly, these counterfactual narratives operate on the same principles as thought experiments do in the sciences.[15]

But that is hardly the end of what literature does. Equally if not more importantly, it multiplies models of reality that operate on subjective and emotional levels, organizing categories of human experience of the contingent world. As Joseph Carroll sums it up, our literary imaginative projections

> direct our behaviour by entering into our motivational system at its very roots—our feeling, our ideas, and our values. We use imaginative models to make sense of the world, not just to 'understand' it abstractly but to feel and perceive our own place in it—to see it from the inside out. (2004, xxii)[16]

That is why, reading fictions, we often feel that they ring true, even though it is not always easy to articulate this feeling in propositional form. This intuitive, not to say instinctive, determination of the (folk-psychological) truth of the story is precisely what lies behind assessing the truth of literary beauty by the suit of evolutionary adaptations. Our brains and minds have been hardwired to spot cheaters, avoid dangers, distinguish friends from foes, seize opportunities to advance our reproductive and other interests—in short, to form a passably reliable picture of the world and act on that picture. This behavioral baseline, expressed across cultures by means of the stories we tell, can furnish literary studies with a yardstick for gauging the truth of narrative representations of behavior.

Naturally, the function of any yardstick is to measure, not to evaluate. The difference underlies the difference between literary studies as a research discipline and literary studies as a procurer and professor of aesthetic appreciations—related but not isomorphic goals. Narrative representations that fail to reflect adaptive economies do not, in and of themselves, signal bad literature. The evolutionary framework for appreciating the bedrock of characters' motivations and of the logic of their actions is not, in and of itself, enough to pass judgment on the artistic and aesthetic value of a literary work. But it provides a way to calibrate the veracity of the characters and, in turn, to calibrate the goals and skills of the storytellers.

In the context, it may not be amiss to say a few words about the work in evolutionary developmental psychology that furnishes more and more details about the key module of our behavioral engagement with other beings. In a series of papers, Michael Tomasello and his collaborators report on their studies of the elementary components of human beings' TOM. Their work into goal-directed (intentional) behavior encompasses studies of normal human infants and autistic children as well as chimps and other primates. The authors mount a strong case that shared intentionality, the framework that also informs *Literature, Analytically Speaking,* is a uniquely human cognitive trait.[17]

No other animals are moved in the same way and to the same degree "to share emotions, experiences, and activities with others of their own kind" (2005, 686). To the extent that the reasoning behind this thesis can be summarized, it can be summarized briefly. Humans are adapted for culture in ways that apes are not. The key adaptation is the ability to understand other agents as *agents,* that is, intentional individuals, and the key factor here is the rate of evolutionary change. *Homo sapiens* separated from apes roughly six million years ago and for four million years after that continued as a very apelike *Australopithecine.* Given this timeline, the conclusion staggers. Our folk psychology, folks—our knack for attributing intentions and beliefs—is likely less than two million years old and possibly considerably less.

The big point is that there was very little time for cognitive adaptations to emerge. The researchers conclude,

> If we are searching for the origins of uniquely human cognition, therefore, our search must be for some small difference that made a big difference—some adaptation, or small set of adaptations, that changed the process of primate cognitive evolution in fundamental ways.[18]

Given the extraordinary speed and the ratcheting effects of this cognitive evolution—perhaps revolution would be a more appropriate term—there are very few agents of change that fit the description. And the most likely of them is the one with which we are intimately familiar: human culture. To be sure, the specific mechanisms of this r/evolutionary metamorphosis are a matter of ongoing debate, as the responses to Tomasello et al. or the special 2008 issue of *Style* devoted to literary evolutionary theory attest. But there is little doubt at this point that shared ("we") intentionality and TOM drive cultural cognition.

Shared intentionality also supplies a good description of the essential elements of the literary process. The production and consumption of fictions permits writers and readers to negotiate responses to the depicted events. This, in turn, feeds into the adaptive function of literature via a creation of storyworlds within which we make sense of our own behavior.

Living in the imagination is a peculiarly human condition, wherein events and actions we read about are synthesized into cognitive projections about human relations extending in space and time. Rarely do we relate to those relations in abstractions, for abstractions are a late part of the human cognitive equipment. Rather, we experience the complex order of things in the narratives we read supercharged with emotions. Fictions, in other words, acquire their dramatic character from readers who emote with imaginary people and, through them, calibrate their own emotions.

And on this my explorations must come to an end, not because there is no more to explore but because we need time to evaluate just how far we have come. Looking back, what is critical from my point of view is that *Literature, Analytically Speaking* advances not merely a series of proposals but a series of arguments. It is not the same, in other words, to say "This is so" as to say "Here are the reasons this is so." It may very well be that some, perhaps even most, of my conclusions largely affirm what many readers and critics have known before. But an intuitive grasp of interpretive principles is not tantamount to giving a step-by-step analysis and evidentiary reasoning for these principles.

If my analyses only confirm what literary critics intuited long ago, this convergence is not to be shrugged off lightly. Confirmation is crucial to the scientific method, or else we would never bother to repeat experiments. This, however, is a big "if." Even a cursory survey of the MLA panels or publishing lists reveals that the theoretical paradigm in literary studies is still poststructuralism augmented in practice by contextless close reading of New Critical vintage. For reasons that should be self-evident by now, neither is compatible with the approach I take and the conclusions I reach.

If only for this reason, I hope that the arguments framed in this book will foster debate about the state of criticism today and about future research into the nature and appreciation of literature—a debate conducted in the spirit of cooperation in which all disciplinary colors blend into one.

# NOTES

## CHAPTER I

1. Hume 2000, 203.

2. Look no further than Rapaport's aptly titled *The Theory Mess: Deconstruction in Eclipse* (2001).

3. For several exceptions to the rule, each of which exemplifies a distinct line of interdisciplinary inquiry, see De Ley 1988, Graves and Frederiksen 1991, Magliano and Graesser 1991, Bruce and Purdy 1994, N. Carroll 1997, Swirski 2000a, Gottschall 2003, Aldama 2008.

4. A notable exception is Petrey (1990), whose first three chapters provide an excellent introduction to the theory's salient points. Among the more recent evocations of speech-act theory in the context of literary studies, Butler 1997 and Miller 2001 are typical in their superficiality.

5. I am thus in full agreement with the direction taken by Livingston (2005). For background on intentions see works by Mele in the bibliography.

6. As such, I implicitly subscribe to Piotr Jaroszynski's hierarchy whereby the "metaphysics of art is a more fundamental domain than esthetics, or even the philosophy of art" (2002, 3). For a dissenting view that attempts to reduce ontological questions to questions of grammar (language use in Wittgenstein's sense) see Tilghman 1973. The *analytic* priority of ontology of art does not, of course, preclude enjoying objects (ancient pottery, religious iconography, and such) aesthetically without, or before, knowing if they are art.

7. See Tanselle 1990. Greetham (1999) carefully distinguishes the provenances of *literary* criticism and *textual* criticism. For a more recent example of the variety of textual scholarship see Hawkins 2006.

8. Mathematically speaking, the name is a misnomer: Fermat's "theorem," lacking proof, was only a conjecture.

9. See Leach and Graham 2007.

10. de Man 1983, ix. For a trenchant critique of Barthes, Derrida, et al. see Livingston, "From Text to Work" (1993a). For a more general critique of the attempted

responses from poststructuralists see Gross and Levitt 1994 and Gross, Levitt, and Lewis 1996.

11. See Doležel 1984. It bears remembering that *Poetics* survives only in fragments of copies of the original work.

12. Dickie 1964; N. Carroll 1990; D. Davies 1991; 1965; Stecker 1996.

13. See Passmore 1951.

14. For a trenchant and all too rare internal critique see R. Levin 1995.

15. Kelly 1998, xi. For statements exemplary of such autarchic tendencies in literary studies see Ingarden 1973 and Shattuck 1998.

16. Kelly 1998, ix.

17. A good introduction of the distinction between works and texts is Livingston's "Texts, Works, and Literature" (1992b).

18. See, for example, W. Koch 1993, Storey 1996, J. Carroll 2004, Gottschall and Wilson 2005, Swirski 2007.

19. For examples of research in empirical aesthetics see Martindale 1990 or Cupchik 1997; for work in psychonarratology, which bridges empirical psychology and narrative aesthetics, see Kuiken, Miall, and Sikora 2004. The classic introduction to theory of mind from the perspective of psychopathology can be found in Baron-Cohen, Tager-Flusberg, and Cohen 2000.

20. Although Premack and Woodruff's data on primates have been challenged by Tomasello et al. (2005), significantly the debate is conducted wholly within the TOM paradigm.

21. Kelly 1998, xii. For a sustained critique of such policies in literary studies see Crews in bibliography.

22. Casti 1989, 59.

23. Lentricchia 1983, 12. Subsequent quotes in this paragraph: Lefkowitz 1996, 301; Kuper 2007, 23; McKendrick 1988, n.p. For more evidence of this nature in history see Palmer 1990, Evans 1997, Marwick 2001; in literary studies see Swirski 2007, Chapter 1.

24. The charge of dryness has been aired for decades; cf. William Elton's roundup of the then popular complaints about the barren, dull, boring, bogus, and desolate character of aesthetics (1954, 2).

25. An exhaustive web coverage of the whole affair can be found at http://www.physics.nyu.edu/faculty/sokal. It is also the subject of *The Sokal Hoax: The Sham That Shook the Academy* (2000), edited by the editors of *Lingua Franca,* which includes a number of subsequent commentaries.

## CHAPTER 2

1. In the latter case, their critique was aimed at Dewey 1934.

2. Zepke 2005, 4.

3. Bruns 2006, 156. For a cogent critique of attempts to formulate a general ontology of literary works see Howell 2002.

4. For a limpid discussion of functionalist and proceduralist definitions of art see Stephen Davies 1991, especially the introduction and Chapter 2. Margolis (1999) provides an indispensable background to the entire matter and a review of the state of the art. Boyd sketches a family-resemblance definition from the evolutionary perspective (2005, 148).

5. For his previous, historicist attempt see Levinson 1979; a good review of the various proposals can be found in Danto 1981.

6. In this he may have been influenced by Dickie (1974), who sees the conferral of aesthetic status as an action type. Currie actually mounts two theses (1989): the Action Type Hypothesis (ATH) in Chapter 3 and the Instance Multiplicity Hypothesis (IMH) in Chapter 4. The two, however, are logically disjointed: neither entails the other. Also, as Levinson points out (1980), Currie does not defend the IMH—which can actually be derived from the ATH under the assumption that the art-creating actions are not uniquely performable, such as in music—but its weaker version. Finally, since the IMH is in the main to counter Wollheim's "dualism" (1968) and Goodman's autographic-allographic distinction (1976), both of which obtain principally in other arts, I exclude it from discussion. Revised here, this part of my research is based on my "Interpreting Art, Interpreting Literature" (2001).

7. Currie derives the concept, it seems, from Imre Lakatos, whose *The Methodology of Scientific Research Programmes* Currie co-edited in 1978 with John Worrall.

8. The distinction was developed originally by Peirce (1931–1958). For a good discussion of the type/token distinction in the context of aesthetics see Jacquette 1994.

9. Goodman 1968, 209. See also the first section in Chapter 3 of the present volume.

10. Norton 2005. For a wider analysis of the biblical transmissions, corruptions, and restorations see Metzger 1992.

11. See Brilliant 2000.

12. See O'Donnell and McDougal 1992.

13. Currie 1989, 63–64. For Currie's multiple appeals to real-life practices and opinions see pages 11, 13, 19, 51, 59.

14. Currie 1989, 41, 42.

15. Nomenclature varies: what we commonly understand as structure has been referred to as significant form by Clive Bell or design by Margolis.

16. Currie 1989, 68.

17. Currie himself evokes the specter of the heuristic starting "to look like writing the history of the universe" (1989, 72). The problem is that his limitation of the heuristic to factors an artist "could have known about even if he did not" still comprises an insuperably large (possibly infinite) set of data.

18. Hamilton 1990, 540.

19. Levinson 1980b, 21; cf. Tolhurst's argument (1984) that found or conceptual art is art because of being "placed" (indicated) by the artist.

20. Such questions are pursued by textual scholars; see Tanselle 1976, Greetham 1999.

21. In his review of Levinson's *Music, Art, and Metaphysics,* Currie succinctly refutes modal objections to the inclusion of the artist's identity (1993, 473), shoring up this aspect of Levinson's theory.

22. The first argument actually supports both versions and may thus be ignored. The second appeals to musicians' intentions during performance—thus, presumably, to readers' intentions while reading. Admitting such a factor detaches the creator from his work and, as such, comes uncomfortably close to functionalism, a move that calls for a great deal of explanation, to say the least.

23. Currie 1993, 473.

24. Currie 1989, 62. For the original evocation of Twin Earths see Putnam 1975. On thought experiments see Swirski 2007. Levinson's review (1992b) is titled "*An Ontology of Art.*"

25. For such pertinence conditions see Swirski 2007, 108–110.

26. Currie 1989, 38.

27. Personal email, 16 June 2008. Faced with the counter-counterargument I develop in the next paragraph, the philosopher typically retreats into modality: the counterfactual is simply *logically* possible (rather than possible in reality), to which I can only reiterate that not all logically possible things are possible in our world.

28. For a still accurate series of arguments about locating a work within a historical and social context see Danto's classic essay, "The Artworld" (1964).

29. See Levinson 1980b, 21–22, and 1992b, 219.

30. Levinson 1992b, 219.

31. For background see the classic studies by Cohen (1958) and Westfall (1980).

32. A good contemporary example is Allen Ginsberg, many of whose self-styled "literary masturbations" from personal journals were later reworked into poems.

33. For accessible and nondoctrinaire discussions of the background for this crucial thesis see Hernadi 1978 and S. Davies 1991.

34. Although Levinson discusses such a possibility briefly in a footnote to "*An Ontology of Art*" (1992b, 220), he never includes it in a formal theory.

35. Other scholars, for example Livingston (2005), use the term "effective" to describe such actual, executive intentions.

36. In this form my theses meet the objections raised by Anderson (1982) and Stephen Davies (1991) against the type of theory espoused by Levinson.

37. See Diffey 1979—an earlier exponent of institutionalism—for a conclusive rebuttal on the grounds, among others, that functionality confuses *approaching* a structure as an artwork with it *being* an artwork.

38. In this I am in profound disagreement with Danto (1986). For an interesting

attempt to quantify maximizing "aesthetic measure" see Birkhoff 1993 (originally published in 1933).

39. For the analysis of various types of literary authorship involving computers see my *Between Literature and Science* (2001a), Chapter 5. On artification see Dissanayake 1988, 1992, 2000.

40. For discussion of interpretability see Danto 1981 and Levinson 1987.

41. For more examples and analysis of the contemporary avant-garde see "Conclusion: Whose Art?" in Swirski 2005a.

## CHAPTER 3

1. For a scathing review of the latter category see Tanselle 1990.

2. Pertinent critiques of the work/text equivocation are supplied by Wilsmore (1987) and David Davies (1991, 2004).

3. Quotes in this and the next paragraph from Bloom et al. 1979: Bloom, 7; Derrida, 84; Miller, 226.

4. Pratt (1977) makes an analogous point on the example of a sentence, "There was a knock on the door," the interpretation of which is clearly inflected by genre, be it horror story, detective story, romance, or pornography.

5. For an illuminating illustration of the role and failings of "taste" see Greetham 1994, especially 297–299.

6. As the third argument takes us outside literary studies, I will not dwell on it here, in a move implicitly sanctioned by Levinson, who wants to extend his reasoning to plays and novels (1980b, 22).

7. See Livingston's "Borgesian assumptions" (2005, 114).

8. Tilghman 1982. The philosophical literature on Borges's story is rich; readers may begin with the short list footnoted in Livingston 2005 on 112–113.

9. See Eco 1994a.

10. Pages 177 and 307 in Harvard 1999 edition; the translation reflects the identical Greek text. For another example, involving Stanislaw Lem's "twin" novels from 1959 and 1976, see Swirski 2005a, Chapter 6.

11. Tanselle 1989, 69.

12. Derrida 1999, 84. Cf. Barthes (1979, 75): "The Text cannot stop, at the end of a library shelf, for example; the constitutive movement of the Text is *traversal (traversée):* it can cut across a work, several works."

13. In Nichol 1948, 338.

14. Ibid.

15. "A faculty committee at Syracuse recently approved a plan to change the name of the major to English and Textual Studies," reports Heller (1988, A16). Similarly, the poststructuralist journal *Glyph* prides itself on dealing in "textual" studies.

16. Young 1982, vii.

17. "Textuist" appears to be an in-house term used among text-editing scholars, presumably in distinction from "textualist."

18. See T. Sanders and J. Sanders 2006, 606–607.

19. For details see Swirski 2007, Chapter 4.

20. Kasser, Meyer, and Wurst (2006) provide a particularly vivid example.

21. Racter 1984. For full analysis of computer authorship see my *Between Literature and Science* (2000a).

22. There are even "texts" from outside the human range, for example animal communication and, fictionally, the neutrino communication from an alien civilization depicted in Lem's *His Master's Voice*.

23. In a more familiar example for Anglo-Saxon readers, the monkeys would produce the *Collected Works of Shakespeare*. Borel's thought experiment was to illustrate Kolmogorov's so-called Zero-One Law.

24. "Valentine. Cease to . . . " (followed by gibberish).

25. Tanselle (1989) analyzes the ontology of art forms such as film, painting, architecture, music, and dance in addition to literature.

26. As such I am in disagreement with Scalise Sugiyama, who maintains that "language is a necessary condition for narrative" (2005, 183).

27. For examples of the syntactic approach see Van Dijk 1972. For the semantic see Brown and Yule 1983; Charolles 1986; or Conte, Petöfi, and Sözer 1989. An early overview of the field can be found in De Beaugrande and Dressler 1981; a much more concise attempt can be found in Shusterman 1992b.

28. Livingston concedes as much (2005, 123n18).

29. Goodman and Elgin 1988, 60; see Livingston's discussion (2005, 115–120).

30. Currie 1991b, 325. For a broader analysis of Currie's thesis see Livingston's "From Text to Work" (1993a).

31. For the pragmatic account of textual individuation see Tolhurst and Wheeler 1979; for a critique along the lines sketched in this section see Currie 1991b.

32. This applies whenever such a copy can be established or at least proposed; see Greetham 1994, 356.

33. On pages 121–134 Livingston reviews objections to competitors, fleshing out the points I make.

34. Greetham 1994, 8. Cf. Gaskell's definition (1985, 321) of the textual grail—the "ideal copy": "the most perfect state of a work as originally intended."

35. All textual scholars emphasize this nonalgorithmic (contextual) element of textual analysis; see, for example, Donaldson 1970, Tolhurst and Wheeler 1979, and Greetham 1999.

## CHAPTER 4

1. Aristotle 1961, 50. See Tooby and Cosmides 2001 for a cogent distinction between fiction and nonfiction from the evolutionary-adaptive point of view.

2. Aristotle 1961, 68.

3. See Cantril, Gaudet, and Herzog 1940.

4. Benedetti 1997.

5. *USA Today* 2007.

6. Benedetti 1997.

7. Quoted in Wheen 2004, 138–139.

8. Thoroughly revised, this and the next section are based on my "The Nature of Literary Fiction" (2000b).

9. Spiegelman 1991a. For an insightful analysis of graphic novels, including Spiegelman's, see Witek 1987.

10. To take only one example, in an eerie reenactment of the Scopes affair, it is illegal to teach evolution in public schools in Kansas.

11. Quinn 1941, 618. For a comprehensive analysis of *Eureka* see my *Between Literature and Science* (2000a), Chapters 2 and 3.

12. Poe's first mesmeric story, "A Tale of the Ragged Mountains," is widely regarded as less accomplished and not as interesting as its two famous successors.

13. For a detailed account of Poe's claims and disclaimers about the assertive content in his mesmeric stories see Mabbott 1978, vol. 3, 1024–1028 and 1228–1233.

14. Thompson 1984, 870.

15. For Lem's views on literature, cognition, and realism see Swirski 1997b, 1999, and 2007.

16. For a thorough analysis of the concept of metatextuality see Margolin 1999.

17. For a succinct statement see Goodman 1978.

18. For useful primers see Austin 1961, 1962; Searle 1969 and 1979, 58–75; Cole and Morgan 1975; Cohen, Morgan, and Pollack 1990; Tsohatzidis 1994; Alston 2000; Vanderveken and Kubo 2002. It may be worth noting that some of Skinner's functional theses about verbal behavior (1957) presage the pragmatic turn taken by Austin.

19. According to the widely accepted schematics introduced by Searle (1979, 58–75), constatives are known as assertives, and the multiplicity of performatives is reduced to four categories—directives ("I order"), commissives ("I pledge"), expressives ("I apologize"), and declarations ("I dub thee").

20. The communicative conditions of felicity fall into three categories: essential, sincerity, and preparatory.

21. Austin's distinction of locution into phones (roughly speaking, sounds), phemes (lexical and syntactic conventions of a language), and rhemes (sense and reference) again lies outside the theory of fiction developed here.

22. This is as good a point as any to complexify the account of the theory. The distinction between constatives and performatives is not as some successors to Austin represent it: clear-cut, permanent, and obvious. In fact, all constatives are at the same time performatives (they can be thought of as a distinct class of performa-

tives), much in line with Austin's later lectures (1962). In literary studies, for a lucid exposition of Austin's initial distinction and his later drive to undermine it see Petrey 1990, Chapters 1 and 2. Although Derrida and other continental philosophers have evoked speech-act theory to make sweeping ontological claims—in which they repudiate truth and referentiality in the name of their performative (and thus, according to them, contingent) nature—Austin's theory and Austin himself do not endorse such construals; see Austin 1962, Lecture 11, especially 145–149.

## CHAPTER 5

1. See Sutrop 2002 for a recent analysis of the concept. I also want to draw attention to Dissanayake's evolution-grounded concept of art as "making special" (1988, 1992); although not limited to fiction, *prima facie* it also seems to be a pragmatic category.

2. See Pratt 1977 and Fish 1980 for relevant critiques of this part of Searle's account.

3. Cf. Currie 1990, 12–18.

4. Currie also rebuts this "functionality principle" (1990, 14).

5. Brown and Steinman 1978, 149. Better-known responses to speech-act theory from the literary-critical standpoint are Hirsch 1975, Beardsley 1978, Maclean 1985, Norris 1985, and Derrida 1988.

6. I find other labels such as "imaginative involvement" less compelling owing to multiple connotations that have little to do with literary-aesthetic context. Moreover, imagining or reading imaginatively is—at least in one obvious sense— also an integral part of reading nonfiction.

7. All page references to the story are from the Mabbott 1978 edition. The discussion of the story is based on my *Between Literature and Science* (2000a, 7–10). For more on the detective-analytic dimension in "The Purloined Letter" see Eddings 1982, Irwin 1986, Blythe and Sweet 1989, Van Leer 1993.

8. Notably Strawson 1964 and Searle 1969. For TOM see Buss 1997; Budiansky 1998; Tomasello 1999; Baron-Cohen, Tager-Flusberg, and Cohen 2000; Baron-Cohen 2005; Tomasello et al. 2005; Focquaert and Platek 2007.

9. For Grice's subsequent publications on the subject see the bibliography of the present volume. For a seminal work on the philosophy of mind that parallels Grice's work in the philosophy of language see Dennett 1978. I am, however, in no way aligned with any particular version of Grice's views; my account is thus quite compatible with Sperber and Wilson's relevance theory (1995).

10. Livingston objects (2005, 180) that while children make fictions, they are too young to exhibit the elaborate constellation of attitudes identified by the Gricean reflexive loop. In my experience children realize that the stories they concoct are fictions and, when queried, can state so; the reflexive interaction may be complex

when spelled out in full bloom, but like walking or sneezing, it is something we mostly do without much explicit awareness. On the Gricean account, however, younger children who may not have developed the sense of make-believe simply do not make fiction; this appears to be confirmed by the research conducted by Tomasello and his group (2005).

11. Tomasello 1999, 517.

12. See also Livingston 2005, 178.

13. The court's decision was intended precisely not to limit writers' freedom to create fiction based on nonfiction.

14. Currie 1990, 41, 202.

## CHAPTER 6

1. For a critique of Iser's approach to the matter see Swirski 1994. The discussion of fictional truth draws on my *Between Literature and Science* (2000a, 14–26).

2. See, for example, Levine and Levine 1976, 502, and Buranelli 1977, 43–44.

3. All page references to Poe are from Mabbott 1978.

4. Among literary critics the best known is Pavel; a notable example of his work is *The Poetics of Plot* (1985). For an introduction to possible worlds semantics see Cresswell 1994, Chihara 1998, and Stalnaker 2003.

5. Although the early Hebrews did forbid fashioning of artistic images of living things, these beliefs were neither Poe's nor the mutual beliefs of contemporary communities. Stecker (1994, 198) also endorses the Mutual Belief Principle.

6. It seems to me that Byrne's argument extends to self-reflexive fictions. For other germane critiques of Currie see Le Poidevin 1995 and David Davies 1996.

7. Examples include Tolhurst 1977; Nathan 1992; Levinson 1992a and 1996, Chapter 10.

8. Cf. Lewis's confession in the closing paragraph to "Truth in Fiction": "But there is a real problem nearby, and I have no solution to offer. Why doesn't the iteration collapse? When the singer pretends to be Ugly Dave pretending to tell the truth about himself, how does this differ from pretending to be Ugly Dave *really* telling the truth about himself? It must be the former, not the latter; else we should conclude that there is no inner fiction and that what is true in the outer fiction— now the only fiction—is that Ugly Dave is duke of everything and tells us so. That would be to miss the point entirely. We must distinguish pretending to pretend from really pretending. Intuitively it seems that we can make this distinction, but how is it to be analyzed?" (1983, 280). On this topic see also Lamarque 1987.

9. From the evolutionary standpoint, it would be indefensible to expect our mental processes to be infallible. Human linguistic programming, which is of greater adaptive importance than our capacity for logical operations, gives no reason to believe that it is immune to illogic.

10. Once again, this type of moderate intentionalism has nothing to do with the old-style intentionalist fallacy and its claims that a work's meaning is uniquely determined by the author.

11. In the same essay Livingston and Mele articulate an analysis of fictional truth homologous to my own.

12. This checks with what Currie argues (1990, 87).

13. See also David Davies 2004.

14. Currie 1990, 69.

## CHAPTER 7

1. Strictly speaking, *God's Grace* was the last novel Malamud published in his lifetime; see Swirski 1998.

2. Nöel Carroll shows why, if there is "thesis projection of nonfictional import—whereby actual authors express their views about life, society, morality, and so forth—and a great deal of literary (indeed artistic) interpretation concerns the identification of such theses, then intentionalist criticism has a wide arena of legitimate activity" (1992, 109). The truth of the premise once again undermines Beardsley's ontological argument.

3. See Swirski 2007.

4. Tomasello 1999, 516.

5. In "What's the Story?" Livingston argues for the shift away from hypothetical intentionalism under the name of the Intentional Heuristic (1993b, 106–109). Stecker (1993, 485) conclusively rebuts Levinson's tripartite defense of hypothetical intentionalism (1992a; also 1996).

6. An excellent statement on why intentions will not go away can be found in Dutton 1987. Readers familiar with the strident pronouncements on the death of the author made by, among others, Barthes and Foucault may wish to consult the many rigorous refutations of these extravagant claims, beginning with Livingston's "Texts, Works, and Literature" and "From Text to Work."

7. Although this argument is often employed by the proponents of hypothetical intentionalism against real intentionalism, both are in fact equally vulnerable to it.

8. Tanselle 1990, 4. For more on "reading off," especially in the context of artistic conventions, see Stephen Davies 1987.

9. Bowers 1959, 8.

10. Even the title metaphor did not escape the knife: in the canonical edition the word "jungle" is completely cut from the first twenty-one and the last nine chapters, and when original sentences are retained, it is often replaced with "city" or the even lamer "forest." For more on *The Jungle* and its troubled history see Swirski 2006.

11. Mulryne 2006, 18.

12. For recent examples of such critical psycho(analytic)-babble see King 2006 and Kucich 2006. For a critique see Swirski 2007, Chapter 1.

13. For an interpretation of the novel as an example of the gothic see Crowley 1995.

14. According to Disch, the novel's 466 pages were culled from well over 700 before it could be published. Such extensive cutting might explain the inconsistencies.

15. Disch, email to the author, 23 September 2007.

16. A brief characterization of these two approaches can be found in the first note on page 205 in Stecker 1994. Cf. also his distinction between content attribution and significance findings (1993, 486–487). Revised here, this section appeared previously in my "Is There a Work in This Classroom?" (2005b).

17. An even longer selection of such self-deconstructing appeals to authorial intentions can be found in Livingston's "From Text to Work" (1993a).

18. Poe's *oeuvre* has been routinely subjected to such egregious readings; see Muller and Richardson 1987.

19. Bowers speaks of "games of intellectual chess" (1959, 17–18).

20. Joseph Carroll 2005, 91.

21. For a full account see Livingston, "What's the Story?" (1993b).

22. See Swirski 2007, 108–109.


CHAPTER 8

1. In Stein 1956, 30.

2. In McCrosson 1966, 14.

3. Longinus's birth is sometimes placed in the third century rather than the first.

4. Stewart 2007, xii.

5. Cited in Stewart 2007, 278. For a more general discussion of physics and art as creative processes sharing aesthetic and compositional demands see Leibowitz 2008.

6. For background see Gebauer 1996, Potolsky 2006.

7. Swirski 2007, 59–67.

8. For a defense and illustration of these precepts see Joseph Carroll's comparative analysis of *The Inheritors* (2004, 163–186). Berger (1997) also provides a good interdisciplinary analysis of the degree to which narratives permeate our popular culture, media, and everyday life.

9. For a review of other theories of art from the evolutionary-adaptive point of view see Boyd 2005. For a recent review of theories of art from a more traditional aesthetic standpoint see Nöel Carroll 2000.

10. See Turner and Poppel 1983; also see Poppel 1989. A good introduction to and illustration of the subfield of chronobiology can be found in Macar, Pouthas, and Friedman 1992.

11. See Morris 2003 for a comprehensive review of the standard theories of realism.

12. See Swirski 2000a, *Between Literature and Science.*

13. A comprehensive analysis of the full spectrum of disciplinary attitudes to literary research can be found in the first chapter, "Literature and Knowledge," of my *Of Literature and Knowledge* (2007).

14. Not that such warnings are anything new; see, for example, Symons 1992.

15. Swirski 2007.

16. See also Koch 1970, Martindale 1990, Storey 1996, and Dutton 2008.

17. See also the mirror neuron research by Rizzolatti and Sinigaglia 2008.

18. Tomasello 1999, 510.

# WORKS CITED

Adams, Robert. 1981. *Beauty in Photography*. New York: Aperture.

Aldama, Frederick Luis, ed. 2010. *Toward a Theory of Narrative Acts (Cognitive Approaches to Literature and Culture)*. Austin: University of Texas Press.

Alston, William P. 2000. *Illocutionary Acts and Sentence Meaning*. Ithaca, NY: Cornell University Press.

Anderson, James. 1982. "Musical Identity." *Journal of Aesthetics and Art Criticism* 40:285–291.

Aristotle. 1961. *Poetics*. Trans. S. H. Butcher; introduction by Francis Fergusson. New York: Hill and Wang.

Austin, John L. 1961. *Philosophical Papers*. Oxford, England: Clarendon.

———. 1962. *How to Do Things with Words*. Cambridge, MA: Harvard University Press.

Bach, Kent, and Robert M. Harnish. 1979. *Linguistic Communication and Speech Acts*. Cambridge, MA: MIT Press.

Bal, Mieke, ed. 1999. *The Practice of Cultural Analysis: Exposing Interdisciplinary Interpretation*. Stanford, CA: Stanford University Press.

Baron-Cohen, Simon. 2005. "The Empathizing System: A Revision of the 1994 Model of the Mindreading System." In *Origins of the Social Mind: Evolutionary Psychology and Child Development*, ed. Bruce J. Ellis and David F. Bjorklund. New York: Guilford.

Baron-Cohen, Simon, Helen Tager-Flusberg, and Donald J. Cohen, eds. 2000. *Understanding Other Minds: Perspectives from Developmental and Cognitive Neuroscience*. 2d edition. Oxford, England: Oxford University Press.

Barrow, John D. 2005. *The Artful Universe Expanded*. Oxford, England: Oxford University Press.

Barthes, Roland. 1974. *S/Z*. Trans. Richard Miller. New York: Noonday Press.

———. 1979. "De l'oeuvre au texte." In *Textual Strategies: Perspectives in Post-Structuralist Criticism*, ed. Josue V. Harari. Ithaca, NY: Cornell University Press.

Batchelor, John, ed. 2006. *Yearbook of English Studies* 36, no. 2.

Beardsley, Monroe C. 1970. *The Possibility of Criticism*. Detroit: Wayne State University Press.

————. 1978. "Aesthetic Intentions and Fictive Illocutions." In *What Is Literature?*, ed. Paul Hernadi. Bloomington: Indiana University Press.

Bell, David F. 1988. *Models of Power: Politics and Economics in Zola's Rougon-Macquart*. Lincoln: University of Nebraska Press.

Benedetti, Paul. 1997. "X-Files Marks the Spot." *Calgary Herald,* 13 September, J14.

Berger, Arthur Asa. 1997. *Narratives in Popular Culture, Media, and Everyday Life*. Thousand Oaks, CA: Sage.

Birkhoff, George David. 1993 [1933]. *Aesthetic Measure*. Cambridge, MA: Harvard University Press.

Blau, Judith R. 2001. "Alley Art: Can We . . . See . . . at Last, the End of Ontology?" In *Handbook of Sociological Theory,* ed. Jonathan H. Turner. New York: Kluwer.

Bloom, Harold, Paul de Man, Jacques Derrida, Geoffrey H. Hartman, and J. Hillis Miller. 1999 [1979]. *Deconstruction and Criticism (Question What You Thought Before)*. New York: Continuum.

Blythe, Hal, and Charlie Sweet. 1989. "The Reader as Poe's Ultimate Dupe in 'The Purloined Letter.'" *Studies in Short Fiction* 26:311–315.

Bonaparte, Marie. 1949. *The Life and Works of Edgar Allan Poe, a Psycho-Analytic Interpretation*. Trans. John Rodker. London: Hogarth.

Borges, Jorge Luis. 1964. *Labyrinths: Selected Stories and Other Writings*. New York: New Directions.

Bowers, Fredson. 1959. *Textual and Literary Criticism*. Cambridge, England: Cambridge University Press.

Boyd, Brian. 2005. "Evolutionary Theories of Art." In *The Literary Animal: Evolution and the Nature of Narrative,* ed. Jonathan Gottschall and David Sloan Wilson. Evanston, IL: Northwestern University Press.

Brilliant, Richard. 2000. *My Laocoön: Alternative Claims in the Interpretation of Artworks*. Berkeley: University of California Press.

Brown, G., and G. Yule. 1983. *Discourse Analysis*. Cambridge, England: Cambridge University Press.

Brown, James R. 1991. *The Laboratory of the Mind*. New York: Routledge.

Brown, Robert L., and Martin Steinmann. 1978. "Native readers of Fiction: A Speech-Act and Genre-Rule Approach to Defining Literature." In *What Is Literature?*, ed. Paul Hernadi. Bloomington: Indiana University Press.

Bruce, Donald, and Anthony Purdy. 1994. *Literature and Science*. Atlanta, GA: Rodopi.

Bruns, Gerald L. 2006. *On the Anarchy of Poetry and Philosophy*. New York: Fordham University Press.

Budiansky, Stephen. 1998. *If a Lion Could Talk: How Animals Think*. London: Weidenfeld and Nicolson.

Buranelli, Vincent. 1977. *Edgar Allan Poe.* Boston: Twayne.

Burkhardt, Armin. 1990. *Speech Acts, Meaning, and Intentions: Critical Approaches to the Philosophy of John Searle.* Berlin: W. de Gruyter.

Buss, Arnold. 1997. "Evolutionary Perspectives on Personality Traits." In *Handbook of Personality Psychology,* ed. Robert Hogan, John Johnson, and Stephen Briggs. San Diego: Academic Press.

Butler, Judith. 1997. *Excitable Speech: A Politics of the Performative.* New York: Routledge.

Byrne, Alex. 1993. "Truth in Fiction: The Story Continued." *Australasian Journal of Philosophy* 71:24–35.

Cantril, Hadley, Hazel Gaudet, and Herta Herzog. 1940. *The Invasion from Mars.* Princeton, NJ: Princeton University Press.

Carroll, Joseph. 2004. *Literary Darwinism: Evolution, Human Nature, and Literature.* New York: Routledge.

———. 2005. "Human Nature and Literary Meaning." In *The Literary Animal: Evolution and the Nature of Narrative,* ed. Jonathan Gottschall and David Sloan Wilson. Evanston, IL: Northwestern University Press.

Carroll, Nöel. 1990. *The Philosophy of Horror: Or, Paradoxes of the Heart.* New York: Routledge.

———. 1992. "Art, Intention, and Conversation." In *Interpretation and Intention,* ed. Gary Iseminger. Philadelphia: Temple University Press.

———. 1997. "Fiction, Non-Fiction, and the Film of Presumptive Assertion: A Conceptual Analysis." In *Film Theory and Philosophy,* ed. Richard Allen and Murray Smith. Oxford, England: Clarendon.

———. 2000. *Theories of Art Today.* Madison: University of Wisconsin Press.

Casti, John L. 1989. *Paradigms Lost: Tackling the Unanswered Mysteries of Modern Science.* New York: Avon.

Charolles, M., ed. 1986. *Research in Text Connexity and Text Coherence: A Survey.* Hamburg, Germany: Buske Verlag.

Chihara, Charles S. 1998. *The Worlds of Possibility: Modal Realism and the Semantics of Modal Logic.* New York: Oxford University Press.

Cioffi, Frank. 1974. "Was Freud a Liar?" *The Listener* 91:172–174.

———. 1985. "Psychoanalysis, Pseudo-Science and Testability." In *Popper and the Human Sciences,* ed. Gregory Currie and Alan Musgrave. Dordrecht, Netherlands: Nijhoff.

Cohen, I. B. 1958. *Isaac Newton's Papers and Letters on Natural Philosophy and Related Topics.* Cambridge, MA: Harvard University Press.

Cohen, Philip R., Jerry Morgan, and Martha E. Pollack, eds. 1990. *Intentions in Communication.* Cambridge, MA: MIT Press.

Cohn, Dorrit. 1999. *The Distinction of Fiction.* Baltimore, MD: Johns Hopkins University Press.

Cole, K. C. 1998. *The University and the Teacup: The Mathematics of Truth and Beauty.* New York: Harcourt Brace.

Cole, Peter, and Jerry L. Morgan, eds. 1975. *Speech Acts.* New York: Academic.

Connor, Steven. 1997. *Postmodernist Culture: An Introduction to Theories of the Contemporary.* 2d edition. Oxford, England: Blackwell.

Conte, M., J. S. Petöfi, and E. Sözer, eds. 1989. *Text and Discourse Connectedness.* Amsterdam: John Benjamins.

Cory, Herbert Ellsworth. 1925. "The Interactions of Beauty and Truth." *Journal of Philosophy* 22 (16 July): 393–402.

Cresswell, M. J. 1994. *Language in the World.* New York: Cambridge University Press.

Crews, Frederick. 1993. Foreword to *After Poststructuralism: Interdisciplinarity and Literary Theory,* ed. Nancy Easterlin and Barbara Riebling. Evanston, IL: Northwestern University Press.

———. 2001. *Postmodern Pooh.* New York: North Point.

———. 2002. *Skeptical Engagements.* http://www.cybereditions.com.

———. 2006. *Follies of the Wise: Dissenting Essays.* Emeryville, CA: Counterpoint.

Crowley, John. 1995. "The Gothic of Thomas M. Disch." *Yale Review* 83, no. 2 (April): 134–146.

Csicsery-Ronay, Istvan. 1986. "Twenty-Two Answers and Two Postscripts: An Interview with Stanislaw Lem," trans. Marek Lugowski. *Science-Fiction Studies* 13 (November): 242–260.

Culler, Jonathan. 1973. *Structuralist Poetics: Structuralism, Linguistics and the Study of Literature.* Ithaca, NY: Cornell University Press.

Cupchik, Gerald C. 1997. "Identification as a Basic Problem for Aesthetic Reception." In *Systemic and Empirical Approach to Literature and Culture as Theory and Application,* ed. Steven Tötösy de Zepetnek and Irene Sywenky. Edmonton, Canada, and Siegen, Germany: University of Alberta RICL-CCS and Siegen University.

Currie, Gregory. 1987. "Fictional Worlds." *Philosophy and Literature* 11:351–352.

———. 1989. *An Ontology of Art.* New York: St. Martin's Press.

———. 1990. *The Nature of Fiction.* Cambridge, England: Cambridge University Press

———. 1991a. "Interpreting Fiction." In *Literary Theory and Philosophy,* ed. R. Freedman and L. Reinhardt. London: Macmillan.

———. 1991b. "Work and Text." *Mind* 100:325–340.

———. 1993. "*Music, Art, and Metaphysics.*" *Philosophy and Phenomenological Research* 53:471–475.

———. 2004. *Arts and Minds.* New York: Clarendon.

Daiches, David. 1969. "Literary Evaluations." In *Problems of Literary Evaluation. Yearbook of Comparative Criticism* 2, ed. L. P. Strelka. University Park: Pennsylvania State University Press.

Danto, Arthur. 1964. "The Artworld." *Journal of Philosophy* 61:571–584.

———. 1973. "Artworks and Real Things." *Theoria* 39:1–17.

———. 1981. *The Transfiguration of the Commonplace.* Cambridge, MA: Harvard University Press.

———. 1986. *The Philosophical Disenfranchisement of Art.* New York: Columbia University Press.

Davies, David. 1991. "Works, Texts, and Contexts: Goodman on the Literary Artwork." *Canadian Journal of Philosophy* 21:331–345.

———. 1996. "Fictional Truth and Fictional Authors." *British Journal of Aesthetics* 36:43–55.

———. 2004. *Art as Performance.* Oxford, England: Blackwell.

Davies, Stephen. 1987. "A Note on Feagin on Interpreting Art Intentionalistically." *British Journal of Aesthetics* 27:178–180.

———. 1991. *Definitions of Art.* Ithaca, NY: Cornell University Press.

De Beaugrande, R., and W. Dressler. 1981. *Introduction to Text Linguistics.* London: Longman.

De Ley, Herbert. 1988. "The Name of the Game: Applying Game Theory in Literature." *SubStance* 55:33–46.

de Man, Paul. 1983. *Blindness and Insight: Essays in the Rhetoric of Contemporary Criticism.* Minneapolis: University of Minnesota Press.

Denuccio, Jerome D. 1990. "Fact, Fiction, Fatality: Poe's 'The Thousand-and-Second Tale of Scheherazade.'" *Studies in Short Fiction* 27:365–370.

Dennett, Daniel. 1978. *Brainstorms: Philosophical Essays on Mind and Psychology.* Brighton, England: Harvester.

Derrida, Jacques. 1988. "Signature Event Context." In *Limited Inc.* Evanston, IL: Northwestern University Press.

———. 1999 [1979]. "Living On: Border Lines." In *Deconstruction and Criticism.* New York: Continuum.

Dewey, John. 1934. *Art as Experience.* New York: Capricorn.

Dickie, George. 1964. "The Myth of the Aesthetic Attitude." *American Philosophical Quarterly* 1:56–65.

———. 1965. "Beardsley's Phantom Aesthetic Experience." *Journal of Philosophy* 62:129–136.

———. 1974. *Art and the Aesthetic: An Institutional Analysis.* Ithaca, NY: Cornell University Press.

Diffey, T. J. 1979. "On Defining Art." *British Journal of Aesthetics* 19:15–23.

Disch, Thomas M. 1991. *The M.D.: A Horror Story.* New York: Berkeley.

Dissanayake, Ellen. 1988. *What Is Art For?* Seattle: University of Washington Press.

———. 1992. *Homo Aestheticus: Where Art Comes From and Why.* Seattle: University of Washington Press.

———. 2000. *Art and Intimacy: How the Arts Began.* Seattle: University of Washington Press.

Doležel, Lubomir. 1984. "Aristotelian Poetics as a Science of Literature." In *Semiosis: Semiotics and the History of Culture, In Honorem Georgii Lotman,* ed. Morris Halle. Ann Arbor: Michigan Slavic Contributions.

Donaldson, Talbot E. 1970. *Speaking of Chaucer.* New York: W. W. Norton.

Dutton, Denis. 1987. "Why Intentions Won't Go Away." In *Literature and the Question of Philosophy,* ed. A. J. Cascardi. Baltimore: Johns Hopkins University Press.

———. *The Art Instinct: Beauty, Pleasure, and Human Evolution.* New York: Bloomsbury, 2008.

Eco, Umberto. 1984. *Postscript to The Name of the Rose.* Trans. William Weaver. San Diego, CA: Harcourt Brace Jovanovich.

———. 1994a. *Apocalypse Postponed.* Ed. Robert Lumley. Bloomington: Indiana University Press.

———. 1994b. *Six Walks in the Fictional Woods.* Cambridge, MA: Harvard University Press.

———. 2006. *On Literature.* Trans. Martin McLaughlin. London: Vintage.

Eddings, Dennis W. 1982. "Poe, Dupin, and the Reader." *University of Mississippi Studies in English* 3:128–135.

Editors of *Lingua Franca.* 2000. *The Sokal Hoax: The Sham That Shook the Academy.* Lincoln: University of Nebraska Press.

Elton, William, ed. 1954. *Aesthetics and Language.* Oxford, England: Basil Blackwell.

Engel, Peter. 1984. "An Interview with Stanislaw Lem." Trans. John Sigda. *Missouri Review* 7:218–237.

Emerson, Ralph Waldo. 1983. *Essays and Lectures.* Ed. Joel Porte. New York: Literary Classics of the U.S., Viking.

Evans, Richard J. 1997. *In Defence of History.* London: Granta.

Feagin, Susan. 1982. "Incompatible Interpretations of Art." *Philosophy and Literature* 6:13–146.

Field, Andrew. 1967. *Nabokov—His Life in Art: a Critical Narrative.* London: Hodder and Stoughton.

Fish, Stanley. 1980. *Is There a Text in This Class?* Cambridge, MA: Harvard University Press.

Focquaert, Farah, and Steven M. Platek. 2007. "Social Cognition and the Evolution of Self-Awareness." In *Evolutionary Cognitive Neuroscience,* ed. Steven M. Platek, Julian Paul Keenan, and Todd K. Shackelford. Cambridge, MA: MIT Press.

Frye, Northrop. 1957. *The Anatomy of Criticism.* Princeton, NJ: Princeton University Press.

Gaskell, Philip. 1985. *New Introduction to Bibliography.* Oxford, England: Oxford University Press.

Gaut, Berys, and Paisley Livingston. 2003. *The Creation of Art: New Essays in Philosophical Aesthetics.* Cambridge, England: Cambridge University Press.

Gebauer, Gunter. 1996. *Mimesis: Culture—Art—Society.* Berkeley: University of California Press.

Goodheart, Eugene. 2007. *Darwinian Misadventures in the Humanities.* Edison, NJ: Transaction.

Goodman, Nelson. 1976. *Languages of Art: An Approach to a Theory of Symbols.* 2d edition. Indianapolis, IN: Hackett.

———. 1978. *Ways of Worldmaking.* Indianapolis, IN: Hackett.

Goodman, Nelson, and Catherine Z. Elgin. 1988. *Reconceptions in Philosophy and Other Arts and Sciences.* Indianapolis, IN: Hackett.

Gorman, David. 1990. "From Small Beginnings: Literary Theorists Encounter Analytic Philosophy." *Poetics Today* 11, no. 3 (Fall): 647–659.

Gottschall, Jonathan. 2003. "Patterns of Characterization in Folk Tales Across Geographic Regions and Levels of Cultural Complexity: Literature as a Neglected Source of Quantitative Data." *Human Nature* 14:365–382.

Gottschall, Jonathan, and David Sloan Wilson, eds. 2005. *The Literary Animal: Evolution and the Nature of Narrative.* Forewords by E. O. Wilson and Frederick Crews. Evanston, IL: Northwestern University Press.

Graves, Barbara, and Carl H. Frederiksen. 1991. "Literary Expertise in the Description of a Fictional Narrative." *Poetics* 20:1–26.

Greetham, David C. 1994. *Textual Scholarship: An Introduction.* New York: Garland.

———. 1999. *Theories of the Text.* Oxford, England: Oxford University Press.

Grice, H. Paul. 1957. "Meaning." *Philosophical Review* 66:377–388.

———. 1968. "Utterer's Meaning, Sentence Meaning, and Word Meaning." *Foundations of Language* 4:225–242.

———. 1969. "Utterer's Meaning and Intentions." *Philosophical Review* 78: 147–177.

———. 1971. "Intention and Uncertainty." *Proceedings of the British Academy* 57: 263–279.

———. 1982. "Meaning Revisited." In *Mutual Knowledge,* ed. N. V. Smith. New York: Academic.

Gross, Paul R., and Norman Levitt. 1994. *The Higher Superstition: The Academic Left and Its Quarrels with Science.* Baltimore, MD: Johns Hopkins University Press.

Gross, Paul R., Norman Levitt, and Martin W. Lewis, eds. 1996. *The Flight from Science and Reason.* New York: New York Academy of Sciences.

Grünbaum, Adolf. 1993. *Validation in the Clinical Theory of Psychoanalysis: A Study in the Philosophy of Psychoanalysis.* Madison, CT: International Universities Press.

Halliday, Michael A. K., and Ruqaiya Hasan. 1976. *Cohesion in English.* London: Longman.

Hamilton, Andy. 1990. "An Ontology of Art." *Philosophical Quarterly* 40: 538–541.

Hawkins, Ann R., ed. 2006. *Teaching Bibliography, Textual Criticism, and Book History.* London: Pickering and Chatto.

Heller, Joseph, and Speed Vogel. 1986. *No Laughing Matter.* New York: Putnam.

Heller, Scott. 1988. "Some English Departments Are Giving Undergraduates Grounding in New Literary and Critical Theory." *Chronicle of Higher Education* 34, no. 47 (August): A15–A17.

Hemingway, Ernest. 1987 [1937]. *To Have and Have Not.* New York: Simon and Schuster.

Hernadi, Paul, ed. 1978. *What is Literature?* Bloomington: Indiana University Press.

Hirsch, E. D. 1975. "What's the Use of Speech-Act Theory?" *Centrum* 3, no. 2:121–124.

———. 1992 [1967]. "In Defense of the Author." In *Intention and Interpretation,* ed. Gary Iseminger. Philadelphia: Temple University Press.

Hofstadter, Douglas. 2007. *I Am a Strange Loop.* New York: Basic.

Holub, Miroslav. 1990. *The Dimension of the Present Moment: Essays by Miroslav Holub.* Ed. David Young. Boston: Faber and Faber.

Homer. 1924. *The Iliad with an English Translation by A. T. Murray, Ph.D., in Two Volumes.* Cambridge, MA: Harvard University Press.

———. 1953. *The Iliad.* Trans. E. V. Rieu. Harmondsworth, England: Penguin.

———. 1984. *Iliad.* Trans. Robert Fitzgerald. New York: Oxford University Press.

———. 1990. *Iliad.* Trans. Robert Fagles. New York: Viking.

———. 1999. *Iliad. Books 1–12.* Trans. A. T. Murray; revised by William F. Wyatt. Cambridge, MA: Harvard University Press.

Horowitz, Tamara, and Gerald J. Massey. 1991. *Thought Experiments in Science and Philosophy.* Savage, MD: Rowman and Littlefield.

Hough, Robert, ed. 1965. *Literary Criticism of Edgar Allan Poe.* Lincoln: University of Nebraska Press.

Howell, Robert. 2002. "Ontology and the Nature of the Literary Work." *Journal of Aesthetics and Art Criticism* 60:67–79.

Hume, David. 2000. *Four Dissertations and Essays on Suicide and the Immortality of the Soul.* South Bend, IN: St. Augustine's Press.

Ingarden, Roman. 1973. *The Literary Work of Art: An Investigation on the Borderlines of Ontology, Logic, and Theory of Literature.* Trans. George G. Grabowicz. Evanston, IL: Northwestern University Press.

Irwin, John T. 1986. "Mysteries We Reread, Mysteries of Rereading: Poe, Borges, and the Analytic Detective Story." *Modern Language Notes* 101:1168–1215.

Iseminger, Gary, ed. 1992. *Intention and Interpretation.* Philadelphia: Temple University Press.

Iser, Wolfgang. 1978. *The Act of Reading*. London: Routledge and Kegan Paul.

Jacquette, Dale. 1994. "The Type-Token Distinction In Margolis's Aesthetics." *Journal of Aesthetics and Art Criticism* 52, no. 3:299–307.

Jaroszynski, Piotr. 2002. *Metaphysics and Art*. Trans. Hugh McDonald. New York: Peter Lang.

Juhl, Peter D. 1980. *Interpretation: An Essay in the Philosophy of Literary Criticism*. Princeton, NJ: Princeton University Press.

Kalderon, Mark Eli, ed. 2005. *Fictionalism in Metaphysics*. Oxford, England: Clarendon.

Kasser, Rodolphe, Marvin Meyer, and Gregor Wurst, eds. 2006. *The Gospel of Judas: from Codex Tchacos*. Washington, DC: National Geographic.

Kelly, Michael, ed. 1998. *Encyclopedia of Aesthetics*. New York: Oxford University Press.

Keneally, Thomas. 1993. *Schindler's List*. New York: Simon and Schuster.

Ketterer, David. 1979. *The Rationale of Deception in Poe*. Baton Rouge: Louisiana State University Press.

King, Richard J. 2006. *Desiring Rome*. Columbus: Ohio State University Press.

Koch, Howard. 1970. *The Panic Broadcast*. New York: Avon.

Koch, Walter A., ed. 1993. *The Biology of Literature*. Bochum, Germany: N. Brockmeyer.

Krausz, Michael, ed. 2002. *Is There a Single Right Interpretation?*. University Park: Pennsylvania State University Press.

Kucich, John. 2006. *Imperial Masochism*. Princeton, NJ: Princeton University Press.

Kuiken, Don, David S. Miall, and Shelley Sikora. 2004. "How Literature Enters Life: Forms of Self-Implication in Literary Reading." *Poetics Today* 25, no. 2:171–203.

Kuper, Adam. 2007. "Anthropology." *Times Literary Supplement,* 30 March, 23.

Lakatos, Imre. 1978. *The Methodology of Scientific Research Programmes*. Ed. John Worrall and Gregory Currie. Cambridge, England: Cambridge University Press.

Lamarque, Peter. 1987. "The Puzzle of the Flash Stockman: A Reply to David Lewis." *Analysis* 47, no. 2:93–95.

Lamarque, Peter, and Stein Haugom Olsen. 1994. *Truth, Fiction, and Literature*. Oxford, England: Oxford University Press.

Leach, Heather, and Robert Graham. 2007. *Everything You Need to Know about Creative Writing*. New York: Continuum.

Lefkowitz, Mary. 1996. "Whatever Happened to Historical Evidence?" In *The Flight from Science and Reason*, ed. Paul E. Gross, Norman Levitt, and Martin W. Lewis. New York: New York Academy of Sciences.

Leibowitz, J. R. 2008. *Hidden Harmony: The Connected Worlds of Physics and Art*. Baltimore, MD: Johns Hopkins University Press.

Lem, Stanislaw. 1976. *The Investigation.* Trans. Adele Milch. New York: Avon.

———. 1983. *His Master's Voice.* San Diego: Harcourt.

———. 1984a. *The Chain of Chance.* Trans. Louis Iribarne. San Diego: Harcourt.

———. 1984b. *Prowokacja.* Krakow, Poland: Wydawnictwo Literackie.

Lentricchia, Frank. 1983. *Criticism and Social Change.* Chicago: University of Chicago Press.

Le Poidevin, Robin. 1995. "Worlds Within Worlds? The Paradoxes of Embedded Fiction." *British Journal of Aesthetics* 35:227–238.

Levin, Harry. 1957. *Contexts of Criticism.* Cambridge, MA: Harvard University Press.

Levin, Richard. 1993. "The New Interdisciplinarity in Literary Criticism." In *After Poststructuralism: Interdisciplinarity and Literary Theory,* ed. Nancy Easterlin and Barbara Riebling. Evanston, IL: Northwestern University Press.

———. 1995. "Negative Evidence." *Studies in Philology* 42 (Fall): 383–410.

Levine, Stuart, and Susan Levine, eds. 1976. *The Short Fiction of Edgar Allan Poe.* Indianapolis, IN: Bobbs-Merrill.

Levinson, Jerrold. 1979. "Defining Art Historically." *British Journal of Aesthetics* 19:232–250.

———. 1980a. "Autographic and Allographic Art Revisited." *Philosophical Studies* 38:367–383.

———. 1980b. "What a Musical Work Is." *Journal of Philosophy* 77:5–28.

———. 1987. "Review of Dickie's *The Art Circle.*" *Philosophical Review* 96: 141–146.

———. 1990. *Music, Art, and Metaphysics: Essays in Philosophical Aesthetics.* Ithaca, NY: Cornell University Press.

———. 1992a. "Intention and Interpretation: A Last Look." In *Interpretation and Intention,* ed. Gary Iseminger, 246–249. Philadelphia: Temple University Press.

———. 1992b. "*An Ontology of Art.*" *Philosophy and Phenomenological Research* 52:215–221.

———. 1996. *The Pleasures of Aesthetics.* Ithaca, NY: Cornell University Press.

Lewis, David K. 1969. *Convention: a Philosophical Study.* Cambridge, MA: Harvard University Press.

———. 1983. "Truth in Fiction." (Oxford University Press) *Philosophical Papers* 1:261–280.

———. 1986. *Counterfactuals.* Oxford, England: Blackwell.

Livingston, Paisley. 1992a. "Literature and Knowledge." In *A Companion to Epistemology,* ed. Jonathan Dancey and Ernest Sosa. Oxford, England: Blackwell.

———. 1992b. "Texts, Works, and Literature." *Spiel* 11:197–210.

———. 1993a. "From Text to Work." In *After Poststructuralism: Interdisciplinarity and Literary Theory,* ed. Nancy Easterlin and Barbara Riebling. Evanston, IL: Northwestern University Press.

————. 1993b. "What's the Story?" *SubStance* 71–72:98–112.

————. 2005. *Art and Intention.* Oxford, England: Oxford University Press.

Livingston, Paisley, and Alfred Mele. 1992. "Intention and Literature." *Stanford French Review* 16:173–196.

Longinus, Cassius. 1965. *On the Sublime.* Trans. T. S. Dorsch. London: Penguin.

Mabbott, Thomas Ollive, ed. 1978. *Collected Works of Edgar Allan Poe.* Cambridge, MA: Harvard University Press.

Macar, Francoise, Viviane Pouthas, and William J. Friedman, eds. 1992. *Time, Action, and Cognition: Toward Bridging the Gap.* Dordrecht, Netherlands: Kluwer Academic.

Maclean, Ian. 1985. "Un Dialogue de Sourds? Some Implications of the Austin-Searle-Derrida Debate." *Paragraph* 5:1–26.

Macmillan, Malcolm. 1991. *Freud Evaluated: The Complete Arc.* Amsterdam: North-Holland.

Magliano, Joseph, and Arthur C. Graesser. 1991. "A Three-Pronged Method for Studying Inference Generation in Literary Text." *Poetics* 20:193–232.

Malamud, Bernard. 1983. *God's Grace.* New York: Avon.

Margolis, Joseph. 1993. "Exorcising the Dreariness of Aesthetics." *Journal of Aesthetics and Art Criticism* 51, no. 2 (Spring): 133–140.

————. 1999. *What, After All, Is a Work of Art? Lectures in the Philosophy of Art.* University Park: Pennsylvania State University Press.

Margolin, Uri. 1999. "Formal, Semantic, and Pragmatic Aspects of Metatextuality: Comparatism Revisited." In *Comparative Literature Now: Theories and Practice / La Litérature comparée à l'heure actuelle. Théories et réalisations,* ed. Tötösy de Zepetnek, Milan V. Dimic, and Irene Sywenky. Paris: Honoré Champion.

Martindale, Colin. 1990. *The Clockwork Muse: The Predictability of Artistic Change.* New York: Basic.

Marwick, Arthur. 2001. *The New Nature of History: Knowledge, Evidence, Language.* Basingstoke, England: Palgrave.

McCrosson, Doris Ross. 1966. *Walter de la Mare.* New York: Twayne.

McKendrick, Neil. 1988. "The Ugly Historians." *New York Times,* 7 February. http://query.nytimes.com/gst/fullpage.html?res=940DE1D8153DF934A3575 1C0A96E948260&sec=&spon=&pagewanted=1.

Melaney, William D. 2001. *After Ontology: Literary Theory and Modernist Poetics.* New York: SUNY Press.

Mele, Alfred R. 1987. "Are Intentions Self-Referential?" *Philosophical Studies* 52:309–329.

————. 1988. "Against a Belief/Desire Analysis of Intention." *Philosophia* 18:239–242.

————. 1989. "Intention, Belief, and Intentional Action." *American Philosophical Quarterly* 26:19–30.

Mele, Alfred R., and Paisley Livingston. 1992. "Intentions and Interpretations." *MLN* 107:931–949.

Mele, Alfred R., and Paul K. Moser. 1994. "Intentional Action." *Nous* 28: 39–68.

Metzger, Bruce M. 1992. *The Text of the New Testament: Its Transmission, Corruption, and Restoration.* 3d edition. New York: Oxford University Press.

Miller, J. Hillis. 2001. *Speech Acts in Literature.* Stanford, CA: Stanford University Press.

Morris, Pam. 2003. *Realism.* New York: Routledge.

Muller, John P., and William J. Richardson, eds. 1987. *The Purloined Poe: Lacan, Derrida, and Psychoanalytic Reading.* Baltimore, MD: Johns Hopkins University Press.

Mulryne, J. R. 2006. "Where We Are Now: New Directions and Biographical Methods." In *Shakespeare, Marlowe, Jonson: New Directions in Biography,* ed. Takashi Kozuka and J. R. Mulryne. Burlington, VT: Ashgate.

Nathan, Daniel. 1992. "Irony, Metaphor, and the Problem of Intention." In *Intention and Interpretation,* ed. Gary Iseminger. Philadelphia: Temple University Press.

Nichol, John W. 1948. "Melville's 'Soiled' Fish of the Sea." *American Literature* 21:338–339.

Norris, Christopher. 1985. "Suspended Sentences: Textual Theory and the Law." *Southern Review* 18, no. 2:123–141.

Norton, David. 2005. *A Textual History of the King James Bible.* Cambridge, England: Cambridge University Press.

O'Connor, Flannery. 1961. *Mystery and Manners.* New York: Noonday.

O'Donnell, Pierce, and Dennis McDougal. 1992. *Fatal Subtraction: The Inside Story of Buchwald v. Paramount.* New York: Doubleday.

Olsen, Stein Haugom, and Peter Lamarque, eds. 2004. *Aesthetics and the Philosophy of Art.* Malden, MA: Blackwell.

O'Rell, Diogenes. 1992. "On the Symmetries of a Grecian Urn." *Mathematical Gazette* 76, no. 476 (July): 269.

Palmer, Bryan D. 1990. *Descent into Discourse: The Reification of Language and the Writing of Social History.* Philadelphia: Temple University Press.

Parker, Hershel. 1984. *Flawed Texts and Verbal Icons: Literary Authority in American Fiction.* Evanston, IL: Northwestern University Press.

Passmore, John A. 1951. "The Dreariness of Aesthetics." *Mind* 60:318–335.

Pavel, Thomas. 1985. *The Poetics of Plot.* Minneapolis: University of Minnesota Press.

Peirce, Charles S. 1931–1958. *Collected Papers of Charles Sanders Peirce.* Ed. Charles Hartshorne and Paul Weiss. Cambridge, MA: Harvard University Press.

Pérez-Reverte, Arturo. 2008. *Un día de cólera.* Buenos Aires: Alfaguara.

Petrey, Sandy. 1990. *Speech Acts and Literary Theory.* New York: Routledge.

Plato. 1999. *Republic.* In *Collected Dialogues.* Ed. Edith Hamilton and Huntington Cairns. Princeton, NJ: Bollingen.

Poe, Edgar Allan. 1997 [1848]. *Eureka: A Prose Poem.* New York: Prometheus.

Ponech, Trevor. 1999. *What Is Non-Fiction Cinema?* Boulder, CO: Westview.

Poppel, Ernst. 1989. "The Measurement of Music and the Cerebral Clock: A New Theory." *Leonardo* 22, no. 1:83–89.

Potolsky, Matthew. 2006. *Mimesis.* New York: Routledge.

Pratt, Mary Louise. 1977. *Toward a Speech-Act Theory of Literary Discourse.* Bloomington: Indiana University Press.

Premack, David, and Guy Woodruff. 1978. "Does the Chimpanzee Have a 'Theory of Mind'?" *Behavioral and Brain Sciences* 4:515–526.

Putnam, Hilary. 1975. *Mind, Language, and Reality.* Vol. 2. New York: Cambridge University Press.

Quinn, Arthur Hobson. 1941. *Edgar Allan Poe: A Critical Biography.* New York: Appleton-Century.

Racter (William Chamberlain and Thomas Etter). 1984. *The Policeman's Beard Is Half Constructed.* New York: Warner.

Rapaport, Herman. 2001. *The Theory Mess: Deconstruction in Eclipse.* New York: Columbia University Press.

Richards, I. A. 2001 [1924]. *Principles of Literary Criticism.* New York: Routledge.

Rizzolatti, Giacomo, and Corrado Sinigaglia. 2008. *Mirrors in the Brain.* Oxford, England: Oxford University Press.

Rossi, Matthew. 2003. *Things That Never Were: Fantasies, Lunatics, and Entertaining Lies.* Austin, TX: Monkey Brain Books.

Sanders, T., and J. Sanders. 2006. "Text and Text Analysis." In *The Encyclopedia of Language and Linguistics,* ed. Keith Brown. 2d edition. London: Elsevier.

Saxe, Rebecca, and Simon Baron-Cohen, eds. 2007. *Theory of Mind.* London: Psychology Press.

Scalise Sugiyama, Michelle. 2005. "Reverse-Engineering Narrative Evidence of Special Design." In *The Literary Animal: Evolution and the Nature of Narrative,* ed. Jonathan Gottschall and David Sloan Wilson. Evanston, IL: Northwestern University Press.

Scharnberg, Max. 1993. *The Non-Authentic Nature of Freud's Observations.* Uppsala, Sweden: Textgruppen i Upsala.

Schelling, Thomas. 1960. *The Strategy of Conflict.* Cambridge, MA: Harvard University Press.

Schiller, Friedrich. 1954. *On the Aesthetic Education of Man.* Ed. Reginald Snell. New Haven, CT: Yale University Press.

Searle, John. 1969. *Speech Acts: An Essay in the Philosophy of Language.* London: Cambridge University Press.

———. 1979. *Expression and Meaning: Studies in the Theory of Speech Acts.* Cambridge, England: Cambridge University Press.

————. 1983. *Intentionality: An Essay in the Philosophy of Mind.* Cambridge, England: Cambridge University Press.

————. 1996a. "Contemporary Philosophy in the United States." In *Blackwell Companion to Philosophy,* ed. Nicholas Bunnin and E. P. Tsui-James. Oxford, England: Blackwell.

————. 1996b. "Literary Theory and Its Discontents." In *Beyond Poststructuralism: The Speculations of Theory and the Experience of Reading,* ed. Wendell V. Harris. University Park: Pennsylvania State University Press.

Shattuck, Roger. "Does It All Fit Together? Evolution, the Arts, and Consilience." *Academic Questions* 11 (1998): 56–61.

Shusterman, Richard. 1989. *Analytic Aesthetics.* Oxford, England: Blackwell.

————. 1992a. "Interpreting with Pragmatist Intentions." In *Interpretation and Intention,* ed. Gary Iseminger. Philadelphia: Temple University Press.

————. 1992b. "Text." In *A Companion to Aesthetics,* ed. David E. Cooper. Oxford, England: Blackwell.

Sibley, Frank. 1959. "Aesthetic Concepts." *Philosophical Review* 68:421–450.

Silvers, Anita. 1987. "Letting the Sunshine In: Has Analysis Made Aesthetics Clear?" *Journal of Aesthetics and Art Criticism* 46:137–149.

Skinner, B. F. 1957. *Verbal Behavior.* New York: Appleton-Century Crofts.

Sorensen, Roy A. 1992. *Thought Experiments.* New York: Oxford University Press.

Sperber, Dan, and Deirdre Wilson. 1995. *Relevance: Communication and Cognition.* Oxford, England: Blackwell.

Spiegelman, Art. 1986. *Maus: A Survivor's Tale.* New York: Pantheon.

————. 1991a. Letter to the editor. *New York Times Book Review,* 29 December, 4.

————. 1991b. *Maus II, A Survivor's Tale: And Here My Troubles Began.* New York: Pantheon.

Stalnaker, Robert C. 2003. *Ways a World Might Be: Metaphysical and Antimetaphysical Essays.* Oxford, England: Clarendon.

Stecker, Robert. 1992. "Incompatible Interpretations." *Journal of Aesthetics and Art Criticism* 50:291–298.

————. 1993. "The Role of Intention and Convention in Interpreting Artworks." *Southern Journal of Philosophy* 31:471–489.

————. 1994. "Art Interpretation." *Journal of Aesthetics and Art Criticism* 52: 193–206.

————. 1996. *Artworks: Definition, Meaning, Value.* University Park: Pennsylvania State University Press.

————. 2003. *Interpretation and Construction: Art, Speech, and the Law.* Malden, MA: Blackwell.

Stein, Jean. 1956. "The Art of Fiction XII: William Faulkner." *Paris Review* 12 (Spring): 29–52.

Stewart, Ian. 2007. *Why Beauty Is Truth: A History of Symmetry.* New York: Basic.

Storey, Robert. 1996. *Mimesis and the Human Animal: On the Biogenetic Founda-tions of Literary Representation.* Evanston, IL: Northwestern University Press.

Strawson, Peter F. 1964. "Intention and Convention in Speech Acts." *Philo-sophical Review* 73:439–460.

*Style.* 2008. Vol. 42, no. 2–3 (Fall, special issue on literary evolutionary studies).

Sutrop, Margit. 2002. "Imagination and the Act of Fiction-Making." *Austral-asian Journal of Philosophy* 80:332–344.

Swirski, Peter. 1994. "Iser's Theory of Aesthetic Response: A Critique." *Reader* 32:1–15.

———. 1997a. "Genres in Action: the Pragmatics of Literary Interpretation." *Orbis Litterarum: International Review of Literary Studies* 52:141–156.

———. 1997b. *A Stanislaw Lem Reader.* Evanston, IL: Northwestern University Press.

———. 1998. "Bernard Malamud: God's Grace." In *Beacham's Encyclopedia of Popular Fiction,* vol. 2. Osprey, FL: Beacham.

———. 1999. "Stanislaw Lem." In *Science Fiction Writers.* New York: Scribner's.

———. 2000a. *Between Literature and Science. Poe, Lem, and Explorations in Aes-thetics, Cognitive Science, and Literary Knowledge.* Montreal: McGill-Queen's University Press.

———. 2000b. "The Nature of Literary Fiction: From Carter to Spiegelman." *M/MLA: Journal of the Midwest Modern Language Association* 33:58–73.

———. 2001. "Interpreting Art, Interpreting Literature." *Orbis Litterarum: In-ternational Review of Literary Studies* 56, no. 1:17–36.

———. 2005a. *From Lowbrow to Nobrow.* Montreal: McGill-Queen's University Press.

———. 2005b. "Is There a Work in This Classroom? Interpretations, Textual Readings, and American Fiction." *International Fiction Review* 32:53–70.

———. 2006. "Upton Sinclair: *The Jungle* (1906); *Oil* (1927)." In *Magill Survey of American Literature,* ed. Tracy Irons-Georges. Revised edition. Pasadena, CA: Salem.

———. 2007. *Of Literature and Knowledge: Explorations in Narrative Thought Ex-periments, Evolution, and Game Theory.* New York: Routledge.

Symons, Donald. 1992. "On the Use and Misuse of Darwinism in the Study of Human Behavior." In *The Adapted Mind: Evolutionary Psychology and the Gen-eration of Culture,* ed. Jerome Barkow, Leda Cosmides, and John Tooby. New York: Oxford University Press.

Tanselle, G. Thomas. 1976. "The Editorial Problem of Final Authorial Inten-tion." *Studies in Bibliography* 29:167–211.

———. 1989. *A Rationale of Textual Criticism.* Philadelphia: University of Penn-sylvania Press.

———. 1990. "Textual Criticism and Deconstruction." *Studies in Bibliography* 43:1–33.

Taylor, Gary. 1987. "Revising Shakespeare." *Text* 3:285–304.

Taylor, Richard P., A. P. Micolich, and D. Jonas. 1999. "Fractal Analysis of Pollock's Drip Paintings." *Nature,* 3 June, 422.

———. 2002. "The Construction of Pollock's Fractal Drip Paintings." *Leonardo* 35, no. 2:203–207.

Thompson, G. R. 1984. *Essays and Reviews.* New York: Library of America.

Tilghman, Benjamin R. 1973. *Language and Aesthetics.* Lawrence: University Press of Kansas.

———. 1982. "Danto and the Ontology of Literature." *Journal of Aesthetics and Art Criticism* 40, no. 3 (March): 293–299.

Tolhurst, William E. 1977. "What a Text Is and How It Means." *British Journal of Aesthetics* 19:3–14.

———. 1984. "Toward an Aesthetic Account of the Nature of Art." *Journal of Aesthetics and Art Criticism* 42:261–269.

Tolhurst, William E., and Samuel C. Wheeler III. 1979. "On Textual Individuation." *Philosophical Studies* 35:187–197.

Tolstoy, Leo. 1991 [1855]. *Tolstoy's Short Fiction.* Ed. and trans. Michael R. Katz. New York: W. W. Norton.

Tomasello, Michael. 1999. "The Human Adaptation for Culture." *Annual Review of Anthropology* 28:509–529.

Tomasello, Michael, Malinda Carpenter, Josep Call, Tanya Behne, and Henrike Moll. 2005. "Understanding and Sharing Intentions: The Origins of Cultural Cognition." *Behavioral and Brain Sciences* 28:675–735.

Tooby, John, and Leda Cosmides. 2001. "Does Beauty Build Adapted Minds? Towards an Evolutionary Theory of Aesthetics." *SubStance* 94–95:6–27.

Tsohatzidis, Savas L., ed. 1994. *Foundations of Speech Act Theory: Philosophical and Linguistic Perspectives.* London: Routledge.

Turner, Frederick, and Ernst Poppel. 1983. "The Neural Lyre: Poetic Meter, the Brain, and Time." *Poetry* 142:277–309.

*USA Today.* 2007. "USA Today/Gallup Poll Results," 9 June. http://www.usa today.com/news/politics/2007-06-07-evolution-poll-results_N.htm? csp=34.

Vanderveken, Daniel, and Susumu Kubo, eds. 2002. *Essays in Speech Act Theory.* Philadelphia: J. Benjamins.

Van Dijk, T. A. 1972. *Some Aspects of Text Grammars.* The Hague: Mouton.

Van Leer, David. 1993. "Detecting Truth: The World of the Dupin Tales." In *New Essays on Poe's Major Tales,* ed. Kenneth Silverman. Cambridge, England: Cambridge University Press.

van Peer, Willie. 1993. "Text." In *The Encyclopedia of Language and Linguistics,* ed. R. E. Asher. Oxford, England: Pergamon.

Vickers, Brian. 1993. *Appropriating Shakespeare: Contemporary Critical Quarrels.* New Haven, CT: Yale University Press.

Walton, Kendall. 1970. "Categories of Art." *Philosophical Review* 66:334–367.

———. 1973. "Pictures and Make-Believe." *Philosophical Review* 82:283–319.

———. 1983. "Fiction, Fiction-Making, and Styles of Fictionality." *Philosophy and Literature* 7:78–88.

———. 1990. *Mimesis as Make-Believe: On the Foundations of the Representational Arts.* Cambridge, MA: Harvard University Press.

———. 2005. *Art and Value.* Oxford, England: Oxford University Press.

Wellek, Rene, and Austin Warren. 1949. *Theory of Literature.* New York: Harcourt Brace.

Westfall, R. S. 1980. *Never at Rest: A Biography of Isaac Newton.* Cambridge, England: Cambridge University Press.

Wheen, Francis. 2004. *How Mumbo Jumbo Conquered the World: A Short History of Modern Delusions.* London: Harper Perennial.

White, Hayden. 1973. *Metahistory: The Historical Imagination in Nineteenth-Century Europe.* Baltimore, MD: Johns Hopkins University Press.

Wilder, Hugh. 1988. "Intentions and the Very Idea of Fiction." *Philosophy and Literature* 12:70–79.

Williams, Austin. 2007. "Is Anyone There?" *Times Literary Supplement,* 19 January, 27.

Williams, Bernard. 1996. "Contemporary Philosophy: A Second Look." In *Blackwell Companion to Philosophy,* ed. Nicholas Bunnin and E. P. Tsui-James. Oxford, England: Blackwell.

Williams, Wirt. 1981. *The Tragic Art of Ernest Hemingway.* Baton Rouge: Louisiana State University Press.

Wilsmore, Susan. 1987. "The Literary Work Is Not Its Text." *Philosophy and Literature* 11:307–316.

Wilson, Edward O. 1998. *Consilience: The Unity of Knowledge.* New York: Knopf.

Wimsatt, William K., and Monroe Beardsley. 1946. "The Intentional Fallacy." *Sewanee Review* 45:469–488.

Witek, Joseph. 1989. *Comic Books as History: The Narrative Art of Jack Jackson, Art Spiegelman, and Harvey Pekar.* Jackson: University Press of Mississippi.

Wollheim, Richard. 1968. *Art and Its Objects.* New York: Harper and Row.

Wolterstoff, Nicholas. 1975. "Towards an Ontology of Artworks." *Nous* 9: 115–142.

———. 1980. *Works and Worlds of Art.* Oxford, England: Clarendon.

Young, Robert. 1982. *Untying the Text: A Post-Structuralist Reader.* Boston: Routledge and Kegan Paul.

Zepke, Stephen. 2005. *Art as Abstract Machine: Ontology and Aesthetics in Deleuze and Guattari.* New York: Routledge.

Zunshine, Lisa. 2006. *Why We Read Fiction: Theory of Mind and the Novel.* Columbus: Ohio State University Press.

# INDEX